The Economics of Trade Unions

Richard B. Freeman and James L. Medoff's now classic 1984 book *What Do Unions Do?* stimulated an enormous theoretical and empirical literature on the economic impact of trade unions. Trade unions continue to be a significant feature of many labor markets, particularly in developing countries, and issues of labor market regulations and labor institutions remain critically important to researchers and policy makers.

The relations between unions and management can range between cooperation and conflict; unions have powerful offsetting wage and non-wage effects that economists and other social scientists have long debated. Do the benefits of unionism exceed the costs to the economy and society writ large, or do the costs exceed the benefits? *The Economics of Trade Unions* offers the first comprehensive review, analysis and evaluation of the empirical literature on the microeconomic effects of trade unions using the tools of meta-regression analysis to identify and quantify the economic impact of trade unions, as well as to correct research design faults, the effects of selection bias and model misspecification.

This volume makes use of a unique dataset of hundreds of empirical studies and their reported estimates of the microeconomic impact of trade unions. Written by three authors who have been at the forefront of this research field (including the co-author of the original volume, *What Do Unions Do?*), this book offers an overview of a subject that is of huge importance to scholars of labor economics, industrial and employee relations, and human resource management, as well as those with an interest in meta-analysis.

Hristos Doucouliagos is Professor of Economics at the Department of Economics, and the Alfred Deakin Institute for Citizenship and Globalisation, Deakin University, Australia.

Richard B. Freeman holds the Herbert Ascherman Chair in Economics at Harvard University. He directs the National Bureau of Economic Research/Science Engineering Workforce Projects and is Senior Research Fellow in Labour Markets at the London School of Economics' Centre for Economic Performance, UK.

Patrice Laroche is Professor of Human Resource Management and Labor Relations at the ISAM-IAE Nancy (Université de Lorraine) and at the ESCP Europe Business School, France.

Routledge Studies in Labour Economics

1 **Youth and the Crisis**
Unemployment, Education and Health in Europe
Edited by Gianluigi Coppola and Niall O'Higgins

2 **Workers and the Global Informal Economy**
Interdisciplinary Perspectives
Edited by Supriya Routh and Vando Borghi

3 **The Political Economy of Employment Relations**
Alternative Theory and Practice
Aslihan Aykac

4 **The Economics of Trade Unions**
A Study of a Research Field and Its Findings
Hristos Doucouliagos, Richard B. Freeman and Patrice Laroche

The Economics of Trade Unions

A Study of a Research Field and Its Findings

Hristos Doucouliagos, Richard B. Freeman and Patrice Laroche

Routledge
Taylor & Francis Group
LONDON AND NEW YORK

First published 2017 by Routledge

2 Park Square, Milton Park, Abingdon, Oxfordshire OX14 4RN
52 Vanderbilt Avenue, New York, NY 10017

Routledge is an imprint of the Taylor & Francis Group, an informa business

First issued in paperback 2020

British Library Cataloguing in Publication Data
A catalogue record for this book is available from the British Library

Library of Congress Cataloging in Publication Data
Names: Doucouliagos, Hristos, author. | Freeman, Richard B. (Richard Barry), 1943- author. | Laroche, Patrice, author.
Title: The economics of trade unions : a study of a research field and its findings / Hristos Doucouliagos, Richard B. Freeman and Patrice Laroche.
Description: Abingdon, Oxon ; New York, NY : Routledge, 2017. | Includes bibliographical references and index.
Identifiers: LCCN 2016042103| ISBN 9781138888302 (hardback) | ISBN 9781315713533 (ebook)
Subjects: LCSH: Labor unions—Economic aspects. | Labor economics. | Industrial relations.
Classification: LCC HD6483 .D68 2017 | DDC 331.88—dc23
LC record available at https://lccn.loc.gov/2016042103

ISBN: 978-1-138-88830-2 (hbk)
ISBN: 978-0-367-66789-4 (pbk)

Typeset in Times New Roman PS
by diacriTech, Chennai

To our friend and meta-analysis mentor, T.D. Stanley, and to all researchers who study union effects.

Contents

Figures

Tables

Introduction

Why study studies of unionism?

> Speaking broadly then it may be said that trade unions have benefited the nation as well as themselves.... Any rise of wages or improvement in the conditions of life, and employment, which they may obtain by these reasonable methods, is likely to make for social well being.
>
> (Alfred Marshall, 1961: 588)

Trade unions – "a continuous association of wage-earners for the purpose of maintaining or improving the conditions of their working lives" (Webb and Webb, 1920: 1) – are the key institution representing workers in capitalism, with impacts on a wide range of outcomes, from employee wages and benefits, job satisfaction, and organizational commitment to the productivity and profitability of plants and to macroeconomic outcomes such as inflation, unemployment, and economic growth.

While most social scientists agree that unions benefit their members, there is considerable disagreement about whether unions have a net positive or negative impact on economies writ large. Contrary to Marshall's view, many social scientists view unions as monopolies that adversely affect firm performance (Hirsch and Addison, 1986) or as an influential interest group that distorts policies in favor of union members at the expense of others (Olson, 1965). Others have taken the view that Adam Smith's principle that self-interested actions can produce socially desirable outcomes can apply in the case of unions. Freeman (1976) and Freeman and Medoff (1984) argue that positive non-wage effects, such as improved communication channels and reduced labor turnover, often offset adverse monopoly effects of unions on wage and non-wage outcomes. Brown and Medoff (1978) present evidence that unions are associated with gains in productivity and benefit firms in that respect.

Unions have been important in capitalist economies since the Industrial Revolution. They provide their members with a voice at work and wider political representation. But after growing in membership and influence in most advanced countries from the Great Depression and World War II through the 1950s and in some countries through the 1960s, unions are now in decline in most advanced countries.[1] Figure I.1 places this pattern in historic perspective in terms of the

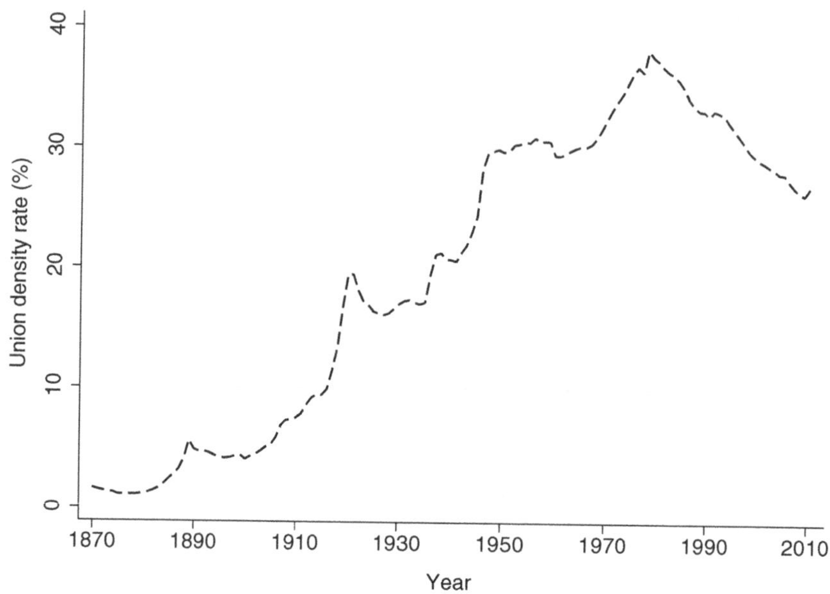

Figure I.1 Union density, 21 OECD economies, 1870–2011

Source: Islam et al. (2016)

average trade union density for 21 OECD countries from 1870 to 2011. Union density increased for most of this period, often in sudden spurts in periods of crisis, but has fallen in virtually every country since the 1980s.

Even in a weakened state, however, unions affect economic outcomes and attract considerable attention from business and government. Business continues to worry about the impact of union wages on labor costs, especially with the entry of China, India, and the former Soviet bloc into the global economy. Policy makers worry about the effects of unions on labor market flexibility and labor market outcomes, such as unemployment (e.g., OECD, 2016). In some countries, unions continue to influence policy development on a wide range of issues, especially through labor and social democratic organizations and political parties. As inequality has become a key economic problem of the twenty-first century, there is increasing recognition that, whatever their effects on economic efficiency, unions are one of the few social institutions with the potential to limit further growth of inequality and to reduce it to more socially desired levels.

Given the huge amount of literature on the economic consequences of unions, some readers may wonder what motivated us to write this book. In *What Do Unions Do?*, Freeman and Medoff (1984) summarized the available evidence base at that time for the United States. Two or so decades later, Bennett and Kaufman (2007) edited a 20-year perspective that reviewed the findings in *What Do Unions Do?* on the basis of ensuing work. Is there truly something new to say about empirical analyses of unions? Yes, there is. There are new things to say and new ways to parse the evidence that adds to what economics and related social sciences can tell us about unions.

There are four reasons for looking anew at the effects of unions.

First, recent decades have witnessed a spread of econometric studies about unions to countries beyond the United States, including developing countries that advanced country researchers largely excluded from consideration. Freeman and Medoff dealt almost exclusively with the United States, and Bennett and Kaufman's edited volume also largely focused on the United States. Globalization of economic activity demands a wider view of union activity and recognition of the variation in unionism and its impacts throughout the world.

Second, the newest work applies more advanced statistical techniques than those used in most studies two to three decades ago. Many employ panel data econometrics that allows analysts to remove person- or establishment-fixed effects from estimates of union impacts. Figure I.2 depicts the growth in the cumulative number of published econometric studies about unions. We use estimates from these studies for our meta-analysis of productivity, productivity growth, physical and intangible capital investment, job satisfaction, and financial performance.[2] From only six studies in the 1970s, the literature bloomed to 125 new studies in the 1990s, with an additional 104 new studies published since 2000. The meta-analyses that constitute the heart of this volume treat 301 studies that report 2,257 estimates of union effects.

Third, the mode of summarizing the findings of diverse studies into a statistically valid assessment of the evidence has advanced considerably. In the early 2000s, Doucouliagos and Laroche (2003a, 2003b, and 2003c) pioneered the use of meta-analysis to combine the results from research studies of union effects into a statistically valid summary picture. As in other areas of science, the techniques of meta-analysis have improved, for example, with new ways to identify and correct for publication selection bias and for assessing replications of extant findings.

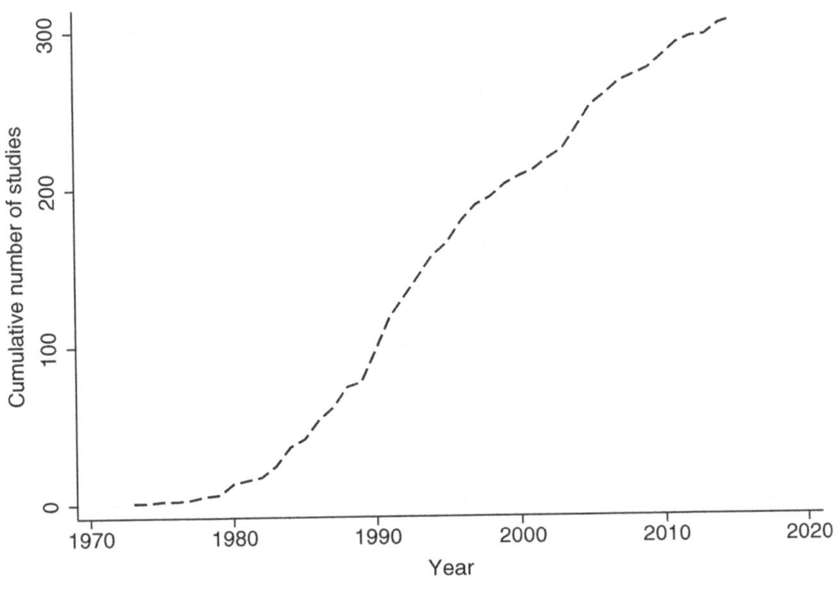

Figure I.2 Cumulative number of studies on the economic effects of unions, 1973–2015

Source: Authors' calculations

This book uses these newer techniques to explore whether prior meta-analyses findings stand up to differences in techniques and whether newer evidence results in fresh insights and inferences about unions as economic institutions.

Fourth, the existence of several meta-analyses on unions provides an opportunity to learn from the findings of meta-analyses on distinct but related topics in a *meta-meta-analysis*. Meta-analysis focuses on drawing inferences from a specific research question. As the name suggests, meta-meta-analysis draws inferences from several related meta-studies, in our case on different outcome variables. Specifically, we use the findings of meta-analyses on the impact of unions on productivity, productivity growth, physical and intangible capital investment, financial performance, labor turnover, organizational commitment, and job satisfaction to provide a more comprehensive picture of what unions do.

Meta-analysis as arbiter in debates

Economic theory often consists of models that allow for a given factor to have competing effects on outcomes – the income effect versus the substitution effect in labor supply behavior being an archetype example. What effect does an increase in wages have on labor supply? Economic theory says it depends on two competing forces: the higher income from increased wages that increases workers' desire for leisure and the higher opportunity cost of leisure from the increased wages. Which effect matters more determines whether time or effort at work are positively or negatively related to changes in wages. The theory poses questions and identifies potential causal lines of impact but cannot resolve the net effect of competing forces. Only empirical analysis can tell whether one effect dominates another in a particular situation.

In the case of the impact of unions on business performance, or indeed of institutions on outcomes more broadly, theory is often highly ambiguous. There are many agents operating under varying constraints and with differing goals. Game theory allows for many potential equilibria. As King Richard III would have said had he been a social scientist, "Empirical estimates, empirical estimates, empirical estimates, my kingdom for some estimates".

We now have many empirical estimates on unionism. The estimates are heterogeneous with differing statistical and economic significance. Some of the variation and difference in significance comes from the lack of statistical power due to small sample sizes in studies of firms. Only a meta-analysis combining the studies can show what the body of work has found and with what statistical precision.

Empirical estimates also vary with outcome variables, data, model, statistical methodology used, country, and time of analysis. They differ because different researchers or the same researcher at different times chooses somewhat different auxiliary variables and/or econometric models. These decisions can produce spurious heterogeneity in reported estimates. If the studies had used exactly the same model and variables, the results might have been similar. Heterogeneity may also be real, as when union effects differ by industry, country, and time. Only a meta-analysis combining and analyzing the studies can identify the sources of this heterogeneity.

The published literature can also suffer from publication selection bias in which researchers choose which of several equally valid estimates to report. This produces a truncated distribution of estimates with artificially inflated effects that leads to possible erroneous inferences (Stanley, 2008; Doucouliagos and Stanley, 2013). Traditional literature reviews are particularly vulnerable to incorrect inferences. Meta-analysis can provide a more rigorous and statistical approach to research synthesis.

This book provides a review of evidence that is more quantitative, complete, statistically systematic, and of course up-to-date than *What Do Unions Do?* or the Bennett and Kaufman 20-year review of findings. It uses state-of-the-art *meta-regression analysis* to identify and quantify associations between unions and dimensions of economic performance, such as productivity, investment, and profitability. Meta-analysis is the scientific way to draw inferences from the diversity of results and to detect possible regularities across studies (Stanley, 2001; Stanley and Doucouliagos, 2012) based on *quantitative* synthesis of a large number of individual studies (Rosenthal, 1984; Schmidt and Hunter, 2015). It is well suited to exploring the multidimensional research on trade unions, synthesizing the knowledge in available estimates, correcting the evidence base for various biases, and drawing inferences from underpowered econometric studies.

Structure of the book

This book consists of eight chapters beyond this introduction.

Chapter 1 gives a scientometric analysis of the literature spawned by *What Do Unions Do?* (Freeman and Medoff, 1984). It analyzes citation and co-citation patterns and keywords to describe quantitatively the contributions of *What Do Unions Do?* over the past 32 years. This chapter was written by Doucouliagos and Laroche, with Freeman absenting himself for reasons the reader will understand.

Chapter 2 lays out the meta-regression methodology that we apply throughout the book. The chapter addresses issues of data collection, research synthesis, publication bias, mis-specification bias, and heterogeneity in empirical findings.

Chapter 3 presents our meta-analysis of the effect of unions on productivity. It updates Doucouliagos and Laroche (2003a) with a new meta-regression analysis of the effect of unions on productivity based on 111 studies.

Chapter 4 presents a new meta-regression analysis of the effect of unions on productivity growth based on 42 studies. It updates Doucouliagos and Laroche (2003b).

Chapters 5 drills down to identify some of the investment channels through which unions impact productivity. We update Doucouliagos and Laroche (2003c) with a new meta-analysis of the link between unionism and physical capital investment from 20 econometric studies and summarize the results of a meta-analysis of 25 studies of investment in intangible capital based on Doucouliagos and Laroche (2013).

Chapter 6 moves beyond the production function methodology to examine the evidence on three forms of employee behavior – turnover, job satisfaction, and organizational commitment – that impact both productivity and worker well-being. It reviews findings from several meta-analyses by other authors and presents a new meta-analysis of 59 studies on the impact of unions on job satisfaction by Laroche (2016).

Chapter 7 explores the classic topic in the study of unions – their impact on wages – and presents a new meta-analysis of the effects of unions on profitability. We update Doucouliagos and Laroche (2009) with findings from 44 econometric studies.

Chapter 8 gives our summary and conclusions and offers suggestions for future research on the effects of unionism.

The book does not cover the entire waterfront of topics on unions. We do not explore the effects of unions on the macroeconomic issues of inflation and employment or on strikes and inequality[3] – nor union effects on social and political issues, such as whether unions lobby successfully for laws that expand their monopoly power, the democratic nature of unionism, and corruption in the union bureaucracy.

The idea to write this book took shape several years ago. Beginning in 2014, the authors began working on the task. All three authors have devoted large parts of their research careers to analyzing the economic effects of unionism. Richard B. Freeman has made a seminal contribution with his path-breaking book with James L. Medoff, as well as in numerous other scientific publications. Nearly 19 years later, Doucouliagos and Laroche pioneered the use of meta-analysis to the growing body of research. We hope that by bringing together our various expertise, we shed additional light on the economic impact of unions.

Notes

1 In the United States, union density has decreased continually since the 1960s (US-BLS, 2016). In the United Kingdom, union membership peaked in 1979 and has since declined. However, in recent years, trade union membership in the United Kingdom has increased in the private sector but declined in the public sector (DBIS, 2015).

2 For the purposes of Figure I.2, we define a study as a published journal paper or book that reports estimates of union effects on one of the outcome variables we review in this book: productivity, productivity growth, physical and intangible capital investment, job satisfaction, and financial performance. Where estimates are provided on more than one outcome variable, we count them as separate studies; e.g., if a journal article reports estimates of the effects of unions on productivity and profitability, we count this as two studies.

3 Macroeconomic effects are explored by Calmfors and Driffill (1988), Pencavel (1991), Flanagan (1999), and Nickell and Layard (1999), among others. Several studies find a negative association between unions and inequality, e.g., Freeman and Medoff (1984), Koeniger et al. (2007), and Koske et al. (2012).

1 A bibliometric analysis of *What Do Unions Do?*[1]

> If I am right that each scientific revolution alters the historical perspective of the community that experiences it, then that change of perspective should affect the structure of post-revolutionary textbooks and research publications. One such effect – a shift in the distribution of the technical literature cited in the footnotes to research reports – ought to be studied as a possible index to the occurrence of revolutions.
>
> (Kuhn, 1962: xi)

The purpose of this chapter is to present a scientometric analysis of *What Do Unions Do?* (Freeman and Medoff, 1984), from 1984 to 2014, with a particular focus on articles published in the 'Industrial and Labor Relations' research area.[2] The aim of the bibliometric analysis is to explore some of the contributions of *What Do Unions Do?* over the past 30 years. We show that this book had an enormous impact on the study of unions. Citations data from the ISI Web of Science reveal that this seminal work has been cited by 1,480 articles, proceedings papers, and book chapters since its publication in 1984; a notable average of 49 citations per annum.[3] This large number of citations suggests that the book has had a major impact on the academic literature across the globe.[4] We investigate the scientific impact of Freeman and Medoff (1984) through a citation analysis and a keywords analysis. Specifically, we explore (1) citation patterns over time, (2) who cites Freeman and Medoff (1984) most frequently, and (3) the main cited themes associated with Freeman and Medoff (1984).

Analysis of citations of Freeman and Medoff (1984) is of interest for several reasons. First, citation counts are a useful measure of academic influence and the depth of citations indicates impact; if only a small number of authors cites their work, then Freeman and Medoff's influence is limited. Second, impact can be assessed by the extent to which a study is cited outside its home discipline. Examination of citations by other disciplines reflects the extent to which the influence of *What Do Unions Do?* spread beyond the domain of industrial relations and labor economics. Third, studying the time trend in citation rates offers another way to assess the book's influence. Most scientific contributions are rarely cited (Lindsey, 1989). However, some landmark studies continue to be cited over time. Hence, we investigate whether citations to Freeman and Medoff (1984) are declining over time.

This chapter has four sections. In the first we give a brief review of Freeman and Medoff's contribution to the economic analysis of trade unions. The second section describes the bibliometric approach employed and data. The third section presents the bibliometric analysis. The last section summarizes the main findings.

Freeman and Medoff's research agenda

In *What Do Unions Do?*, Freeman and Medoff consider a variety of issues related to the economic effects of unions, with the primary concern being the contribution of union voice to the functioning of the economy. Freeman and Medoff argue that unions can play a beneficial role in improving workplace performance by stabilizing the workforce, increasing workers' productivity, and reducing pay inequality. This line of research was developed in a series of articles that highlighted the importance and role of union voice on workers' behavior and consequently on different economic outcomes (Brown and Medoff, 1978; Freeman, 1976, 1980, 1981, 1984; Freeman and Medoff, 1979a, 1979b, 1981, 1982). Table 1.1 summarizes Freeman and Medoff's major studies for the period 1976 to 1984, including *What Do Unions Do?*, a summary of the findings of each study, and the number of citations received as of July 2015.

Freeman's (1976) article was the starting point to the whole analysis. This article was written in honor of Hirschman's (1970) *Exit, Voice, and Loyalty* book. The American Economic Association asked Freeman to say what *Exit, Voice, and*

Table 1.1 Freeman and Medoff's contributions to the study of the economic effects of unions, 1976–1984

Study	*Summary*	*Citations*
Freeman (1976). Individual mobility and union voice in the labor market. *The American Economic Review: Papers and Proceedings*.	Examines the non-wage effects of unions using Hirschman's exit-voice framework.	141
Brown & Medoff (1978). Trade unions in the production process. *The Journal of Political Economy*.	Examines the effect of unions on productivity. Unionization has a significant positive effect on output per worker.	208
Freeman & Medoff (1979a). New estimates of private sector unionism in the United States. *Industrial and Labor Relations Review*.	Presents new estimates of two measures of unionism in the US: percent of private sector workers covered by union agreements and percent who are union members. Estimated coverage is higher on average than estimated membership percentage.	183

Study	*Summary*	*Citations*
Freeman & Medoff (1979b). The two faces of unionism. *The Public Interest.*	In addition to raising wages, unions have significant non-wage effects. By providing workers with a voice both at the workplace and in the political arena, unions affect positively the functioning of the economy.	63
Freeman (1980). Unionism and the dispersion of wages. *Industrial and Labor Relations Review.*	Examines the effects of unions on the dispersion of wages in the private sector in the USA. Unionism reduces wage dispersion.	173
Freeman (1981). The effect of unionism on fringe benefits. *Industrial and Labor Relations Review.*	Analyzes the impact of unions on fringe benefits for production workers. The union fringe benefits effect exceeds the wage effect; standard union wage studies understate the union effect on total compensation.	161
Freeman & Medoff (1981). The impact of the percentage organized on union and nonunion wages. *The Review of Economics and Statistics.*	Disentangles the relation between the percentage of workers organized and the wages received by union and non-union workers. The percentage organized has a strong positive association with the wages of unionized manufacturing workers.	81
Freeman & Medoff (1982). Substitution between production labor and other inputs in unionized and nonunionized manufacturing. *The Review of Economics and Statistics.*	Provides estimates for US manufacturing of the constant output elasticity of demand for unionized and non-unionized production workers and of the elasticity of substitution between these workers and other inputs. The substitution between production labor and other inputs is generally lower in union than non-union settings.	40
Freeman (1984). Longitudinal analyses of the effects of trade-unions. *Journal of Labor Economics.*	Examines how measurement error biases longitudinal estimates of union effects. Longitudinal analysis confirms the significant impact of unionism found in cross-section studies.	164
Freeman & Medoff (1984). *What Do Unions Do?*	Summarizes several years of research by Freeman and Medoff on unionism, concluding that on balance unions are socially desirable institutions.	1,480

Source: Table lists the main publications by Richard Freeman and James Medoff, from 1976 to 1984. Citations collected from ISI Web of Science as of July 2015.

Loyalty meant to labor market analysis. Freeman's article attracted Jim Medoff's attention. This led to their collaboration and the *What Do Unions Do*? program.

Freeman and Medoff advance a new perspective on unionism that focuses on the collective voice and institutional response dimension of unions (hereafter CV/IR). Specifically, Freeman and Medoff argue that there is no single union/non-union wage differential and that the social cost of union monopoly wage gains is relatively modest. According to Freeman and Medoff, the claim that unions increase wage inequality is incorrect. On the contrary, unions reduce inequality, for example by adopting pay policies that limit managerial discretion in wage-setting, increasing the relative pay (wages and benefits) of the unskilled and compressing earnings (Jarrell and Stanley, 1990; Kahn, 2000). Freeman and Medoff also highlight how union voice determines rules and working conditions by instituting grievance and arbitration procedures and by negotiating clauses desired by workers. The notion of 'collective voice' or 'employee voice' draws upon the perspective of Hirschman's *Exit, Voice, and Loyalty* (1970). As a result of voice, workers are less willing to quit their jobs and unionized workforces are more stable compared to non-unionized workforces. Freeman and Medoff also observe that unionized workers report themselves less satisfied with their jobs than non-union workers. This is said to arise because unions stimulate worker discontent in order to be more effective in negotiations with management. Freeman and Medoff claim, however, that unionism does not restrain productivity. They show that unionized workplaces are often more productive than non-unionized workplaces. This higher productivity is attributed to lower employee turnover and improved managerial performance in response to unionization. Nevertheless, Freeman and Medoff acknowledge that unionism can have a negative effect on firms' profitability, when pay increases are not sufficiently offset by higher labor productivity associated with unionism, especially in highly concentrated sectors of the economy. Freeman and Medoff also address the view that unions in the United States are non-democratic institutions run by corrupt bosses. They consider this depiction to be a myth, as most unions are highly democratic, even if corruption exists in some instances.

Freeman and Medoff's work challenges the traditional economics view of unionism. They argue that while labor unions have a monopoly face, they also have a collective voice face. By comparing the effects of these two faces on productivity, income distribution, and other economic outcomes, Freeman and Medoff argue that in net terms, labor unions are socially desirable institutions. Many consider *What Do Unions Do?* to be one of the most influential labor relations books (Blanchflower and Bryson, 2004). The book provides a wide-ranging collection of quantitative studies available (at that time) on the effect of unionism on the economy and society, and it also offers a new conceptual framework for thinking about these issues. Some of the findings were controversial, challenging the prevailing negative assessment of the economic impact of unionism.

Not surprisingly, key claims made by Freeman and Medoff in their book generated considerable discussion and drew criticism. For example, numerous publications have challenged their ideas. Twenty years after the publication of *What Do*

Unions Do?, a book entitled *What Do Unions Do? A Twenty-Year Perspective* was published in 2007, compiling academic articles originally published in a special issue of the *Journal of Labor Research* (Bennett and Kaufman, 2007). One purpose of this book was to address critical questions on the economic and social effects of unions, considering the additional theoretical and empirical research on unionism since the publication of *What Do Unions Do?*. This book also incorporates some international evidence of the effects of unions and broadened the discussion to non-economic effects of unions, such as social justice and democracy in industry. Some authors were critical of *What Do Unions Do?*, focusing on the negative monopoly face of unionism and contesting the arguments of positive collective voice effects. Others provided evidence that supported the two faces of unionism perspective.

Approach and data

We examine the extent to which *What Do Unions Do?* is cited, particularly in industrial relations, and the content of the citations, through a bibliometric study of the leading industrial relations journals from 1984 to 2014. Many of the ideas covered in *What Do Unions Do?* were also presented in earlier studies; recall Table 1.1. Hence, by focusing predominantly on citations of *What Do Unions Do?*, we understate the influence of the CV/IR paradigm.

The aim of bibliometric analysis is to examine patterns in the literature using citation and co-citation analysis (Diodato, 1994). Analysis of citations is motivated by the idea that authors cite prior studies that are relevant to their own arguments and analysis (Garfield, 1979; Zuckerman, 1987). Consequently, articles that are cited more are likely to exert greater influence in a research field. Co-citation analysis involves scrutinizing a pair of articles cited by a specific research article on the notion that being cited together signals that the content of the cited articles are connected. Some proximity of the content of the two cited articles to the citing document may be inferred. The rationale is the same for distinguishing clusters of authors or topics covered, allowing a better understanding of how different analyses relate to one another (see White and Griffith, 1981; White and McCain, 1998). Assuming that the references cited in a given article reflect content similarity and influence, we identify the influence of Freeman and Medoff (1984) by determining links among authors and themes and topics covered. We do not explore whether citing authors approved or criticized *What Do Unions Do?* nor the articles on which the book itself relied. We focus only on whether this book was cited.

All the data were collected from ISI Web of Science. We searched this database for articles published in industrial and labor relations journals citing *What Do Unions Do?*. This search identified 1,480 research works (articles, conference proceedings, chapters in books) published between 1984 and 2014. The relevant information in these papers was collected and analyzed using *Bibexcel* and *Ucinet*. Specifically, we analyze authorship of the papers citing Freeman and Medoff, the citations and co-citations of the top articles referencing their work, and the keywords used in each of these articles.

Analysis

We present three types of analysis: citation analysis, co-citation analysis, and keyword analysis.

Citation analysis

The influence of Freeman and Medoff's ideas and their relevance for industrial and labor relations research is highlighted in Tables 1.2, 1.3, and 1.4. Table 1.2 lists the top ten most cited authors in one of the most reputed industrial relations journal, the *Industrial and Labor Relations Review* (*ILRR*). Freeman is the most cited author in the *ILRR* during the period 1985–2006 (Casey and MacMillan, 2008). Table 1.3 lists the top 20 cited authors in the ISI Web of Science Industrial and Labor Relations research area; Freeman is one of the most cited authors. Taken together, Tables 1.2 and 1.3 indicate the impact of Freeman's research on unions in industrial relations research.

The 1,480 citing articles included in our survey were written by 418 different authors. The most frequent citing authors were Addison (18 articles), Bryson (18 articles), Kaufman (18 articles), Schnabel (15 articles), Fiorito (14 articles), and Kleiner (14 articles). The top 20 authors citing *What Do Unions Do?*

Table 1.2 The ten most cited authors in the *Industrial and Labor Relations Review*, 1985–2006

1985–1995		*1996–2006*	
Number of cites	*Author*	*Number of cites*	*Author*
136	**Freeman, RB**	103	**Freeman, RB**
73	Kochan, TA	62	Card, D
59	US Census Bureau	46	Blau, FD
57	US Bureau of Labor Statistics	44	Farber, HS
44	Ehrenberg, RG	43	Katz, LF
42	Brown, C	40	Osterman, P
42	Ashenfelter, O	38	Bound, J
41	Farber, HS	37	Heckman, JJ
41	Heckman, JJ	35	Brown, C
36	US Department of Labor	34	Lazear, EP

Source: Casey and McMillan (2008: 128).

Table 1.3 Top 20 authors in the Industrial and Labor Relations research area

Authors	*Web of Science number of citations*
Neumark, D	2,233
Borjas, G	1,526
Card, D	1,409
MacDuffie, JP	1,304
Hirsch, BT	1,235
Osterman, P	1,216
Freeman, RB	1,194
Kahn, LM	1,067
Thomas, D	927
Addison, JT	836
Cappelli, P	829
Blau, FD	793
Summers, LH	763
Ehrenberg, RG	758
Kochan, TA	758
Bound, J	745
Welch, F	745
Krueger, AB	737
Blanchflower, DG	728
Kalleberg, AL	722

Note: Top 20 authors from a total of 42,283 authors.

Source: ISI Web of Science, July 2015.

are listed in Table 1.4. Not surprisingly, most of these authors are scholars in the fields of industrial and labor relations or labor economics. They are also well known for their studies on the economic effects of unions or the effects of unions on human resources practices. For instance, John T. Addison published 18 articles citing *What Do Unions Do?*. Addison's central interest is the effects of unions on firm performance, especially with his co-author Barry T. Hirsch. Their book published in 1986, titled *The Economic Analysis of Unions:*

New Approaches and Evidence, is also a landmark for scholars studying labor unions and their economic effects, providing a complete survey of the existing literature on this topic at that time. It is worth noting that Hirsch and Addison (1986: 208) conclude that "the evidence of a union productivity effect is underwhelming", challenging the Freeman and Medoff conclusion. Another industrial relations expert, Alex Bryson, extended Freeman and Medoff's work in the

Table 1.4 Top 20 authors citing *What Do Unions Do?*

Author	*Number of citations*	*Proportion of 1,480 citations (%)*
Addison, JT	18	1.22
Bryson, A	18	1.22
Kaufman, BE	18	1.22
Schnabel, C	15	1.02
Fiorito, J	14	0.95
Kleiner, MM	14	0.95
Drago, R	12	0.82
Hirsch, BT	12	0.82
Freeman, RB	11	0.75
Heywood, JS	11	0.75
Kalleberg, AL	11	0.75
Masters, MF	11	0.75
Machin, SJ	9	0.61
Wagner, J	9	0.61
Bacon, N	8	0.54
Blanchflower, DG	8	0.54
Budd, JW	8	0.54
Delaney, JT	8	0.54
Mitchell, DJB	8	0.54
Clark, GL	7	0.48

Source: ISI Web of Science, July 2015.

British context, focusing largely on the effects on employees. Bruce Kaufman, an expert in human resource management, employee representation, and institutional economics, with a deep interest in the history of economic and management thought on industrial relations, is another researcher whose citations show the influence of Freeman and Medoff's contributions. In *The Origins and Evolution of the Field of Industrial Relations in the United States* (1993), Kaufman situated their work in the historic development of the field. Kaufman is also the co-editor with James T. Bennett of the book *What Do Unions Do? A Twenty-Year Perspective*. In this book, he presents a neutral point of view on the different theoretical perspectives on the economic effect of unions and underlines the importance of Freeman and Medoff's contribution to the theory and understanding of unions. He considers that Freeman and Medoff forced economists and policy makers "to carefully reconsider the case for and against unionism and have, possibly, moved the verdict in a modestly more favorable direction" (Bennett and Kaufman, 2007: 41).

The 1,480 citing articles have been published in a total of 165 journals. These journals represent 45 disciplines, with the most frequent citing areas being industrial and labor relations (655 citing articles), economics (408 citing articles), management (178 citing articles), and sociology (163 citing articles); see Table 1.5, column (1). Table 1.5, column (2), shows that most of the citations of *What Do Unions Do?* are in the business and economics research area, with a significant proportion in sociology, and government and law. These data indicate the widespread influence of *What Do Unions Do?*, particularly in the field of industrial and labor relations, economics, and management.

Table 1.6 lists the top 15 journals with articles that cite *What Do Unions Do?*. Nine of the 15 journals containing the largest number of citing articles were from the industrial relations and labor field. We conclude from Tables 1.5 and 1.6 that while most of the influence of *What Do Unions Do?* has been within industrial relations, this book has also attracted attention outside its home discipline. This can also be seen from Table 1.7, which lists the top 40 most cited articles that reference *What Do Unions Do?*. Arthur's (1994) *Academy of Management Journal* article is the most cited article citing *What Do Unions Do?*. It is worth noting that these 40 articles were published in the main academic journals of their field, especially in management, economics, and sociology. Importantly, the top 27 of these top 40 articles were not published in an industrial relations journal. That is, even though *What Do Unions Do?* is one of the most cited works in industrial relations, its influence extends beyond this primary research field, as indicated by the most cited articles that reference it. For example, 12 of the 40 most cited articles were from the management discipline or industrial psychology. In recent years, the management discipline has embraced Freeman and Medoff's research. In particular, the 'high-performance workplace practices' literature mobilizes the contribution of *What Do Unions Do?* on employee voice and especially its relationship with firm performance;

Table 1.5 Top 10 ISI Web of Science disciplines and research areas

Web of Science category	*Number of citations (1)*		*Number of citations (2)*
Discipline		*Research area*	
Industrial and labor relations	655	Business and economics	1,171
Economics	408	Sociology	163
Management	178	Government and law	122
Sociology	163	Psychology	75
Business	65	Social sciences other topics	55
Political science	62	Public administration	49
Law	60	Mathematical methods in social sciences	21
Psychology applied	56	History	19
Public administration	34	International relations	16
Social sciences interdisciplinary	29	Health care sciences and services	15

Source: ISI Web of Science, July 2015.

e.g., Evans and Davis (2005), Wood and Wall (2007), Gill (2009), Budd et al. (2010), and the special issue of *Human Resource Management* dealing with the employee voice (Wilkinson and Fay, 2011).

Figure 1.1 illustrates the annual number of published articles citing *What Do Unions Do?*, during the period 1984–2014. Evidently, *What Do Unions Do?* continues to attract considerable attention from scholars even 30 years after its publication, with an average of 49 citations per annum. Indeed, it appears that there has been renewed interest in this work in recent years. For example, the impact of voice in organizations is still a highly topical issue, with several articles published on this topic in recent years, especially in the management field.[5]

Co-citation analysis

The influence of *What Do Unions Do?* can also be determined through co-citations. This involves examining which studies are cited together. Figure 1.2 illustrates the co-citations among the top 30 most-cited articles referencing *What Do Unions Do?*. The co-citations correspond to the relationship between the different articles cited, and the thickness of the line connecting them illustrates the strength of the tie. The thicker the line between two articles, the larger the number of co-citations.

Table 1.6 Top 15 academic journals citing *What Do Unions Do?*

Journal	*Number of citations*	*Proportion of 1,480 (%)*	*Journal Impact Factor 2014*	*5-year Impact Factor*	*Category*
Journal of Labor Research	129	8.72	0.277	0.598	ILR
Industrial & Labor Relations Review	108	7,30	0.888	1.525	ILR
Industrial Relations: A Journal of Economy and Society	96	6.49	1.040	1.679	ILR
British Journal of Industrial Relations	78	5.27	0.954	1.672	ILR
Relations Industrielles/ Industrial Relations	47	3.18	0.218	0.467	ILR
International Journal of Human Resource Management	28	1.89	0.916	1.375	MGT
Journal of Labor Economics	24	1.62	1.893	3.177	ILR
Economic and Industrial Democracy	21	1.42	0.791	1.193	ILR
Social Forces	19	1.28	N/A	N/A	SOC
Work and Occupations	17	1.14	1.222	1.632	ILR
American Sociological Review	16	1.08	4.390	6.824	SOC

(*continued*)

Table 1.6 Top 15 academic journals citing *What Do Unions Do?* (*continued*)

Journal	*Number of citations*	*Proportion of 1,480 (%)*	*Journal Impact Factor 2014*	*5-year Impact Factor*	*Category*
Journal of Industrial Relations	13	0.88	0.922	0.682	ILR
Human Resource Management	13	0.88	1.293	2.705	MGT
Applied Economics	13	0.88	0.613	0.679	ECO
American Journal of Sociology	13	0.88	3.545	5.326	SOC

Notes: Category denotes Web of Science category. ILR = Industrial and Labor Relations; MGT = Management; SOC = Sociology; ECO = Economics.

Source: ISI Web of Science, July 2015.

Table 1.7 Top 40 most cited articles referencing *What Do Unions Do?*

	Author(s)	*Title*	*Journal*	*Citations*
1	Arthur (1994)	Effects of human resource systems on manufacturing performance and turnover	*Academy of Management Journal*	865
2	Prendergast (1999)	The provision of incentives in firms	*Journal of Economic Literature*	753
3	Delaney & Huselid (1996)	The impact of human resource management practices on perceptions of organizational performance	*Academy of Management Journal*	722
4	Edelman (1992)	Legal ambiguity and symbolic structures: Organizational mediation of civil-rights law	*American Journal of Sociology*	488

	Author(s)	*Title*	*Journal*	*Citations*
5	Akerlof & Yellen (1990)	The fair wage-effort hypothesis and unemployment	*Quarterly Journal of Economics*	429
6	Brown & Medoff (1989)	The employer size wage effect	*Journal of Political Economy*	407
7	Bielby & Baron (1986)	Men and women at work: Sex segregation and statistical discrimination	*American Journal of Sociology*	380
8	Edelman (1990)	Legal environments and organizational governance: The expansion of due-process in the American workplace	*American Journal of Sociology*	373
9	Jackson & Schuler (1995)	Understanding human-resource management in the context of organizations and their environments	*Annual Review of Psychology*	299
10	Bulow & Summers (1986)	A theory of dual labor-markets with application to industrial policy, discrimination, and Keynesian unemployment	*Journal of Labor Economics*	292
11	Coff (1999)	When competitive advantage doesn't lead to performance: The resource-based view and stakeholder bargaining power	*Organization Science*	291

(*continued*)

Table 1.7 Top 40 most cited articles referencing *What Do Unions Do?* (*continued*)

	Author(s)	*Title*	*Journal*	*Citations*
12	Black & Lynch (2001)	How to compete: The impact of workplace practices and information technology on productivity	*Review of Economics and Statistics*	281
13	Koch & McGrath (1996)	Improving labor productivity: Human resource management policies do matter	*Strategic Management Journal*	260
14	Rusbult et al. (1988)	Impact of exchange variables on exit, voice, loyalty, and neglect: An integrative model of responses to declining job-satisfaction	*Academy of Management Journal*	256
15	Pfeffer & Baron (1988)	Taking the workers back out: Recent trends in the structuring of employment	*Research in Organizational Behavior*	232
16	Wall et al. (2004)	On the validity of subjective measures of company performance	*Personnel Psychology*	222
17	Abraham & Farber (1987)	Job duration, seniority, and earnings	*American Economic Review*	219
18	Acemoglu & Pischke (1999a)	The structure of wages and investment in general training	*Journal of Political Economy*	215
19	Shaw et al. (1998)	An organization-level analysis of voluntary and involuntary turnover	*Academy of Management Journal*	206

	Author(s)	*Title*	*Journal*	*Citations*
20	Withey & Cooper (1989)	Predicting exit, voice, loyalty, and neglect	*Administrative Science Quarterly*	205
21	Voos & Sherman (2000)	Breaking the iron law of oligarchy: Union revitalization in the American labor movement	*American Journal of Sociology*	176
22	Katz and Summers (1989)	Industry rents: Evidence and implications	*Brookings Papers on Economic Activity*	173
23	Card (1996)	The effect of unions on the structure of wages: A longitudinal analysis	*Econometrica*	170
24	Wallerstein (1999)	Wage-setting institutions and pay inequality in advanced industrial societies	*American Journal of Political Science*	150
25	Cappelli & Sherer (1991)	The missing role of context in OB: The need for a meso-level approach	*Research in Organizational Behavior*	145
26	Walder (1992)	Property-rights and stratification in socialist redistributive economies	*American Sociological Review*	140
27	Weeden (2002)	Why do some occupations pay more than others? Social closure and earnings inequality in the United States	*American Journal of Sociology*	133
28	Bartel (1994)	Productivity gains from the implementation of employee training-programs	*Industrial Relations*	132

(*continued*)

Table 1.7 Top 40 most cited articles referencing *What Do Unions Do?* (*continued*)

	Author(s)	*Title*	*Journal*	*Citations*
29	Shaw et al. (2005)	Alternative conceptualizations of the relationship between voluntary turnover and organizational performance	*Academy of Management Journal*	130
30	Cooke (1994)	Employee participation programs, group-based incentives, and company performance: A union-nonunion comparison	*Industrial & Labor Relations Review*	129
31	Marini (1989)	Sex-differences in earnings in the United States	*Annual Review of Sociology*	128
32	Fuchs et al. (1998)	Economists' views about parameters, values, and policies: Survey results in labor and public economics	*Journal of Economic Literature*	120
33	Prendergast & Taper (1996)	Favoritism in organizations	*Journal of Political Economy*	119
34	Blau & Beller (1988)	Trends in earnings differentials by gender, 1971–1981	*Industrial & Labor Relations Review*	119
35	Adler & Cole (1993)	Designed for learning: A tale of 2 auto plants	*Sloan Management Review*	116
36	Rose (1987)	Labor rent sharing and regulation – evidence from the trucking industry	*Journal of Political Economy*	116

	Author(s)	*Title*	*Journal*	*Citations*
37	Murnane & Cohen (1986)	Merit pay and the evaluation problem – why most merit pay plans fail and a few survive	*Harvard Educational Review*	114
38	Marwell (2004)	Privatizing the welfare state: Nonprofit community-based organizations as political actors	*American Sociological Review*	107
39	Davis & Haltiwanger (1991)	Wage dispersion between and within United States manufacturing plants, 1963–86	*Brookings Papers on Economic Activity*	106
40	Acemoglu & Pischke (1999b)	Beyond Becker: Training in imperfect labour markets	*Economic Journal*	105

Source: ISI Web of Science, July 2015.

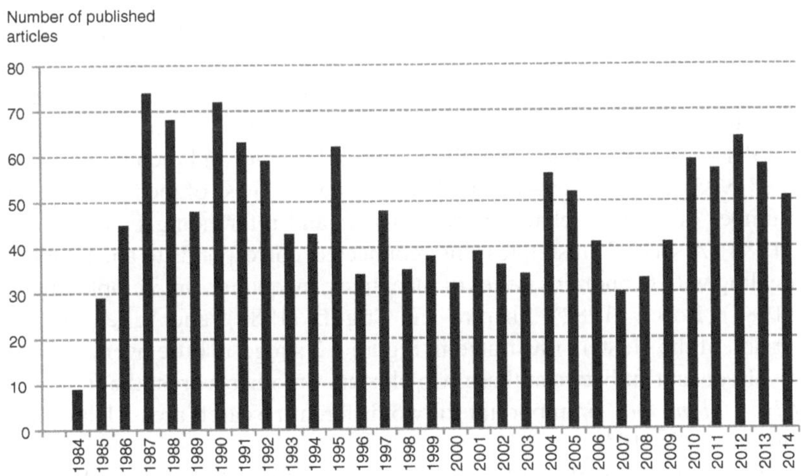

Figure 1.1 Published articles citing *What Do Unions Do?*, 1984–2014

Source: ISI Web of Science, July 2015.

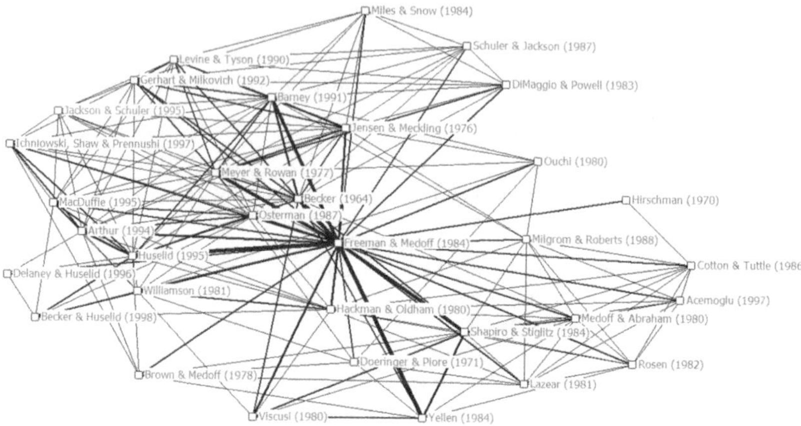

Figure 1.2 Co-citations among the top 30 most cited studies referencing *What Do Unions Do?*

Source: ISI Web of Science, May 2015. Analyses and graphs with *Ucinet*.

The six articles that are cited most often with Freeman and Medoff (1984) are Becker (1964), Meyer and Rowan (1977), Shapiro and Stiglitz (1984), Yellen (1984), Barney (1991), and Huselid (1995).

It is also informative to analyze clusters, or subsets of the network in which scholars are more closely and intensely tied to one another (Borgatti et al., 2002). A cluster is a group of studies that tend to be cited together; studies included in a cluster tend to be similar within the cluster (e.g., in terms of themes) and dissimilar to those in different clusters. We use a one-dimensional clique overlap computed using *Ucinet* (Everett and Borgatti, 1998). At least two main clusters can be observed from Figure 1.2. One cluster corresponds to a network involving several authors dealing with HRM issues and firm performance. This cluster includes Barney (1991), Arthur (1994), Huselid (1995), Jackson and Schuler (1995), MacDuffie (1995), and Ichniowski et al. (1997). The thickness of the ties indicates a large number of studies related to one another and referencing Freeman and Medoff (1984). A second cluster, less interconnected, corresponds to a network of articles dealing with economics issues of incentives, inequality, or unemployment: Lazear (1981), Rosen (1982), Shapiro and Stiglitz (1984), and Yellen (1984). A comparison of the clusters illustrated in Figure 1.2 suggests little overlap; there is a relatively distant fit between these two clusters. In other words, the influence of *What Do Unions Do?* is important in two different research areas: labor economics and strategic HRM.

Figure 1.3 shows networks of the co-authors of the top 30 most cited papers within the Industrial and Labor Relations research, referencing Freeman and Medoff (1984), i.e., co-authorship networks formed within this research area, among the top 30 most cited articles. *Ucinet* was used to draw the structural networks. Each set of connected authors have at least one article together.

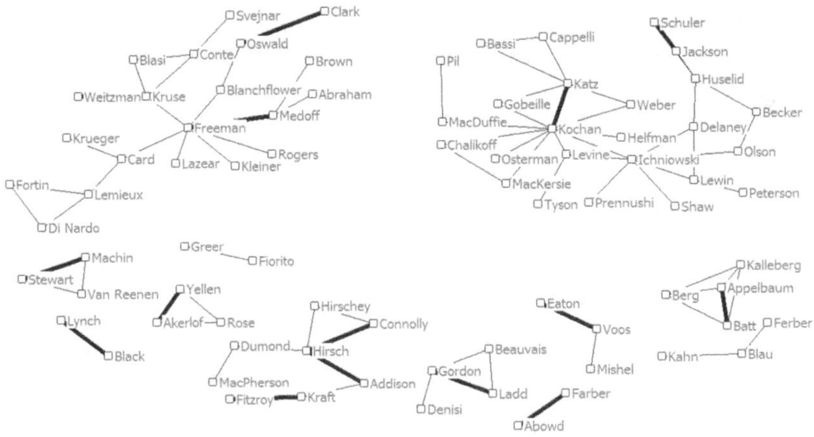

Figure 1.3 Networks among the most influential authors within the Industrial and Labor Relations research area citing *What Do Unions Do?*

Source: ISI Web of Science, May 2015. Analyses and graphs with *Ucinet*.

The thickness of the tie binding authors indicates a larger number of articles involved. Examining the network displayed, different clusters can be observed that correspond to different networks involving several authors. It is worth noting that Freeman and Medoff themselves continued to produce several studies on labor unions and workers' voice that extend their earlier work. With economists such as David Card and Ed Lazear, they have published several articles that extend our knowledge on unions and their effects on workers, firms and labor markets. In particular, Freeman published several contributions on employee voice, especially two books: *What Workers Want* with Joel Rogers in 1999 and *What Workers Say* with Peter Boxall and Peter Haynes in 2007 (the latter is not listed in Figure 1.3).

Another group of scholars provide new insights on union activities and workplace experience. Research by Thomas Kochan, Harry Katz, and Robert B. MacKersie offer a general framework for analyzing industrial relations issues. They integrate the classical theories of industrial relations systems with the literature on strategy, structure, and decision making. They highlight the role played by the environment, institutional structures and history in the analysis of employment relations processes and outcomes. Their key premise is that choice and discretion on the part of labor, management and government can affect the structure and the processes of industrial relations systems. Likewise, several studies deal with the different managerial responses to unions and extend the analysis to non-economic considerations. Since the publication of Kochan et al.'s book *The Transformation of American Industrial Relations* in 1986, management scholars have argued for the superior performance of commitment systems, with a particular focus on the effect of human resource practices on firm performance (Huselid, 1995; Delaney and Huselid, 1996; and Ichniowski et al., 1997).

Another interesting research stream explores the effects of high-performance workplace practices on plant performance and worker outcomes. Scholars such as Eileen Appelbaum, Rosemary Batt, Fritz K. Pil, and John Paul MacDuffie, among others, investigate workplace practices by studying their effects on organizations and workers in US manufacturing. They published several articles referencing *What Do Unions Do?*, emphasizing that employee voice continues to be a pillar of the employment relations literature. Besides these studies in management and industrial relations, there is another set of scholars in labor economics working on the impact of unions without being in the same cluster as Freeman. Barry T. Hirsch and John T. Addison are labor economists working on the economic effects of unions with a distinctive effort to broaden the research by including a significant international component. John T. Addison published several articles on work councils in Germany with Claus Schnabel and Joachim Wagner (e.g., Addison and Schnabel, 1997; Addison et al., 2001, 2004).

Content analysis

One conclusion that can be drawn from citation and co-citation analysis is that the diversity of authors and research works that cite *What Do Unions Do?* confirms the book's relevance and impact for a large breadth of research fields. We can dig deeper into influence by examining the main issues covered by articles citing *What Do Unions Do?*. As the authors supply keywords, we can code and analyze the content of each article. We built a list of major keywords to analyze the content of each article, as suggested by Furrer et al. (2008). We make the reasonable assumption that keywords reflect the content of the paper, or at least the content that authors prefer to highlight. The grouping of keywords leads to 47 major keywords. The analysis of the frequency of major keywords among the 30 most cited papers referencing *What Do Unions Do?* indicates that 'wages (or earnings or compensation)' was the most frequent keyword, followed by 'performance', 'productivity', 'human resource management', 'strategy', and 'discrimination'. Figure 1.4 shows that the largest frequency of keywords revolves around financial dimensions (wages and profits), followed by productivity. Given the focus of Freeman and Medoff's work, it is not surprising that these topics received so much attention.

Figure 1.5 illustrates the proximity between keywords used by the top 40 articles that reference *What Do Unions Do?*; this reveals the strength of the connection between keywords. Greater proximity between keywords is evident when a larger number of articles use the keywords together. For example, the keywords 'performance' and 'strategy' are closer in the articles citing Freeman and Medoff (1984). A cluster may be observed, including issues related to 'human resource management', 'strategy', 'turnover', 'productivity', and 'performance'. This cluster focuses on Freeman and Medoff's work on firm performance. Another cluster centers around the keywords 'wage', 'earnings', 'inequalities', and 'discrimination'.

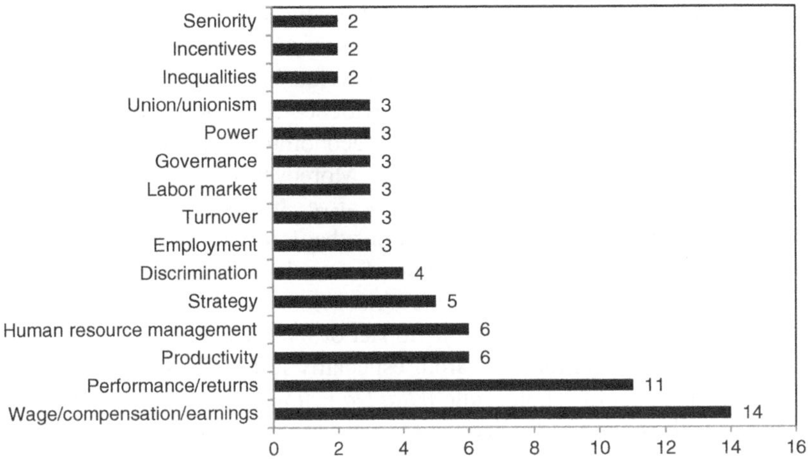

Figure 1.4 The top 15 most frequently used keywords of studies citing *What Do Unions Do?*

Note: Figures next to bars report the frequency count.

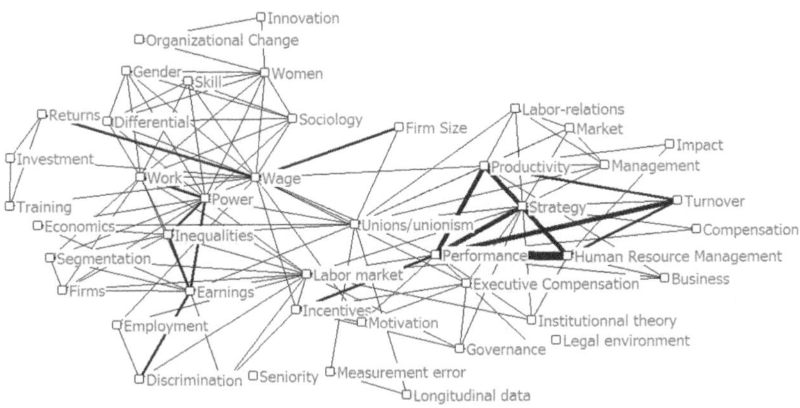

Figure 1.5 Frequency of major keywords among the 40 most cited articles referencing *What Do Unions Do?*

Source: ISI Web of Science, May 2015. Analyses and graphs with *Ucinet*.

Summary

This chapter describes some of Freeman and Medoff's contributions to social science research, specifically the influence of their book, *What Do Unions Do?*. The use of a bibliometric approach to examine citation patterns, the topics covered and the linkage between authors permits us to understand how the academic community received and used Freeman and Medoff's contributions. Freeman and Medoff's (1984) work on the economic effects of unionism offers new insights on the impact of unions on wages, job satisfaction, turnover, productivity, profits, and legal environment. The feature of the book is that it reviewed the quantitative evidence based on samples of thousands of individuals and establishments. The book has drawn an extraordinary amount of evidence concerning what unions do to wages and also on other economic and non-economic dimensions such as productivity and profits in the American context. Moreover, the general conclusion of the book is clearly controversial and provocative, at least, for those who consider unions to be merely monopoly institutions that interfere with labor markets. Freeman and Medoff challenged this view of unionism. They argue that union voice effects lead to net positive economic outcomes.

Our bibliometric study shows that the impact of *What Do Unions Do?* extends well beyond industrial relations research, especially into management research. A considerable diversity of scholars cite *What Do Unions Do?* for primarily one of four reasons: (1) the notion of 'collective voice' or 'employee voice', (2) a general reference to organizational performance, (3) union wage differentials, and (4) the controversial conclusion on the net positive effects of unions on productivity in the United States. A closer examination of the actual citation contexts revealed that some of these citations appear to have been mechanical with little effort to extend the work done, as if such citation in itself guaranteed authority. Having said this, it is interesting to note how the work of Freeman and Medoff (1984) has dispersed in the academic literature. For example, recent work on high-performance work practices has a growing impact in the management literature – as well as the industrial and labor relations literature – and this literature continues to cite intensely Freeman and Medoff. For instance, the most cited papers in the period 1980–2015 involve research dealing with the effects of workplace practices on organizational performance (MacDuffie, 1995; Ichniowski et al., 1996). Freeman and Medoff's (1984) book has had a significant impact on this stream of the management literature on high-performance work practices.

More generally, our study illustrates how a bibliometric approach enables scholars to learn more about the influence of seminal research. However, it should be noted that our bibliometric analysis does not distinguish the reason why a citation is made. Some authors may cite Freeman and Medoff (1984) in disagreement, whereas others may cite in agreement. In the analysis presented here, keywords were used as proxies for the article content. However, a more in-depth content analysis of the articles that cite Freeman and Medoff's book could shed additional light. Assessing the impact of any given work requires going beyond mere citation counts (Anderson, 2006; Golden-Biddle et al., 2006). The number of citations do not reveal how subsequent work has refined or extended the theory and analysis presented by Freeman and Medoff. Hence, extending our citations-based analysis to an exploration of the cited content could provide a richer understanding of the true contribution of this seminal work.

Freeman and Medoff's book has had enormous impact in labor economics and industrial relations. Their direct impact is evident in the number of citations to their work and also indirectly through citations of authors that reference their work. It is no exaggeration to say that *What Do Unions Do?* is now a 'classic' for anyone interested in labor unions. Freeman and Medoff's book continues to attract citations and future bibliometric research may reveal an even larger impact over time.

What Do Unions Do? represents a milestone in our understanding of trade unions and their impact on the economy. We hope that the ensuing chapters will assist other scholars to build upon and extend knowledge of this fundamental institution of employment relations.

In the following chapter, we discuss the meta-regression methodology.

Notes

1 This chapter was written by Doucouliagos and Laroche. Our high praise for *What Do Unions Do?* reflects our appreciation of Freeman and Medoff's scholarship.

2 We use the ISI Web of Science definition of Industrial and Labor Relations research area.

3 Data collected from ISI Web of Science, July 2015.

4 *What Do Unions Do?* is cited by scholars from 44 different countries. Of the 1,480 citations: 915 come from scholars from the United States, 202 from the United Kingdom, 147 from Canada, 78 from Australia, 69 from Germany, 25 from France, 18 from South Korea, 17 from Norway, and 17 from Italy.

5 See, for example, Dundon and Gollan (2007), Naus et al. (2007), and Klaas et al. (2012).

2 Research synthesis through meta-regression analysis

In this chapter we describe the meta-regression analysis used in this book.[1] Meta-regression analysis differs from traditional literature reviews – which are qualitative and narrative, and rely predominantly on the reviewers' subjective assessment (Stanley, 2001) – by offering a *quantitative* research synthesis. An extensive reference literature lays out the details of meta-analysis, including Rosenthal (1984), Hedges and Olkin (1985), Cook et al. (1992), Borenstein et al. (2009), Stanley and Doucouliagos (2012), and Schmidt and Hunter (2015), among others. Here we treat the basic issues of data collection, research synthesis, detection and correction of publication and mis-specification biases, and modeling of heterogeneity.

The form of meta-analysis most suited for economics is *meta-regression analysis*. The meta-regression model has been developed to analyze the multi-dimensional nature of the research process (Stanley and Jarrell, 1989; Stanley, 2001). One of the earliest and pioneering applications of meta-regression analysis in economics is Jarrell and Stanley (1990) on the union-nonunion wage gap. There are now hundreds of studies applying meta-regression analysis to a diverse range of economic issues. Stanley (2001), Doucouliagos and Stanley (2013), and Ioannidis et al. (2017), provide partial reviews of the growing list of meta-regression analysis applications in economics.

In this book we use meta-regression analysis to:

1 calculate meta-averages that summarize the evidence base,
2 correct the evidence base for publication selection bias and mis-specification bias, and
3 identify and seek to understand the sources of heterogeneity in reported union effects.

With meta-regression, all three aims can be achieved simultaneously.

Meta-regression analysis makes use of the extant evidence base of the *population* of *comparable* empirical studies on the economic impact of unions. This evidence allows us to comprehensively analyze the effect of unions on a particular outcome variable, such as productivity or profitability, and compare this association across industry, country, and time. The section "The core challenge of inference" explains the value of meta-regression analysis in statistical inference. The section "Collecting and coding meta-data" discusses the collection and coding of the meta-data. The section "Effect size" shows how to calculate effect sizes while the section "Meta-averages" shows the calculation of meta-averages. The section "Multiple meta-regression analysis" explains how multiple meta-regression analysis treats heterogeneity in estimates. The section "Summary" concludes.

The core challenge of inference

Empirical analysis begins with hypothesis formulation and data collection or exploration, and then proceeds to model construction to estimate what the data might teach us, and statistical analysis to make valid inference from the data. The existence of more and larger data sets, development of increasingly sophisticated nonparametric as well as parametric estimators available in accessible software packages such as R or Stata, and greater computing power to use these techniques on data have made the process easier than before. Researchers can now analyze data on laptops in a short time that would have been unimaginable to researchers studying the effects of unions using mainframes in the 1970s or 1980s. But there remain substantive problems in drawing causal inferences from the data due to endogeneity of key explanatory variables. Gold standard random assignment controlled experiments are near impossible to conduct in union research.

The post–Freeman and Medoff literature on unionism has produced a large growing number of estimates on the relation between unions and outcomes in an ever growing number of journals and other publication outlets. How can we draw valid inferences from the diverse studies?

Traditional reviews of any literature suffer from what Stanley (2001: 145) calls "casual methodological speculation" that relies on qualitative judgment of reviewers. Absence of a statistical method for weighing different estimates rules out formal hypothesis testing and makes traditional reviews prone to potential bias from the reviewers' personal perspective. Only a quantitative review can test a hypothesis or claim about what the empirical studies show in a scientifically rigorous manner. Just as scores are necessary to determine winners in athletic contests, some form of quantitative scoring is essential to determine what a large body of econometric studies truly finds and the winners in hypothesis contests.[2]

The quantitative way to score estimates from many studies is to apply meta-statistical analysis. Meta-analysis is used to "summarize, evaluate and analyze empirical economic research" (Stanley, 2001: 131). It turns the variation in estimates of key parameters or relations that arise from methodological and data differences into statistics that summarize the central tendency and variation across studies. It helps us understand the reasons for the variation in the reported effects of unions across studies. A key justification for meta-regression analysis is that it allows researchers to combine the results of numerous under-powered studies (Ioannidis et al., 2017) to obtain the statistical power necessary for reaching valid conclusions (Schmidt and Hunter, 2015).

A good traditional review can find parallels and differences among studies, place studies into historical perspective, and suggest new hypotheses to account for differences or similarities in results in ways that at least up until now computer algorithms cannot do. Meta-analysis can also achieve some of these tasks. Meta-regression analysis of large numbers of studies is arguably as necessary in assessing what a body of research has uncovered as statistical summary is necessary for each study to analyze its data.

Collecting and coding meta-data

The first step in any meta-regression analysis is to identify the relevant population or random sample of comparable studies. Our analysis focuses on published studies, excluding working papers and other unpublished studies and reports. To the extent that results presented in unpublished material, such as manuscripts and working papers, change when they reach their published form, they are less reliable than those in published material.

Including only published studies raises questions of whether publication suppresses part of the evidence base. Assume a study estimates that unions increase or decrease wages by 90%. The estimates are so huge as to raise questions about the empirical strategy or possible data errors in the analysis. Such a study is likely to receive an especially tough review and unlikely to be published. But it is more likely that researchers seeing such results would themselves review their statistics carefully and possibly decide that "something is wrong" even if they cannot identify it. Stanley and Doucouliagos (2012) note that in many cases publication bias is actually reporting bias, which can just as easily occur with working papers as with final journal publications. From this perspective, excluding unpublished studies from the data does not create selection bias in a meta-regression analysis.

A key issue in meta-regression analysis is the comparability of estimates across studies. It is standard practice in meta-regression analysis to include studies that use different measures of the dependent and independent variables. Union density rates, measures of collective bargaining coverage, and dichotomous dummy variables for unionism are alternate ways to measure union activity and union presence. In many cases, researchers have no choice in the measures and must use the data that is available. When researchers have a choice, they often explore alternatives and report results which are representative of their entire body of statistical results. But in other cases, they may report the results from particular models that fit their priors or that have exceptionally strong statistical significance.

Some of these problems – differences in the data used, in measuring variables, and in model construction – are in our view a strength of the research. They provide robustness tests of findings in a world in which random assignment controlled experiments is not possible so that things invariably differ, be it measures of variables, estimated effects from different plausible models, and most importantly, environmental context in which economic agents operate, be it industry, firm, or country. In social science, replication with the exact same data tests for differences in the computer code of researchers, possible differential treatment of outliers, or difference in the underlying algorithms that produce the statistics. But the only way to know if results generalize broadly is to evaluate many studies that differ in data, measures, models, sectors, firms, or countries. Just as biologists do not expect to find a given drug to have the exact same effect on people as on mice or on people with different genetics, social scientists studying unions do not expect to find the same estimated effect of unions in different countries. The critical research issue in meta-regression analysis is to quantify the differences among studies and differentiate how much they are due to differing research methodology as opposed to differences in the economic world.

The inputs for meta-regression analysis are estimates of union effects and information on the econometric specification, data, and estimator used to produce them, with study differences coded as *moderator* variables. All the meta-regressions we present adhere to the MAER-Net guidelines on conducting and reporting meta-analysis in economics (Stanley et al., 2013).

Effect size

Effect size measures the quantitative association between two variables, one treated as the effect of the other. Union studies report the relation between unions and outcomes in various ways – as regression coefficients often from log transformations of the outcome variable, as correlations, and so on – which must be put on the same scale for quantitative analysis. As most measures of association of variables are fairly simple transformations of each other, the decision of which measure to choose is largely a matter of convenience. In this book, we measure effect size in two ways: (1) the partial correlation coefficient and (2) the percentage union effect.

Partial correlation

The partial correlation is our main measure of association between unionization and outcome variables. The partial correlation measures the strength and direction of an association between two variables, holding all other variables constant. It provides us with a comparable measure of the effect of unions on an outcome variable – say, for concreteness, physical capital investment – holding constant other factors such as growth and firm size that might also affect that outcome.

As the studies that we review report regression coefficients, standard errors, *t*-statistics, or levels of statistical significance rather than partial correlations, we transform them into partial correlations. The algebra of statistics allows us to do that directly from the *t*-statistics, and where *t*-statistics are not reported, from the reported levels of statistical significance, or from reported regression coefficients and standard errors, per Stanley and Doucouliagos (2012).

The formula used to calculate partial correlations is, $t/\sqrt{(t^2 + df)}$ where t is the t-statistic and df is degrees of freedom. We also require the standard error of the partial correlation, SE. This can be calculated as $SE = \sqrt{(1 - r^2) / df}$.

Like zero order correlation coefficients, partial correlation coefficients are restricted to values between +1.00 and –1.00, which means that reported correlations will tend to have non-normal sampling distributions. Accordingly, many researchers prefer to convert correlation coefficients into their associated *z*-scores using the Fisher *z*-transformation (see Stanley and Doucouliagos, 2012). For our data sets, it does not matter substantively if partial correlation coefficients are used directly or if the *z*-transformation is applied.

We prefer partial correlations to simple correlations because they control for covariates and thus help identify the marginal impact of unions. There is also a practical reason for using partial correlations. Economics studies focus on multivariate regressions, and many studies in industrial relations and human resource management do not report simple correlations.

Percentage union effect

The percentage union effect measures the impact on performance due to unionization measured in percentage or the near-equivalent natural log (ln) differential units. In wage studies, it links studies of union wage effects to the ln wage curve that dominates labor economics. In productivity studies, it links studies of union productivity effects to the Cobb-Douglas production function that is the workhorse in productivity analysis. We calculate percentage union effects where the data is available. Because analysts in some disciplines do not normally report percentage effects, partial correlation gives us a much larger number of data points, and we focus largely on it.

Data dependence

We calculated the partial correlation coefficient between unionism and an outcome variable from each of the published studies in our data. Where studies report more than one set of results, we have a choice in summarizing the findings. We can calculate the average of all comparable estimates, often known as the 'Average-set'. Or we can use all comparable estimates, often known as the 'All-set'. Doucouliagos and Laroche (2003a and 2003b) used one estimate from each study, typically the author's preferred estimate or an average of all estimates. Meta-analysis in economics has evolved over time to use all comparable estimates, the All-set. We adopt this approach in this book.

The use of several estimates from a given study raises issues of data dependence, as such estimates are likely to be statistically related to each other. This can affect standard errors and inflate the level of statistical significance. To deal with this issue, we use cluster-adjusted standard errors, correcting for data dependence within studies (Stanley and Doucouliagos, 2012), and apply the wild bootstrap, which can give more accurate standard errors if the number of clusters (studies in our case) is small or if the number of estimates per study vary greatly (see Cameron et al., 2008; Gallet and Doucouliagos, 2014; McKinnon and Webb, 2015).[3]

Meta-averages

With a population of comparable estimates of union effects, meta-regression analysis combines all the estimates into a *meta-average* that summarizes what the evidence base has established. There are alternative ways to construct such averages, ranging from simple unweighted averages, weighted averages, and weighted averages that correct for various biases in the analysis. Conditional meta-averages can be derived by modeling heterogeneity in reported estimates. The meta-averages we use in this book are listed and described below.

The *unweighted average* averages all comparable effect sizes, or partial correlations (r) in our case, without allowance for differences in the estimated precision of effects or for any possible bias in the estimated effects. Estimation is through an OLS regression of the partial correlations on a constant. By treating all estimates the same, unweighted meta-averages can be unreliable for statistical inference.

Fixed-effect and random-effects weighted averages are more useful summary statistics. The *fixed-effect weighted average, FEE-WLS*, is estimated using weighted least squares (*WLS*) with the inverse variance of estimates as weights constructed from the partial correlation's estimated standard error (*SE*). The inverse of the standard error is an estimate of precision. The inverse of the squared standard error gives the individual weight assigned to each estimate, that is, $1 / (SE_i^2)$. Here we report estimates using these inverse variance weights. Another weighting scheme uses the number of observations in a sample as weights on the notion that an estimate of 1,000 observations is more important than one of 100 observations, so we also report estimates weighted by sample size.[4]

The *FEE-WLS* involves estimating the following regression:

$$r_i = \beta_0 + \varepsilon_i, \tag{2.1}$$

where β_0 is the estimated meta-average. Estimated without weights, OLS regression of Eqn (2.1) estimates the unweighted average. Estimated with inverse variance weights, OLS regression of Eqn (2.1) gives the *unrestricted FEE-WLS* (Stanley and Doucouliagos, 2015)[5] estimate of a single average effect size. If, however, there is heterogeneity in union effects, the appropriate model to deal with heterogeneity is the multiple MRA described in the section below titled "Multiple meta-regression analysis".

The main rival to the *FEE-WLS* model is the *random-effects weighted average, REE-WLS*, estimated typically by *REML*.[6] The *REE-WLS* uses weights that treat between-study heterogeneity as well as individual study estimation error. It is a popular estimator, especially in medical research, but can lead to biased estimates of the meta-average. Stanley and Doucouliagos (2015 and 2016) show that the unrestricted *FEE-WLS* estimator has better coverage probabilities and is preferable in situations of heterogeneity, which is present in studies of unions, and when estimates are subject to publication bias which cannot be ruled out a priori.[7] Hence, while we report estimates of *REE-WLS* for the sake of completeness, we rely on unrestricted *FEE-WLS* for making inferences.[8]

Publication selection bias corrected weighted average

Publication selection bias occurs when authors selectively report estimates using criteria that are unrelated to methodological and scientific considerations, such as preferential reporting of estimates that are statistically significant or that conform to the researcher's priors or expectations. A researcher with a prior expectation that unions decrease productivity may report results from model specifications that show statistically significant adverse productivity effects while finding some reason to discard models that are inconsistent with such priors. Similarly, a researcher who believes that research producing statistically significant results is more likely to be published might choose to report results from specifications that produced statistical significance rather than equally plausible specifications that yielded statistically insignificant results.

A fruitful way to detect and adjust meta-analysis for publication selection bias is to conduct an 'Egger-type' meta-regression test of whether the distribution of reported estimates is symmetrical (Egger et al., 1997; Stanley, 2008; Stanley and Doucouliagos, 2012). Visually this can be seen in a funnel plot that illustrates the association between an effect size and its estimated precision. Research studies free of publication selection bias will tend to have a symmetric funnel plot, with estimated effect sizes randomly distributed around the 'true' effect and where the range around the effect shrinks with larger sample sizes. Pronounced gaps in the distribution, for example, one side of the distribution is missing are a warning sign of publication selection bias (Stanley and Doucouliagos, 2012; Doucouliagos and Stanley, 2013). We present funnel plots in the individual chapters.

In economics, the most commonly used Egger-type regression is the *FAT-PET* (Stanley, 2005 and 2008). This involves a simple WLS regression of an estimated effect on a constant and its standard error:

$$r_{ij} = \beta_0 + \beta_1 SE_{ij} + \varepsilon_{ij}, \tag{2.2}$$

where r_{ij} is the ith estimated partial correlation from the jth study, SE_{ij} is its standard error, and ε_{ij} is the sampling (or estimation) error. The reported effect sizes will be positively correlated with their standard errors if there is publication selection bias, which can be found through the 'funnel-asymmetry test' (*FAT*) (Stanley, 2008), a test of whether estimates are or are not evenly distributed around the average at different standard errors. Given some selection bias, the existence of a genuine empirical effect beyond publication selection bias can be tested via the precision-effect test (*PET*) (Stanley, 2008), which tests for the existence of real effects corrected for any asymmetry in the distribution of reported estimates. The *FAT* involves testing $\beta_1 = 0$, while the *PET* involves testing $\beta_0 = 0$. Hence, Eqn. (2.2) provides a framework for investigating the existence of publication selection bias and for correcting the evidence base for the effects of publication selection and then identifying the existence of a genuine empirical effect (Stanley, 2008; Stanley and Doucouliagos, 2012).

When the *FAT* test on β_1 shows the existence of publication bias, via the relation of the estimated partial correlations with their standard errors, and the *PET* test on β_0 shows a genuine non-zero partial correlation, there is still a problem in estimating the genuine effect linking the variables. Stanley (2008) shows that the Eqn. (2.2) meta-regression provides a biased estimate of the underlying genuine effect reflected in the mean of the distribution of partial correlations because publication bias means that some correlation coefficients from the true distribution are "missing" in the reported data set and publication bias is likely to be a more complex function of the standard error than the linear process suggested by Eqn. (2.2). Stanley and Doucouliagos (2012, 2014) show through simulations that replacing *SE* with SE_i^2, in MRA model Eqn. (2.2) will often give a better estimate of the size of the genuine effect, corrected for publication bias:

$$r_{ij} = \gamma_0 + \gamma_1 SE_{ij}^2 + v_{ij}. \tag{2.3}$$

Eqn. (2.3) provides the best Taylor polynomial approximation to the expected value of a truncated distribution, called Precision-Effect Estimate with Standard Error (*PEESE*) (Stanley and Doucouliagos, 2012; 2014). Stanley and Doucouliagos (2012; 2014) recommend the *FAT-PET-PEESE* methodology that involves initially estimating the *FAT-PET*. If there is evidence of a genuine empirical effect beyond publication bias, they recommend that researchers estimate *PEESE* to derive a more accurate estimate of the underlying empirical effect.

Eqns. (2.2) and (2.3) are estimated using unrestricted WLS because the error terms (ε_{ij} and v_{ij}) will be heteroscedastic rather than independently and identically distributed (see Stanley and Doucouliagos, 2012).

Multiple meta-regression analysis

Empirical studies use specifications that introduce different control variables, use data at different levels of aggregation, time periods, industries and countries, and statistical estimators from different regression or other statistical packages. Meta-regression analysis takes the findings of regression analyses from the existing pool of studies and uses regression models to model heterogeneity among the studies and to detect whether these study characteristics are associated in any way with the estimated study outcomes. This enables a quantitative assessment of the impact of differences in research design, methodology, data, and estimation on reported study outcomes; this is not possible in a traditional narrative and qualitative literature review.

We use meta-regression analysis to identify moderator variables and to explore the impact of specification on the estimated union effects. We are, however, also interested in deriving conditional estimates of the effect of unions. The advantage of meta-regression analysis is its multivariate context. Meta-regression analysis allows researchers to identify, for example, the association between data aggregation (e.g., firm- versus industry-level data) and estimated union-performance effects, while controlling for other study characteristics, such as whether estimates correct for endogeneity. Meta-regression analysis offers a rich framework through which an existing body of empirical literature can be reviewed.

The basic multiple meta-regression equation takes the following form:

$$r_{ij} = \mathbf{x}'_{ij}\beta + u_{ij}, \tag{2.4}$$

where r_{ij} is again the ith partial correlation from the jth study, $\mathbf{x}_{ij}$ is a vector of explanatory (also known as moderator) variables, β is the vector of parameters to be estimated, and u_{ij} is the error term. The preferred estimator is again unrestricted WLS (Stanley and Doucouliagos, 2016). Eqn. (2.4) quantifies the effect of differences in data, specification, measurement, and estimator, on reported union effects. Some of these differences are due to economic factors, such as differences between countries and over time, while others are due to research design, such as differences in the econometric specification. The elements of the $\mathbf{x}$ vector will vary according to the union effect under investigation. Details of the moderators used are provided in the subsequent individual chapters.

Model reduction

A common problem in meta-regression analysis is that there is often a very large list of potential moderator variables that can be included in the meta-regression model. This can be an issue in cases where there are a relatively small number of observations. There is little guidance in the field as to the specification of the meta-regression model. Our approach is to choose the variables that theory and econometric practice suggests may be important moderating factors and for which there is sufficient variation in the research design and data used. The individual chapters discuss the chosen models.

We commence with general models that include all the moderator variables and then proceed to reduce these models, following a general-to-specific modelling strategy (see Stanley and Doucouliagos, 2012). The reason for this model reduction is to gain greater clarity in the underlying relationships. Model reduction is carried out in two ways: (1) sequentially removing moderator variables that are statistically insignificant, and (2) removing groups of variables. We use Wald tests to validate the meta-regression model reductions. Both approaches lead to the same specific meta-regression models. The individual chapters report both general and specific models.

Summary

Meta-regression offers a scientific basis for reviewing the evidence base of union effects or other claimed relations between variables. It involves a search for comparable studies, the coding of estimates and research dimensions, calculation of meta-averages, detection and correction for publication bias, and analysis of heterogeneity. These are by now well established in the field, and our methodology follows current best practice.

In the following chapter we apply meta-regression analysis to investigate the impact of unions on productivity levels.

Notes

1 Parts of this chapter borrow heavily from the various studies we have co-authored over the years, especially Doucouliagos and Laroche (2003a), Doucouliagos et al. (2005), and Stanley and Doucouliagos (2012).

2 However, even this may prove to be insufficient to eliminate subjectivity. For example, meta-analysis can also be prone to subjective choices and biases; see the discussion in Doucouliagos et al. (2012) on the value of a statistical life literature as one example.

3 Doucouliagos and Laroche (2009) use an alternative multi-level model strategy to accommodate data dependence.

4 Other weights can be used, such as journal impact factors or some other weight for study quality differences.

5 This is different to more conventional fixed-effect estimates that produce identical averages but with more narrow confidence intervals; see Stanley and Doucouliagos (2015; 2016) for details.

6 This is the approach taken, for example, in Stata's **metareg** routine. However, as we will nearly always need to adjust standard errors for data dependence, we estimate the *REE-WLS* model directly rather than through canned routines; **metareg** does not adjust standard errors for data dependence.

7 Doucouliagos and Stanley (2013) argue that wherever theoretical contests exist, then publication selection bias is less likely. Given the intense debates between neoclassical economists and economists supporting the CV/IR theory, then we would expect to find relatively little publication bias in this literature. Nevertheless, as the individual chapters will show, there is some publication selection bias in the union effects literature.

8 Note that the terms fixed- and random-effects in meta-analysis relate to the weights used for the calculation of the meta-averages and thus have a different meaning than the same terms in panel data analysis. However, fixed-effects and random-effects panel estimation can also be used in meta-regression analysis when studies report more than one estimate (Stanley and Doucouliagos, 2012).

3 Unions and productivity

Direct estimates

> What effect do differences in the material conditions and social relations of production associated with trade unions have on the productivity of otherwise-comparable workers utilizing the same amount of capital?
>
> (Brown and Medoff, 1978: 356–7)

This and the next three chapters apply meta-regression analysis to evaluate the impact of unions on productivity. This chapter examines direct estimates of the effects of unions on productivity. The direct estimates of the effects of unions on productivity growth are examined in Chapter 4. Chapters 5 and 6 drill further to identify some important investment (physical and intangible capital) and behavioral channels (labor turnover, job satisfaction, and organizational commitment), through which unions impact productivity.

Researchers have studied union productivity effects in a variety of industries, predominantly manufacturing, construction, mining, and education. Most studies use data from the United States and to a lesser degree the United Kingdom. Some studies give positive estimates. Some give negative estimates. And others show no significant effects. To make sense of the disparate studies requires careful quantitative assessment of measures, specifications, methods, and samples. Do results differ because of researcher decisions about modelling and data that create the appearance of heterogeneity in a world that truly has a single union effect? Or do results differ because in reality unions have different effects on productivity in different circumstances? No one with knowledge of the differences among industries, unions, and companies, much less countries, expects a single union effect for every industry, country, or time period. But how much of the heterogeneity among reported union effects findings is due to real differences as opposed to the artifact of studies?

This chapter investigates this question using the tools of meta-regression analysis summarized in the preceding chapter. The chapter updates and re-estimates Doucouliagos and Laroche (2003a) to assess the estimated effects of unions on the *level of labor productivity* at a point in time. We quantify the average effect of unions on productivity and explore the causes of heterogeneity in the reported estimates.

Unions and productivity levels

In traditional (neoclassical) economic analysis, unions distort labor market outcomes through their using monopoly power to raise wages and benefits above competitive market levels. They also limit management control of employment practices by introducing rules such as seniority in hiring and firing and establishing grievance and arbitration systems to resolve disagreements between management and workers. The traditional story also claims that unions contribute to unemployment and the associated output losses.[1] In contrast to these arguments, Freeman (1976) and Freeman and Medoff (1984), among others, argue that unions can raise productivity by providing workers with a means of expressing discontent as an alternative to 'exiting', by opening up communication channels between workers and management, and by inducing managers to alter methods of production and adopt policies that improve efficiency. These non-wage effects have the potential to offset efficiency losses arising from unionization.

In their assessment of the extant evidence for the United States of 16 estimated productivity effects from eight studies, Freeman and Medoff (1984) concluded that unions have a positive effect on productivity. The meta-analysis by Doucouliagos and Laroche (2003a) using a larger data base, by contrast, found an overall zero union effect, with a negative association between unions and productivity in the United Kingdom balancing a positive association for manufacturing in the United States. Doucouliagos et al.'s (2005) meta-analysis, which focused on publication selection bias, confirms the absence of any union effect on productivity on average.

Using an updated and larger data set in this chapter, we conclude that the impact on productivity varies by country and industry. For manufacturing, we find no effect for the United States, confirm the finding of an adverse effect for the United Kingdom, and find a positive effect for developing countries. In the case of other industries, we find positive productivity effects for construction, mining, and education. Taken together, the different industry and country effects yield a zero productivity effect overall.

Theory review

To begin, we review briefly the main theoretical arguments on the impact of unions on productivity (see Addison, 1982 and 1985; Addison and Barnett, 1982; Freeman and Medoff, 1984; Kuhn, 1985; Hirsch and Addison, 1986; Turnbull, 1991; and Belman, 1992, among others). As is often the case in economics, the theory recognizes potential positive or negative effects but is ambiguous about which dominates in the world. The key theoretical contribution of *What Do Unions Do?* was to develop a conceptual framework that encompasses the broad range of possibilities via the so-called two faces view of unionism (Freeman and Medoff, 1984): the traditional *monopoly face* and the *collective voice/institutional response face*.

The monopoly face of unionism refers to adverse wage and non-wage effects associated with monopoly distortions of otherwise perfectly functioning firms or markets. One of the most well established effects of unions is their ability to increase wages above competitive levels (Lewis, 1963) – a finding corroborated by Jarrell and Stanley's (1990) meta-analysis of the union–non-union wage gap, as we elaborate later in Chapter 7. Similarly, union rent seeking acts as a tax on the return on investment, which reduces R&D spending and tangible and intangible investments, and innovation (Connolly et al., 1986; and Hirsch and Link, 1987), with a detrimental impact on the dynamic path of productivity.

Unions can also adversely impact productivity by restricting managerial discretion in allocating labor. For example, unions may force firms to adopt inefficient personnel hiring and firing practices, closed-shop arrangements, impose restrictive work practices, or limit layoffs and thus raise employment above the optimal level. They may obstruct the introduction of new technology (McKersie and Klein, 1983). Strike activity and non-cooperative behavior can also reduce productivity (Flaherty, 1987).[2]

The other dimension of unions is the collective voice and institutional response face (CV/IR) emphasized by Freeman and Medoff (1984). The CV/IR model draws on Hirschman's (1970) exit-voice dichotomy. In this framework, "voluntary quits become the labor market expression of exit and unions become the institution for the expression of (collective) voice" (Turnbull, 1991: 137). By providing workers with a means of expressing discontent at the workplace, unions can reduce excessive quits and absenteeism. By representing workers' collective preferences to management, unions give workers an alternative to resignation or apathy. This channel is important because excessive labor turnover can reduce workplace productivity through a direct loss of firm-specific training as well as reduced worker effort (Freeman, 1976; Addison and Barnett, 1982).

Opening of communication channels between management and workers can result in integrative rather than distributive bargaining (Dworkin and Ahlburg, 1985). By providing information to a firm about the collective preferences of employees, unions can enable the firm to choose a better mix among working conditions, workplace rules, and employee remuneration. This can produce a more satisfied, cooperative, and productive workforce. There may also exist important public goods in the workplace, such as workplace safety. By providing voice, unions may invest in such public goods to the benefit of the organization. But as with any public good, the incentives to free ride may lead to relatively little union investment in public goods (Olson, 1965).

The older industrial relations literature stressed that unions could induce a 'shock effect' that lead managers to alter production methods and adopt more efficient personnel policies (Slichter et al., 1960). Union activities could also improve worker morale and motivation by reducing the potentially arbitrary nature of decisions regarding promotions or layoffs with seniority rules that require management to give preference to more senior workers among those with equal competency. Employees were more likely to perceive their employer as fair when it had a rule-based system for assignments or promotions than when it allowed supervisors to choose favorites among workers, which would raise morale and motivation and productivity (Leibenstein, 1966). Union seniority rules were expected to spur workers to try harder and to make older workers more willing to accept efficient changes in workplace operations (Rees, 1962). The CV/IR model operates in the context where employers imperfectly monitor employees' behavior and where opportunistic managers may make decisions that benefit them personally but not in the firm's interest. If a bottle of whiskey 'gift' leads a supervisor to promote A instead of B, restricting managers' discretion has the potential to improve the firm's performance.

The increase in wages associated with unionism should also affect productivity. Higher wages should induce the firm to substitute capital for labor, raising the capital-to-labor ratio and increasing labor productivity but reducing allocative inefficiency and raising total production costs. Going beyond the simple substitution story, the CV/IR framework "may be interpreted as a hypothesis that internal organization matters, and as an extension of modern organization theory which abandons the standard textbook neoclassical economic perception of the firm as a machine" (Addison and Barnett, 1982: 147).

The two faces of unions are not incompatible. As Hirsch (1997: 37) notes, "The monopoly and collective voice faces of unionism operate side-by-side, with the importance of each being very much determined by the legal and economic environment in which unions and firms operate. For these reasons, an assessment of union's effects on economic performance hinges on empirical evidence".

Empirical evidence, empirical evidence, my kingdom for evidence.

Studies on unionization and productivity

Most econometric studies of union impacts on productivity estimate a reduced form production function of the following generic form:

$$\ln(Y/L)_i = \beta_0 + \beta_k \ln(K/L)_i + \beta_u U_i + \boldsymbol{\gamma}'\mathbf{Z}_i + \varepsilon_i, \tag{3.1}$$

where Y is a measure of output, L and K are measures of labor and capital input, U is a measure of unionization, β_u is the key coefficient of interest, and **Z** is a vector of other variables. Several studies estimate a version of the Brown and Medoff (1978) model:

$$\ln(Y/L)_i \cong \ln A + \alpha \ln(K/L)_i + (\alpha + \beta - 1)\ln L_i + \beta(c-1)P_i + \varepsilon_i, \tag{3.2}$$

where P is the ratio of unionized to non-unionized labor. Equations (3.1) and (3.2) extend readily to panel data with fixed effects or (rarely done) random effects.

Most studies choose the Cobb-Douglas specification, though several estimate the Translog version. Some studies allow the elasticity of output with respect to capital to vary between union and non-union firms. Others allow for interactions between U and other variables. The variables in the **Z** vector can affect estimated union effects significantly. If higher wages due to unions induce firms to substitute skilled labor for unskilled labor and capital for labor, it is important to control for labor quality and capital intensity, so it is important to assess how a study treats these variables.[3]

Going outside the production function framework, the potential effect of productivity on whether or not a firm is unionized requires careful investigation. Unions might find it advantageous to organize more productive firms and sectors. Alternatively, unions may be more effective in unionizing poorly managed or struggling firms as DiNardo and Lee (2004) note. Moreover, if a money measure of output – the value of production or sales – is improperly deflated to reflect real output, the estimate of output can be distorted by price effects originating from higher unionized wages. Although the endogeneity of inputs muddies interpretation of almost all production function analysis, the vast majority of the econometric estimates do not address the issue. Following Doucouliagos and Laroche (2003a), we take a conservative approach in interpreting meta-analysis estimates of the 'effect' of unions as reflecting association within a production function framework rather than causation. In the multiple MRA we test whether results from the few studies that address endogeneity give results that differ from other studies.

Compilation of data

The starting point for meta-regression analysis is the compilation of published econometric studies of the relationship between unions and productivity. Doucouliagos and Laroche (2003a) identified 73 studies for their meta-analysis, which Doucouliagos et al. (2005) extended to 77 studies. For this book, we did an extensive computer and manual search for studies in English or French in a number of databases[4], in references lists and individual and institutional webpages between January 2015 and June 2015. Keywords in the search included 'unions', 'collective bargaining', 'productivity', 'productivity growth', 'growth', 'performance', 'production function', 'two faces of unionism', as well as 'What do unions do?' and 'Freeman and Medoff'. We also searched industry classifications such as 'mining', 'manufacturing', 'construction', and 'education'. Our search turned up 111 econometric studies with a total sample size of 293,016. The construction of our data and reporting of results conforms closely to the reporting guidelines by Stanley et al. (2013) that are designed to regularize and codify meta-analysis.

We entered into our evidence base studies that estimate the association between unions and productivity, with productivity as the dependent variable and unionism as one of a set of explanatory variables. We excluded studies that were (a) unpublished; (b) did not provide information from which to calculate effect sizes; (c) focused on the relation between corporatist economic policies and economic performance without estimates relating to unionization; (d) estimated the association between labor relations climate and productivity through strike activities, grievances procedures, and Quality of Working Life; (e) used managers' perceptions of performance; (f) relate solely to works councils; and (g) estimated union interaction terms from which we could not derive the total union productivity effect[5]; and (h) analyzed the union relation to productivity *growth* effect rather than to the level of productivity (productivity growth effects are analyzed in Chapter 4).

Effect size

We calculated the partial correlation coefficient for all the published estimates in our data and collected information on the percentage union-productivity effect from many studies. We place greater weight on the partial correlation measure of the union-productivity effect, because some studies focused on statistical significance (e.g., *t*-statistics) rather than economic impact (percentage impact on productivity), giving more reliable information on the former. Also, many studies include unions as a control variable and did not report the percentage differential nor provide sufficiently clear information from which to calculate it. As noted in Chapter 2, analyzing partial correlations facilitates comparisons with other meta-analysis of workplace interventions and performance.

Most studies in our data set report more than one set of results. As noted in Chapter 2, we can construct two types of estimates from these reports: an average of comparable estimates, so that each study contributes one averaged estimate (the 'Average' data set); and all comparable estimates; this is the larger, 'All' data set. Given current practice in meta-analysis, we focus on the results from the All-set.

Influential observations

It is necessary to eliminate influential outlier observations from the data. Such observations are typically the result of reporting and coding errors and can potentially distort MRA coefficients. We identify influential observations by examining standardized residuals. We do this by first estimating a *FAT-PET* (i.e., funnel-asymmetry test and precision-effect test; see Stanley and Doucouliagos, 2012) meta-regression, as discussed in Chapter 2:

$$r_{ij} = \beta_0 + \beta_1 SE_{ij} + \varepsilon_{ij}, \tag{2.2}$$

where r_{ij} is the ith estimate of the partial correlation reported in the jth study, SE_{ij} is its corresponding standard error, and ε_{ij} is the error term. After estimating Eqn. (2.2), we identified outlier observations as those that had a meta-regression standardized residual greater than 3.5. This process identifies eight influential observations, i.e., 1 percent of the data.[6] We remove these from subsequent analysis, leaving a total 710 observations for the MRA.

The 111 studies from which we obtained the 710 observations are listed in alphabetical order in Table 3.1, together with the country to which the data relate, the sample size, the median *t*-statistic, and the median partial correlation coefficient (r). The table shows a wide range of results, with 60 percent (428 of the 710) giving a positive association and 40 percent (282) a negative association.

Table 3.1 Econometric studies of unions and productivity levels

Author(s)	*Country*	*N*	*Median t-statistic*	*Median r*	*Author(s)*	*Country*	*N*	*Median t-statistic*	*Median r*
					North America				
Allen (1984)	US	81	3.11	0.36	Allen (1985)	US	102	1.53	0.24
Allen (1986a)	US	44	1.15	0.20	Allen (1986b)	US	151	1.44	0.18
Allen (1988a)	US	387	2.50	0.23	Allen (1988b)	US	42	2.77	0.48
Argys & Rees (1995)	US	3169	1.60	0.03	Arthur (1994)	US	30	–2.24	–0.41
Baldwin (1992)	Canada	167	–1.70	–0.14	Bartel (1994)	US	155	1.95	0.16
Batt (1999)	US	202	–0.57	–0.04	Black & Lynch (1996)	US	1346	0.85	0.04
Black & Lynch (2001)	US	638	–0.21	–0.01	Boal (1990)	US	249	0.09	0.01
Bronars et al. (1994)	US	960	0.17	0.01	Brown & Medoff (1978)	US	341	3.62	0.20
Byrne et al. (1996)	US	128	–1.51	–0.15	Byrnes et al. (1988)	US	197	2.52	0.25
Cavalluzzo & Baldwin (1993)	US	83	2.27	0.26	Caves & Barton (1990)	US	268	–1.54	–0.10
Chezum & Garen (1998)	US	8152	–1.74	–0.02	Chintrakarn & Chen (2011)	US	672	–1.51	–0.06

Author(s)	*Country*	*N*	*Median t-statistic*	*Median r*	*Author(s)*	*Country*	*N*	*Median t-statistic*	*Median r*
Clark (1980a)	US	104	1.60	0.16	Clark (1980b)	US	465	1.61	0.16
Clark (1984)	US	4681	–2.00	–0.03	Conte & Svejnar (1988 & 1990)	US	155	2.07	0.17
Cooke (1994)	US	841	2.59	0.09	Craig & Pencavel (1995)	US	170	0.25	0.02
Datta et al. (2005)	US	118	–1.98	–0.19	DiNardo & Lee (2004)	US	28785	–0.53	–0.01
Eberts (1984)	US	3251	2.19	0.04	Edwards & Field-Hendrey (1996)	US	96	1.18	0.13
Ehrenberg et al. (1983)	US	256	0.30	0.02	Freeman (1988)	US	650	3.57	0.04
Gittell et al. (2004)	US	489	1.86	0.09	Graddy & Hall (1985)	US	60	–1.47	–0.19
Grimes & Register (1990)	US	1626	3.63	0.09	Grimes & Register (1991)	US	2062	2.26	0.05
Hirsch (1990a)	US	3146	–9.08	–0.17	Hirsch (1991a)	US	6248	–2.53	–0.10
Hosios & Siow (2004)	Canada	658	0.02	0.01	Huselid (1995)	US	855	1.00	0.04

(continued)

Table 3.1 Econometric studies of unions and productivity levels (*continued*)

Author(s)	*Country*	*N*	*Median t-statistic*	*Median r*	*Author(s)*	*Country*	*N*	*Median t-statistic*	*Median r*
Ichniowski *et* al. (1997)	US	2190	–1.11	–0.02	Katz et al. (1987)	US	33	1.45	0.26
Kaufman & Kaufman (1987)	US	37	–0.50	–0.09	Kim et al. (2010)	Various	106	1.98	0.20
Kleiner & Petree (1988)	US	490	2.43	0.12	Koch & McGrath (1996)	USA	319	0.70	0.04
Kurth (1987)	US	50	–3.19	–0.46	Lovell et al. (1988)	USA	26	–2.49	–0.48
Maki (1983)	Canada	183	2.13	0.16	Maki & Meredith (1986)	Canada	220	0.89	0.06
Mefford (1986)	US	126	2.24	0.21	Milkman (1997)	US	2684	2.58	0.05
Mitchell et al. (1990)	US	886	1.77	0.09	Mitchell & Stone (1992)	US	83	–2.64	–0.30
Moshiri & Simpson (2011)	Canada	21598	10.00	0.07	Nelson & Gould (1988)	US	46	1.49	0.24
Noam (1983)	US	1100	0.34	0.01	Pantuosco & Ullrich (2010)	US	96	–2.16	–0.28
Peltzman (1993)	US	50	0.40	0.05	Peltzman (1996)	US	50	–1.90	–0.29

Author(s)	*Country*	*N*	*Median t-statistic*	*Median r*	*Author(s)*	*Country*	*N*	*Median t-statistic*	*Median r*
Register (1988)	US	389	3.31	0.23	Register & Grimes (1991)	US	1229	2.01	0.06
Schuster (1983)	US	474	1.56	0.25	Steelman et al. (2000)	US	50	3.90	0.50
Warren (1985)	US	26	–3.12	–0.56	Wilson (1995)	US	237	0.51	0.07
Zigarelli (1994)	US	532	5.43	0.24					
United Kingdom									
Caves (1980)	UK/US	47	–1.59	–0.25	Conyon & Freeman (2002)	UK	942	–0.70	–0.03
Davies & Caves (1987)	UK/US	168	–1.50	–0.17	Dickerson et al. (1997)	UK	98	0.53	0.06
Kersley *et al.* (2006)	UK	429	–1.04	–0.07	Machin (1991)	UK	208	–0.53	–0.04
Monastiriotis (2007)	UK	180	0.79	0.07	Pencavel (1977)	UK	56	–3.71	–0.46
Robinson & Wilson (2006)	UK	372	–2.38	–0.13	Wilson & Cable (1991)	UK	260	–2.04	–0.13
Continental Europe									
Coutrot (1996)	France	4289	2.44	0.05	Damiani & Ricci (2011)	Italy	23058	8.67	0.06

(continued)

Table 3.1 Econometric studies of unions and productivity levels (*continued*)

Author(s)	*Country*	*N*	*Median t-statistic*	*Median r*	*Author(s)*	*Country*	*N*	*Median t-statistic*	*Median r*
Doucouliagos & Laroche (2007)	France	1486	–5.12	–0.13	Fairris & Askenazy (2010)	France	1008	–0.98	–0.04
Fitzroy & Kraft (1987)	Germany	123	2.80	0.26	Hübler & Jirjahn (2003)	Germany	816	–2.12	–0.08
Jirjahn & Muellery (2014)	Germany	20276	–1.22	–0.01	Kleiner & Ay (1996)	Sweden & OECD	406	–0.02	–0.07
Laroche (2004)	France	1275	0.67	0.02	Lucifora & Origo (2015)	Italy	27555	–0.78	–0.01
Wolf & Zwick (2008)	Germany	2778	1.87	0.04	Zwick (2004)	Germany	2085	0.94	0.03
Zwick (2006)	Germany	2090	4.33	0.10					
				Australasia, Japan, and Korea					
Brunello (1992)	Japan	979	0.27	0.01	Guthrie (2001)	New Zealand	136	1.04	0.09
Kleiner & Lee (1997)	Korea	184	–0.13	–0.01	Lee & Rhee (1996)	Korea	144	–2.33	–0.20
Morishima (1991)	Japan	69	1.00	0.13	Moriwaka (2010)	Japan	27431	6.24	0.09
Muramatsu (1984)	Japan	515	2.26	0.14	Tachibanaki & Noda (2000)	Japan	1616	–1.88	–0.05

Author(s)	*Country*	*N*	*Median t-statistic*	*Median r*	*Author(s)*	*Country*	*N*	*Median t-statistic*	*Median r*
Torii (1992)	Japan	124	–0.14	–0.01	Valadkhani (2003)	Australia	32	–2.05	–0.40
				Developing countries					
Anwar & Sun (2015)	China	40752	3.68	0.07	Budd *et al.* (2014)	China	406	3.66	0.19
Cassoni *et al.* (2005)	Uruguay	4849	2.39	0.04	Fairris (2006)	Mexico	10149	2.82	0.04
Lu *et al.* (2010)	China	2628	4.16	0.08	Menezes-Filho *et al.* (2005)	Brazil	2529	–2.28	–0.05
Saavedra & Torero (2005)	Peru	1030	0.07	0	Standing (1992)	Malaysia	2597	4.51	0.09
Urízar & Lée (2005)	Guatemala	316	–2.08	–0.17					

Notes: Calculated by the authors from the primary econometric studies. The table reports medians for all comparable estimates, combining estimates from various measures of unionization and productivity. N denotes total sample size used in the study; *r* denotes partial correlation.

The next two tables give the distribution of the number of estimates by country (Table 3.2) and by industry (Table 3.3). These tables also report the simple unweighted average of estimates and the fixed-effect (*FEE-WLS*) weighted average, estimated using unrestricted WLS. As these are unconditional averages with no corrections for publication bias, we use them as baseline estimates. Most studies (65 percent) are of the United States, and nearly half relate to manufacturing (46 percent). Relatively little is known about the impact of unions for most countries. There is, however, an emerging literature on the impact of developing countries which we explore in the meta-regressions.

The unconditional averages in Table 3.2 suggest that overall, unions have a small positive effect on productivity when all estimates are combined; see Column (3), with clear country differences. The weighted average partial correlation is zero for the United States, Germany, and Italy and France combined, negative for the United Kingdom, and positive for Canada, Japan, and developing countries. The averages in Table 3.3 suggest no effect for manufacturing in the United States but a small positive effect in manufacturing elsewhere. Unionization has a positive correlation in non-manufacturing industries in the

Table 3.2 Number of estimates and meta-average by country

	Number of estimates (studies) (1)	*Simple unweighted average (2)*	*FEE-WLS weighted average (3)*
All countries	710 (111)	0.049*** (3.01)	0.016* (1.76)
US	458 (62)	0.078*** (3.58)	0.003 (0.52)
UK	65 (10)	–0.102*** (–4.03)	–0.066*** (–3.79)
Germany	27 (6)	0.059 (1.55)	0.013 (0.70)
Japan	22 (6)	0.086** (3.47)	0.076*** (11.87)
Italy & France	23 (6)	–0.040 (–0.90)	0.009 (0.33)
Canada	21 (5)	0.090 (2.13)	0.072*** (18.99)
Developing	82 (9)	0.014 (0.71)	0.020*** (3.61)
Other	10 (6)	–0.064 (–0.68)	0.016 (0.35)

Notes: Column 1 reports the number of estimates and the number of studies for each country (in brackets). Column 2 reports the simple unweighted meta-average for each country. Column 3 reports the fixed-effect (*FEE-WLS*) weighted average using inverse variance weights (unrestricted WLS). Figures in brackets in columns (2) and (3) are *t*-statistics using standard errors adjusted for within study clustering. *Developing* includes China, Brazil, Guatemala, Malaysia, Mexico, Peru, and Uruguay. *Other* includes Australia, Korea, New Zealand, Sweden, and studies that pool estimates from several countries.

***, **, and * denote statistical significance at the 1%, 5%, and 10% levels, respectively.

Table 3.3 Number of estimates and meta-average by industry

	Number of estimates (studies) (1)	*Simple unweighted average (2)*	*FEE-WLS weighted average (3)*
Manufacturing only – All	324 (52)	0.022 (1.20)	0.001 (0.17)
Manufacturing only – US	169 (24)	0.044 (1.56)	–0.007 (–1.34)
Manufacturing only – non-US	155 (28)	–0.001 (–0.06)	0.013** (2.36)
Other – All	386 (63)	0.071*** (2.92)	0.043*** (3.30)
Other – US	289 (41)	0.098*** (3.29)	0.040** (2.45)
Other – non-US	97 (22)	–0.011 (–0.45)	0.044** (2.60)
Various	144 (26)	0.024 (0.87)	0.045** (2.64)
Services	75 (11)	0.017 (0.37)	0.029 (1.50)
Education	71 (14)	0.129 (1.54)	0.050* (1.92)
Construction	51 (7)	0.260*** (6.30)	0.267*** (6.79)
Mining	36 (4)	0.030 (0.40)	–0.004 (–0.37)

Notes: Column 1 reports the number of estimates and the number of studies for each industry (in brackets). Column 2 reports the simple unweighted meta-average for each industry. Column 3 reports the *FEE-WLS* weighted average using inverse variance weights (unrestricted WLS). Figures in brackets in columns (2) and (3) are *t*-statistics using standard errors adjusted for within study clustering. *Various* denotes estimates that pool data from several industries. *Other* refers to non-manufacturing plus studies that include data from various industries. All observations for *Construction* are for the US. All but two observations for *Mining* are for the US. All but four observations for *Education* are for the US. All but one estimate for Services are for the US.

***, **, and * denote statistical significance at the 1%, 5%, and 10% levels, respectively.

United States and elsewhere, and this appears to be driven by estimates relating to construction and, to a lesser extent, education. Figures 3.1 and 3.2 are funnel plots of the data, calculated for the average estimate of each study and for all estimates from all studies, respectively. Figures 3.3 and 3.4 are funnel plots for estimates for all manufacturing and other industries, respectively, where other

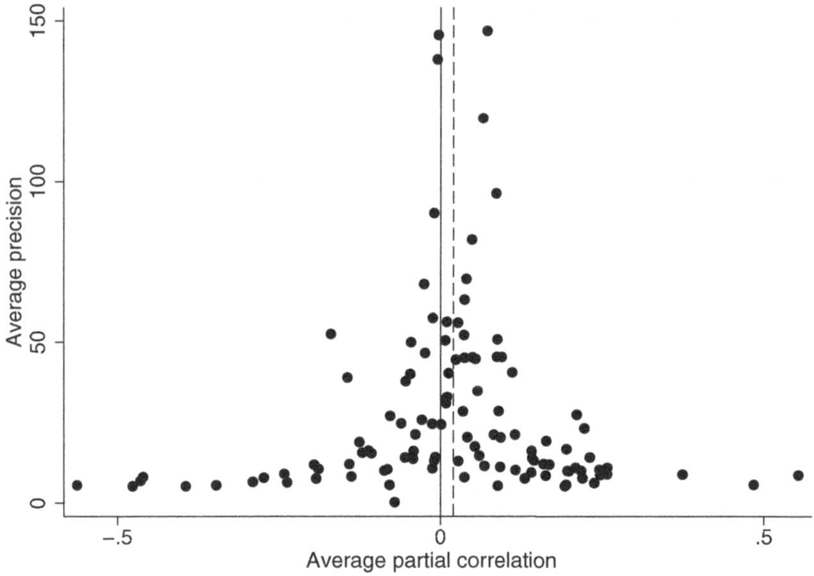

Figure 3.1 Funnel plot of unions and productivity, average estimate

Notes: The plot uses the average estimate per study. Solid and dashed vertical lines denote zero and the unweighted average correlation (0.02), respectively.

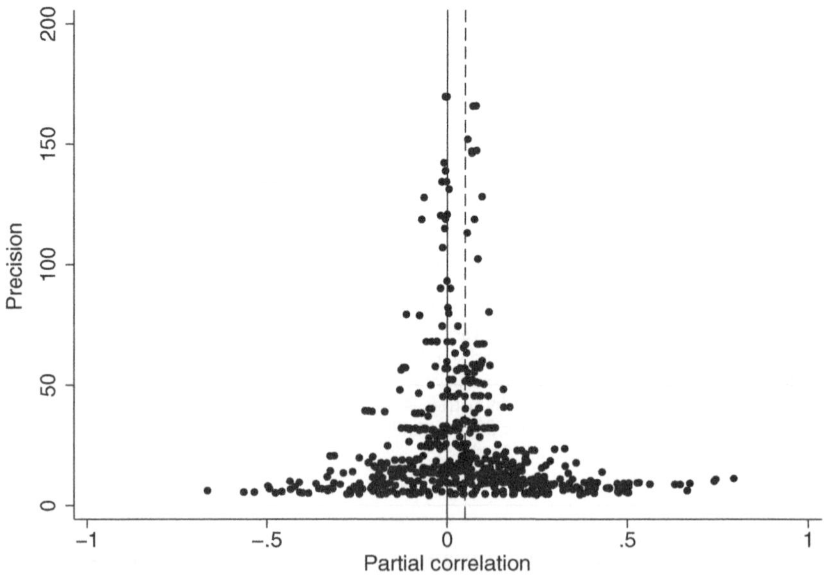

Figure 3.2 Funnel plot of unions and productivity, all estimates

Notes: Solid and dashed vertical lines denote zero and the unweighted average correlation (0.05), respectively.

refers to non-manufacturing plus estimates for various industries combined, some of which might be manufacturing. The funnel plots illustrate the wide variation in the reported union-productivity effects as measured by partial correlations. Figures 3.1 and 3.2 further suggest a bimodal distribution, with one mean centered on zero and another centered on a positive correlation. We show below that this distribution can, at least partly, be explained by country and industry differences.

Figures 3.5 and 3.6 examine the time series pattern in the reported union-productivity estimates for manufacturing and other industries, respectively. The partial correlations become, on average, more negative over time in manufacturing, but there is no change in other industries. This is confirmed when we condition for other moderating variables in the MRA.

Study quality

While we included the 111 studies in our data set as being of sufficient quality for the meta-analysis, there are likely differences in the quality of studies that deserve attention. Many researchers assign quality to the publication outlet. Of the 111 studies listed in Table 3.1, 15 were published in the *Industrial and Labor Relations Review*, 9 in *Industrial Relations*, 3 in the *British Journal of Industrial Relations*, 6 in leading management journals (*Academy of Management Journal*,

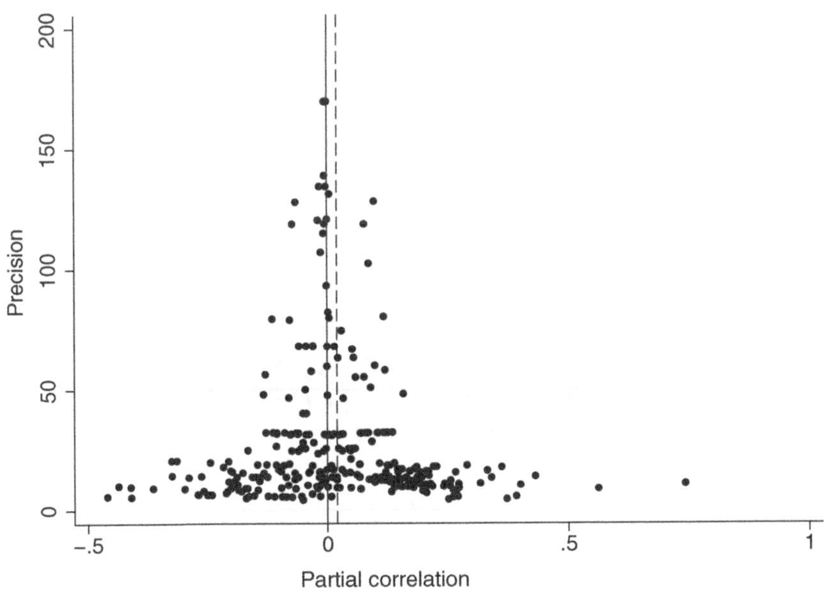

Figure 3.3 Funnel plot of unions and productivity, manufacturing

Notes: Solid and dashed vertical lines denote zero and the unweighted average correlation (0.02), respectively.

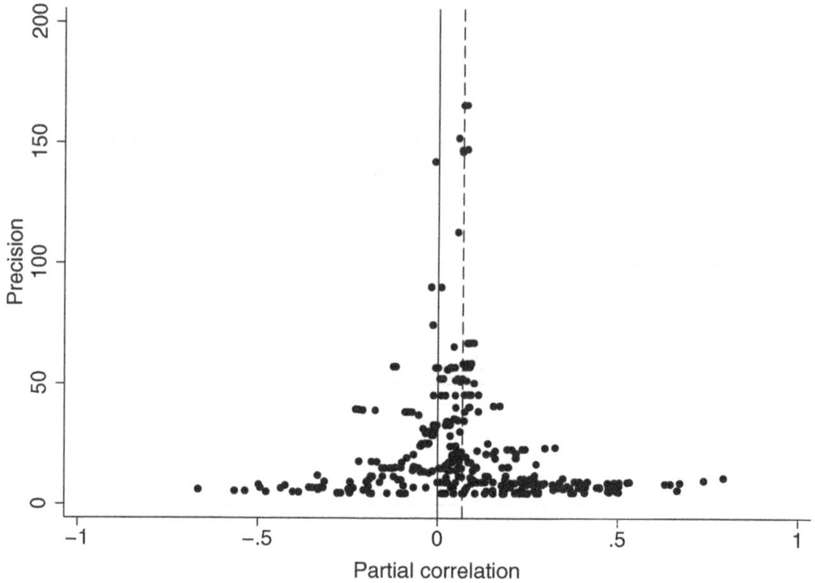

Figure 3.4 Funnel plot of unions and productivity, other industries

Notes: Solid and dashed vertical lines denote zero and the unweighted average correlation (0.07), respectively.

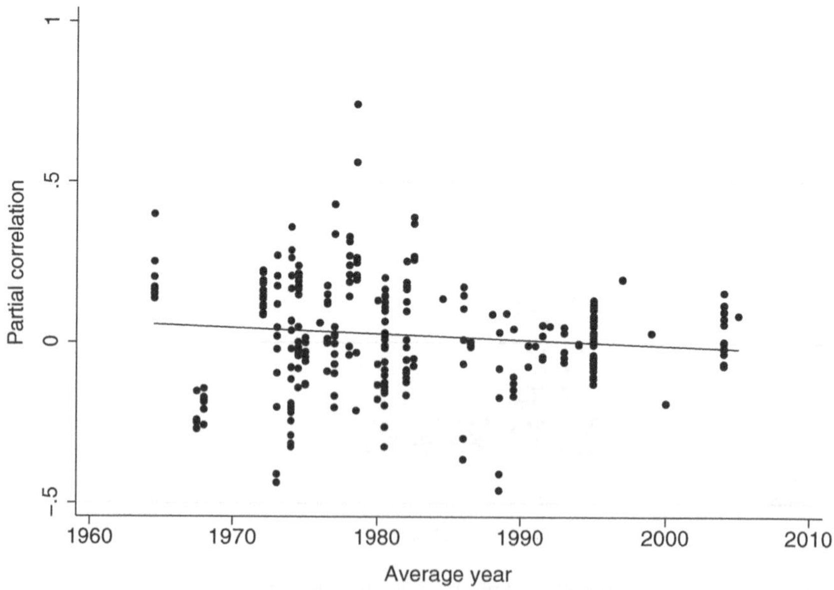

Figure 3.5 Unions and productivity partial correlations, manufacturing, chronological order

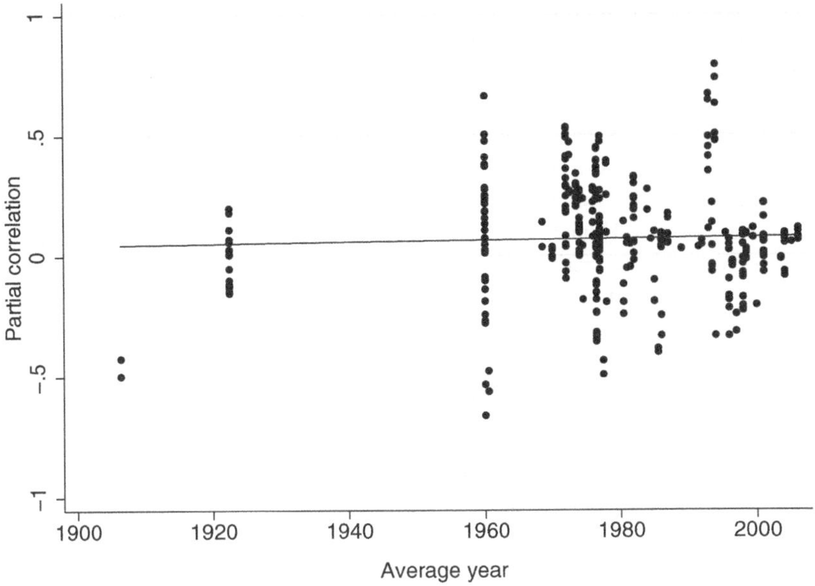

Figure 3.6 Unions and productivity partial correlations, other industries, chronological order

Management Science, and *Strategic Management Journal*), and 11 in leading economics journals (*Journal of Political Economy*, *American Economic Review*, *Review of Economics and Statistics*, and *Quarterly Journal of Economics*). Hence, the published empirical literature is of a very high quality, according to 'industry standards'. As it is not obvious that estimates reported in other journals will be more biased and less deserving of inclusion in the meta-analysis (see Stanley and Doucouliagos, 2012), we eschew weighting studies by impact factors or other journal related measures of publication outlet.[7]

Instead, we measure quality of the estimates by their statistical precision as reflected by the inverse of an estimate's standard error (see Hedges and Olkin, 1985 and Stanley and Doucouliagos, 2012). By weighing estimates by their precision, we are able to rank estimates (and studies) on the basis of an objective measure of quality.

The unconditional average correlation between unions and productivity

Depending on the balance between the productivity enhancing/collective voices and institutional response effects and productivity diminishing monopoly effects, the *net* impact of unions on productivity is likely to be country, industry, and time specific. Accordingly, we conduct the meta-analysis separately for manufacturing and other industries, and explore country and time differences.

Table 3.4 gives unconditional meta-averages of union productivity effects for manufacturing (Panel (a)) and for all other industries, including combined industry samples, (Panel (b)). The table includes all countries and distinguishes the United States and non–United States. Column (1) reports the *FEE-WLS* fixed-effect weighted least squares. Column (2) reports the *REE-WLS* random-effects weighted least squares. While the *REE-WLS* is a very popular estimator, Stanley and Doucouliagos (2015) show that it produces biased estimates when there is publication selection bias. Hence, we prefer the *FEE-WLS*. Column (3) reports meta-averages corrected for selection bias (the *PET*) while Column (4) reports estimates of the degree of publication selection bias (the *FAT*). Finally, Column (5) gives the *PEESE* estimates. All meta-averages are estimated with weighted least squares.

Table 3.4 Unconditional meta-average partial correlation, unions and productivity, manufacturing and other industries

	FEE-WLS weighted average (1)	*REE-WLS weighted average (2)*	*FAT-PET, selection bias corrected weighted average (PET) (3)*	*FAT-PET, publication selection bias (FAT) (4)*	*PEESE corrected weighted average (5)*
			(a) Manufacturing		
All estimates (n = 324; k = 52)	0.001 (0.17)	0.022 (1.40)	–0.005 (–1.15)	0.453 (1.59)	–0.001 (–0.13)
US estimates (n = 169; k = 24)	–0.007 (–1.34)	0.040 (1.54)	–0.014* (–1.91)	0.685 (1.68)	–0.009 (–1.48)
Non-US estimates (n = 155; k = 28)	0.013** (2.36)	0.007 (0.45)	0.015 (1.64)	–0.107 (–0.23)	0.015** (2.57)
			(b) Other		
All estimates (n = 386; k = 63)	0.043*** (3.30)	0.065*** (2.90)	0.038** (2.21)	0.243 (0.61)	0.040*** (2.93)
US estimates (n = 289; k = 41)	0.040** (2.45)	0.095*** (3.20)	0.005 (0.32)	1.008** (2.45)	0.029* (1.95)
Non-US estimates (n = 97; k = 22)	0.044** (2.60)	0.005 (0.24)	0.069*** (3.49)	–1.941** (–2.21)	0.049*** (2.95)

Notes: The columns report the fixed-effect, random-effects, the *PET*, the *FAT*, and *PEESE* unconditional meta-averages, respectively. All columns are estimated using WLS, using inverse variance weights. Column (3) reports the *PET* coefficient; publication bias corrected average. Column (4) reports the *FAT* coefficient; degree of publication bias. Figures in brackets are *t*-statistics using standard errors adjusted for clustering of observations within studies. Panel (a) uses only data for manufacturing. Panel (b) uses data for other industries, including samples that include various industries; n and k denote number of observations and studies, respectively.
***, **, and * denote statistical significance at the 1%, 5%, and 10% levels, respectively.

With two exceptions, the meta-averages in Table 3.4 suggest no association between unions and productivity in manufacturing. The exceptions are that *PET* finds a small negative association for the United States at a low level of statistical significance (Column (3), Panel (a)), while the *PEESE* finds a positive effect for non-US estimates with a small correlation (Column (5), Panel (a)). In contrast, there is a small positive correlation for the *Other* group, which is larger outside the United States (Column (5), Panel (b)). The *FAT* coefficients suggest no publication bias in the manufacturing sample, but publication bias in the *Other* sample in favor of positive correlations for the United States and negative correlations elsewhere.

Meta-regression analysis of heterogeneity

Figures 3.1 to 3.4 show widely varying estimates. Heterogeneity in reported empirical effects can reflect genuine underlying differences where the union effect varies among industries and countries, or it can be an artifact from research design choices such as how the researcher measured inputs and outputs or specified the equation. Both genuine and artificial heterogeneity can be analyzed using meta-regression. Recall from Chapter 2 that the meta-regression model takes the following form:

$$r_{ij} = \mathbf{x}'_{ij}\boldsymbol{\beta} + u_{ij}, \tag{2.4}$$

where again r_{ij} is the ith partial correlation from the jth study, $\mathbf{x}_{ij}$ is a vector of explanatory (or moderator) variables, $\boldsymbol{\beta}$ is the vector of parameters to be estimated, and u_{ij} is the error term. Eqn. (2.4) can be used to identify moderator variables, of which there are potentially many. We have opted for a parsimonious specification with a few moderator variables that capture the salient features of the estimates.[8] We conduct the MRA separately for manufacturing and for all other sectors.

Moderator variables

We include in the MRA the following moderator variables.[9]

1 The partial correlation's standard error, *SE*, to detect and correct for publication selection bias within a multiple MRA, applying the *FAT-PET* model that identifies and corrects publication selection bias conditional on other factors.
2 Other input variables in the production function. Most studies include a measure of capital, but several do not. *Capital* is a binary variable for the inclusion of capital in the estimated production function. Some studies include a measure of technology and other intangible forms of capital; the variable *Tech* controls for this in the MRA. *LabQuality* is a binary variable for estimates that control for labor quality differences. These three variables – *Capital, Tech,* and *LabQuality* – can also be viewed as indirect channels through which unions impact productivity. We also enter a binary variable *Participation,*

which is 1 for estimates that control for employee participation, defined as any scheme that includes direct participation of employees in decision making or any financial participation scheme such as profit-sharing and employee share ownership. To the extent that unions create such programs, they are an indirect channel that we differentiate from unionism per se. To the extent that firms introduce them as a substitute for unionism, we control for participation programs as we would for capital or labor skill inputs. Thus our estimated effect of unions on productivity is for firms/establishments with the same capital, technology, labor quality, and direct employee participation schemes.

3 Indicators for measures of output. Studies of manufacturing productivity use value added, physical output, or efficiency scores. Value added in current dollars could be influenced by unions' impact on wages, which the firm passes on to consumers through higher prices. This would likely overstate the union-productivity effect. On the other hand, if physical output data are used with no allowance for price movements, there is a risk of failing to control for changes in output quality. Some studies avoid this problem by assessing the difference in technical efficiency levels between unionized and non-unionized firms from either Data Envelopment Analysis or Stochastic Frontier Analysis. We make value added measures the base and include the binary variables *Physical* and *Efficiency* to control for the effect of using deflated value added or technical efficiency in the reported union-productivity and correlation.

4 Indicators in the measurement of unionization. Some studies use a continuous union density or collective bargaining coverage measure while others use a dummy variable for union presence (*UnionDummy*). We make the continuous measure the base and explore whether the dummy variable for union presence affects correlations.

5 Indicators for the level of aggregation. Some studies use data at the establishment, plant or firm level. Others use industry-level data. Some use provincial/state-level data. Others use data at the nation level. We make firm-level data the base, and add dummy variables for *Industry*, *State*, and *Nation*, to explore the impact of more aggregate data. It is possible that countrywide data may hide important differences among industries, and that industry data may hide important differences among firms. While production function analysis applies best at the plant level, the impact of unions at the industry and national level will capture potential interactions or spillovers that may increase or decrease union effects.

6 Indicators for country and industry. We explore differences between the United States and other nations by using several country dummy variables (Canada, Japan, United Kingdom, Germany, Italy and France combined, developing countries, and all other countries), with the base being the United States. *Developing* includes China, Brazil, Guatemala, Malaysia, Mexico, Peru, and Uruguay. *Other* includes Korea, Australia, New Zealand, Sweden, and also studies that pool estimates from several countries. For the meta-analysis of other industries (Table 3.7) we explore industry differences by making estimates for several industries combined (including manufacturing)

as the base and including four industry dummy variables: construction, mining, education, and services.

7 Indicators for the use of panel data (*Panel*), with cross-sectional data as the base. The use of panel data enables researchers to eliminate establishment (or industry) fixed effects and correct biases that might arise from unobserved time-invariant effects. Comparing panel data to cross-sectional data estimates can also potentially inform on differences between partial equilibrium and general equilibrium effects. Panel data also can help deal with endogeneity and identify lines of causality.

Finally, we consider time variation and labor-market regulations that differ across country and time. While some studies explore differences in the union effect over time, most do not. One advantage of meta-analysis is that it can be used to explore time variation among studies. We do this by calculating the average year of the data used by primary studies (*AveYear*).[10] We also include a measure of the average degree of labor market regulation, *LabReg*, to explore whether the union-productivity correlation is moderated by the degree of labor market regulation at the time the samples were taken. The data for this series come from the *Economic Freedom of the World* from the Fraser Institute. This series scores labor market regulations and institutions favorable to unions or workers as inimical to economic freedom while scoring rule of law and policies that protect capital as enhancing economic freedom.[11] Regardless of whether one views labor regulations as restrictions on markets or protections of workers, the index effectively classifies countries by the extent of those regulations (Chor and Freeman, 2005) and thus is a potentially informative moderator variable for analyzing country differences in the estimated effects of unions on outcomes. *LabReg* is an index taking into account: the existence and size of the minimum wage, the degree of hiring and firing regulation, the degree of centralization of collective bargaining, and the mandated cost of hiring and firing. It is our measure of the degree to which labor market institutions deviate from the ideal competitive market. The series ranges from 1 to 10, with 10 being the least regulated and 1 the most regulated. By taking advantage of the time variation in samples and the institutional context at the time samples were taken, we can explore new dimensions in the union-productivity association even when *none* of the primary studies entered that dimensions in their regressions. The *LabReg* index turns out to be important, at least for manufacturing. With the exception of the average year of data and the average degree of labor market regulation, all the other explanatory variables in the meta-regression are dummy variables.

Unions and productivity in manufacturing industries

Table 3.5 presents four sets of MRA estimates relating to the union-productivity correlation in manufacturing. Column (1) reports the general results with all 21 moderating variables included (plus the constant). Many of these are not statistically significant. Adopting a general-to-specific strategy (Stanley and

Doucouliagos, 2012), we remove any variable with a *p*-value greater than 0.1. A Wald test confirms that these redundant variables can be eliminated from the MRA (*p*-value = 0.20). The resulting specific model is reported in Column (2). These are our preferred results.

Table 3.5 Unions and productivity, multiple MRA, manufacturing

	Mean (Standard deviation)	*General, FEE-WLS*	*Specific, FEE-WLS*	*Specific, N weights FEE-WLS*	*Specific, REE-WLS*
		(1)	*(2)*	*(3)*	*(4)*
SE	0.07 (0.05)	1.018** (2.52)	1.328*** (3.89) [0]	1.230*** (3.70)	0.170 (0.35)
AveYear	1.84 (10.26)	–0.003* (–1.87)	–0.003*** (–3.11) [0.005]	–0.004*** (–3.21)	–0.009*** (–3.33)
LabReg	0.06 (1.08)	0.025*** (3.48)	0.021*** (3.63) [0.010]	0.021*** (3.58)	0.005 (0.35)
Developing	0.20 (0.40)	0.100** (2.67)	0.099*** (4.32) [0]	0.100*** (4.53)	0.129** (2.17)
Canada	0.04 (0.20)	0.024 (0.47)	–	–	–
Japan	0.04 (0.19)	–0.006 (–0.22)	–	–	–
UK	0.15 (0.36)	–0.169*** (–4.29)	–0.194*** (–6.24) [0.005]	–0.189*** (–6.20)	–0.212*** (–7.68)
Germany	0.02 (0.14)	0.090 (1.14)	–	–	–
ItalyFrance	0.01 (0.11)	0.087* (1.73)	0.070*** (2.00) [0.075]	0.067* (1.92)	0.021 (0.25)
Other	0.01 (0.10)	–0.125 (–1.25)	–0.154* (–1.96) [0.400]	–0.147* (–1.88)	–0.187 (–1.64)
Physical	0.15 (0.36)	0.042 (1.46)	–	–	–
Efficiency	0.07 (0.26)	–0.012 (–0.17)	–	–	–

	Mean (Standard deviation)	*General, FEE-WLS*	*Specific, FEE-WLS*	*Specific, N weights FEE-WLS*	*Specific, REE-WLS*
		(1)	*(2)*	*(3)*	*(4)*
Capital	0.77 (0.42)	–0.012 (–1.04)	–0.015* (–1.70) [0.215]	–0.014 (–1.57)	–0.024 (–1.02)
Tech	0.17 (0.38)	–0.076*** (–3.75)	–0.075*** (–5.60) [0.005]	–0.074*** (–5.43)	–0.084** (–2.61)
LabQuality	0.32 (0.47)	–0.001 (–0.04)	–	–	–
Participation	0.23 (0.42)	0.057** (2.58)	0.076** (4.19) [0]	0.078** (4.32)	0.116*** (3.64)
UnionDummy	0.48 (0.50)	–0.004 (–0.28)	–	–	–
State	0.01 (0.10)	–0.039 (–0.58)	–0.036** (–2.06) [0.065]	–0.036** (–2.05)	–0.010 (–0.26)
Industry	0.15 (0.36)	0.044 (0.85)	–	–	–
Endogeneity	0.12 (0.32)	0.027* (1.91)	0.036*** (4.13) [0]	0.035*** (4.16)	0.042 (1.15)
Panel	0.73 (0.44)	–0.041*** (–3.41)	–0.045*** (–3.93) [0.005]	–0.045*** (–4.02)	–0.022 (–0.86)
Constant		–0.002 (–0.07)	–0.005 (–0.29) [0.715]	–0.003 (–0.21)	0.054 (1.16)
Studies/ Observations		50/321	50/321	50/321	50/321
Adjusted R^2		0.24	0.25	0.24	0.31

Notes: The dependent variable is the partial correlation between unions and productivity. All columns estimated with unrestricted WLS, using inverse variance weights. Column (1) reports results of the general model with all moderator variables included. Column (2) reports the specific model after removing any variable with a *p*-value greater than 0.1 in Column (1); Wald-test for redundant variables is 1.48 with *p*-value of 0.20. Column (3) uses sample size weights. Column (4) uses random-effects weights. Figures in round brackets are absolute *t*-statistics using standard errors adjusted for clustering of observations within studies. Figures in square brackets reported in Columns (2) are *p*-values derived from applying the wild bootstrap to correct for uneven number of observations within studies and within study dependence. Lack of data on *LabReg* reduces the number of studies to 50.
***, **, and * denote statistical significance at the 1%, 5%, and 10% levels, respectively.

Because the number of estimates varies among studies, with some studies reporting a single estimate and others reporting many, we correct for data dependence using cluster adjusted standard errors. The associated *t*-statistics are reported in round brackets. We also use the wild bootstrap procedure (Cameron et al., 2008) to correct for data dependence, which, as noted in Chapter 2, is important when there is a small number of clusters (studies in our case) and/or the number of estimates is unequal between clusters. The regression coefficients are identical but the corrected *p*-values reported in square brackets differ. For the sake of brevity, we report these only in Column (2). The application of the wild bootstrap leads to the same inferences as those given by more standard methods of dealing with clustering. The variable *Other* is an exception; this is a residual country category and of little significance to our analysis. For the purpose of robustness, in Column (3) we use sample size weights rather than inverse variance weights and we report the random-effects MRA in Column (4).

Several interesting results emerge from the MRA:

Publication selection bias. The statistical significance of *SE* indicates publication bias in estimates of the correlation between unionization and productivity in manufacturing. The positive sign on *SE* suggests preferential reporting in favor of positive union-productivity effects in manufacturing. The size of the coefficient exceeds 1. According to Doucouliagos and Stanley's (2013) guidelines, there is substantial publication bias in the manufacturing sample with *FAT* coefficients between 1 and 2. This confirms the need to investigate and correct publication selection bias in our evidence base.

Time variation. The estimated negative coefficient on *AveYear* suggests that, conditional on all other dimensions of data and modeling, the estimated union-productivity effect becomes less positive/more negative over time. This may reflect a genuine structural change in the impact of unions over time. Alternatively, it may reflect an artifact with earlier studies having a preference to report more positive productivity effects[12] and later studies responding to this bias, so that as the evidence base accumulates, it reveals the genuine association.

Labor regulation. The positive coefficient on regulation (*LabReg*) indicates that union-productivity correlations are more positive/less negative in less regulated markets. This finding is consistent with the idea that labor market regulations insulate insiders from competition, giving them greater bargaining power that can produce adverse productivity effects; and is also consistent with the view that unions and management are more willing to cooperate toward joint maximization of output in more competitive markets. In any case, these results confirm that context and labor institutions matter.

Country differences. The MRA indicates significant country differences. The coefficient on *UK* is negative, indicating a more adverse effect of unions on productivity in manufacturing in the United Kingdom than in the base country, the United States. The coefficients for *Developing* and *ItalyFrance* are positive, indicating that unions have a less negative/more positive productivity effect in developing countries and Italy/France than in the United States.

Modeling choices. In terms of data aggregation, provincial-level data results in larger adverse effects, while panel data also results in larger negative/smaller positive correlations. In addition, some variables that are related to the union productivity effect are not statistically significant in the MRA, e.g., the country dummies *Canada* and *Japan*. The *UnionDummy* variable for measuring unionism is also not statistically significant. Turning to the mode of estimation, *Endogeneity* has a positive coefficient in the preferred MRA model (Column (2)), indicating that estimates that treat unionism as endogenous produce more positive effects. This supports the DiNardo and Lee (2004) view that unions organize badly managed firms.

Econometric specification. With regard to specification, the MRA indicates that controlling for capital (*Capital*) or technology (*Tech*) results in larger negative/smaller positive productivity effects. However, the result for *Capital* is not statistically significant when we apply the wild bootstrap to correct standard errors. Controlling for labor quality (*LabQuality*) does not have a noticeable impact on the unionization and productivity correlation, possibly due to insufficient variation in labor quality and/or poor measurement of labor quality. In contrast to these results, controlling for employee participation (*Participation*) results in more positive unionization-productivity correlations.

Conditional meta-average

The MRA coefficients can be used to estimate the union-productivity correlation for different countries. Table 3.6 presents these estimates for the United States, the United Kingdom, developing countries, and for Italy and France combined. We construct these meta-averages under two assumptions regarding labor market regulation: in Column (1) we evaluate at the country sample means of labor market regulation and in Column (2) we evaluate at maximum labor market flexibility. In deriving these estimates, we assume that a well-constructed model will use panel data, address endogeneity, and control for capital stock, technology, and employee participation in the econometric specification.

Doucouliagos (2011) gives guidelines for interpreting the size of partial correlations. In the case of labor economics research, a partial correlation less than $\pm$ 0.048 can be regarded as small, a partial correlation greater than $\pm$ 0.112 can be regarded as moderate, and a partial correlation greater than $\pm$0.234 can be regarded as large. We conclude from Table 3.6 that unions have no effect on productivity in manufacturing in the United States, a moderate to large negative effect in the United Kingdom, a small to moderate positive effect in developing countries, and a small positive effect in Italy and France.

Table 3.6 Unions and productivity, conditional meta-average correlation, by country and degree of labor market regulation, manufacturing

	Labor market regulation at sample means (1)	*Most liberal labor markets (2)*
US	–0.023 (–1.32)	0.021 (1.14)
UK	–0.212 (–6.04)***	–0.169 (–4.44)***
Developing	0.077 (2.38)**	0.121 (3.28)***
Italy & France	0.044 (1.33)	0.088 (2.07)**

Notes: Predictions based on coefficients from Column (2), Table 3.5, controlling for endogeneity, panel data, technology, capital stock, and employee participation. Column (1) evaluates at the sample mean of labor market regulation. Column (2) evaluates at the most liberal labor market regime. Standard errors adjusted for clustering.

*** and ** denote statistical significance at the 1% and 5% levels, respectively.

Unions and productivity in other industries

Table 3.7 repeats the multiple MRA for education, construction, mining, services, as well as for mixtures of industries, including manufacturing. The format of the table is similar to Table 3.5.

These results show some differences from those for manufacturing. First, the coefficient on *SE* is not statistically significant, implying that the estimates on other industries are free of publication selection bias. Second, neither the average year nor the labor regulation variables are statistically significant, indicating that the partial correlations do not vary over time nor with different labor regulations. Labor regulations appear to be important for moderating the union-productivity effect only in manufacturing industries.

Country differences are found in the other industries sample, though these are different from those in manufacturing. The indicators *Developing* and *Other* are not statistically significant, probably due to a small number of observations. *Canada* has a positive and statistically significant coefficient, while *UK* and *ItalyFrance* both have negative coefficients; union-productivity effects are slightly higher in Canada and lower in the United Kingdom and Italy and France than in the United States, for the various industries sample.

Both *Construction* and *Education* have statistically significant positive coefficients. Consistent with the results for manufacturing, inclusion of technology in the production function results in less positive productivity effects and studies that use panel data also yield less positive results. Finally, studies that use physical output or efficiency scores find larger negative effects.

Table 3.7 Unions and productivity, multiple MRA, other industries

	Mean (Standard deviation)	*General, FEE-WLS*	*Specific, FEE-WLS*	*Specific, N weights, FEE-WLS*	*Specific, REE-WLS*
		(1)	*(2)*	*(3)*	*(4)*
SE	0.09 (0.06)	0.432 (0.68)	–	–	–
AveYear	–2.22 (19.19)	0.001 (0.47)	–	–	–
LabReg	–0.09 (1.54)	–0.001 (–0.14)	–	–	–
Developing	0.05 (0.21)	–0.035 (–0.59)	–	–	–
Canada	0.02 (0.13)	0.072 (1.23)	0.058*** (3.58) [0.100]	0.057*** (3.50)	–0.008 (–0.11)
UK	0.04 (0.19)	–0.103*** (–3.41)	–0.108*** (–6.80) [0.005]	–0.105*** (–8.33)	–0.120** (–2.57)
Germany	0.05 (0.23)	0.009 (0.15)	–	–	–
ItalyFrance	0.05 (0.22)	–0.079*** (–3.02)	–0.063*** (–4.33) [0.005]	–0.060*** (–4.40)	–0.123*** (–2.77)
Other	0.02 (0.13)	–0.073 (–1.11)	–	–	–
Construction	0.13 (0.34)	0.137** (2.06)	0.188*** (5.43) [0.015]	0.182*** (5.38)	0.183*** (4.62)
Mining	0.09 (0.29)	0.056 (1.45)	–	–	–
Education	0.18 (0.39)	0.100** (2.41)	0.052** (2.44) [0.035]	0.049** (2.44)	0.115* (1.74)
Services	0.19 (0.40)	0.007 (0.47)	–	–	–

(continued)

Table 3.7 Unions and productivity, multiple MRA, other industries (*continued*)

	Mean (Standard deviation)	*General, FEE-WLS*	*Specific, FEE-WLS*	*Specific, N weights, FEE-WLS*	*Specific, REE-WLS*
		(1)	*(2)*	*(3)*	*(4)*
Physical	0.48 (0.50)	–0.106** (–2.38)	–0.080*** (–7.27) [0.005]	–0.080*** (–7.29)	–0.078** (–2.39)
Efficiency	0.05 (0.22)	–0.091* (–1.71)	–0.124*** (–3.88) [0.005]	–0.122*** (–3.94)	–0.022 (–0.27)
Capital	0.74 (0.44)	0.018 (0.42)	–	–	–
Tech	0.14 (0.35)	–0.077 (–1.52)	–0.054*** (–3.21) [0.07]	–0.054*** (–3.26)	–0.057* (–1.70)
LabQuality	0.39 (0.49)	0.021 (0.98)	–	–	–
Participation	0.17 (0.38)	–0.011 (–0.67)	–	–	–
UnionDummy	0.61 (0.49)	–0.018 (–0.29)	–	–	–
State	0.09 (0.29)	–0.001 (–0.14)	–	–	–
Nation	0.12 (0.32)	–0.129 (–1.07)	–	–	–
Industry	0.09 (0.28)	0.017 (0.31)	–	–	–
Endogeneity	0.05 (0.22)	0.060 (1.25)	–	–	–
Panel	0.34 (0.47)	–0.048* (–1.90)	–0.044** (–2.63) [0.07]	–0.041** (–2.66)	–0.066** (–2.12)
Constant		0.089 (1.31)	0.109*** (9.68) [0.000]	0.107*** (10.42)	0.114*** (4.57)

	Mean (Standard deviation)	*General, FEE-WLS*	*Specific, FEE-WLS*	*Specific, N weights, FEE-WLS*	*Specific, REE-WLS*
		(1)	*(2)*	*(3)*	*(4)*
Studies/ Observations		61/363	63/386	63/386	63/386
Adjusted R^2		0.40	0.39	0.39	0.45

Notes: The dependent variable is the partial correlation between unions and productivity. Columns (1) and (2) estimated with unrestricted WLS, using inverse variance weights. Column (1) reports results of the general model with all moderator variables included. Column (2) reports the specific model after removing any variable with a p-value greater than 0.1 in Column (1); Wald-test for redundant variables is 0.123 with p-value of 0.28. Column (3) uses unrestricted WLS with sample size weights. Column (4) uses random-effects weights. Figures in round brackets are absolute t-statistics using standard errors adjusted for clustering of observations within studies. Figures in square brackets reported in Columns (2) are p-values derived from applying the wild bootstrap to correct for uneven number of observations within studies and within study dependence. Lack of data on *LabReg* reduces the number of studies to 61 in Column (1).
***, **, and * denote statistical significance at the 1%, 5%, and 10% levels, respectively.

Conditional meta-average

We use the MRA coefficients to estimate the union-productivity correlation for various industries, conditioning on technology and the use of panel data, which produce larger negative/smaller positive results. Column (1) of Table 3.8 reports the conditional meta-averages for the United States with output measured in value terms. Studies that include several industries together do not establish a statistically significant correlation but there is a robust positive correlation for education, and an even larger correlation for construction. Column (2) reports meta-averages when physical output measures productivity. In Column (3) we report meta-averages for the United Kingdom with productivity measured in value terms. The results presented in Columns (2) and (3) are largely out-of-sample predictions, especially for the United Kingdom, and thus with a potentially high error rate (Stanley and Doucouliagos, 2012). These meta-averages suggest a small adverse productivity effect for various industries but the positive effect for construction remains. Because Column (1) results are largely in-sample, we have greater confidence in them. On the basis of the Doucouliagos (2011) guidelines, we conclude that the average correlations between unionism and productivity are small to moderate in education and moderate to large in construction.

To see if these effects are of economic significance, we calculate productivity differentials from the estimated partial correlations by running a Robust regression of the estimated union-productivity evaluated at 100 percent unionization against the partial correlations. This produces a slope coefficient of 110, with a t-statistic of 45.34. Assuming that this linear relationship holds, each 0.1 partial correlation increment represents an 11 percent productivity differential for firms/industries that are 100 percent unionized – a counterfactual far removed from the

Table 3.8 Unions and productivity, conditional meta-average correlation, other industries

	US, value added (1)	*US, physical output (2)*	*UK, value added (3)*
Various industries	0.012 (0.75)	–0.069*** (–3.65)	–0.096*** (–4.39)
Construction	0.200*** (5.17)	0.120*** (3.10)	0.092** (2.25)
Education	0.063** (2.40)	–0.017 (–0.67)	–0.044 (–1.43)

Notes: Predictions based on coefficients from Column (2), Table 3.7, controlling for panel data and technology. Standard errors adjusted for clustering.
*** and ** denote statistical significance at the 1% and 5% levels, respectively.

data. The predicted conditional meta-averages in Tables 3.6 and 3.8, however, suggest that that some of the productivity differentials are of economic significance at current union levels. For example, the –0.21 partial correlation between unions and productivity in UK manufacturing (Table 3.6, Column (1)) translates to a 23 percent productivity disadvantage for unionized firms in the United Kingdom. Similarly, the 0.20 correlation between unions and productivity in construction (Table 3.8, Column (1)) translates into a 22 percent productivity advantage for unionized firms.

Summary

Neither economic theory nor sociological nor organization theory establishes an unambiguous association between unions and productivity. Empirical research provides estimates of the association between unions and productivity levels. Assessing all the evidence available to us when we wrote this book, our meta-regression analysis suggests a near zero association between unions and productivity with important country and industry variation: a negative association in the United Kingdom and positive effects for construction and education in the United States, and for manufacturing in developing countries.

Our methodology detected substantial publication selection bias in studies of manufacturing productivity. The bias gives a more positive correlation in the effect of unions on the levels of productivity. Identifying and correcting such bias is important for an accurate understanding of the effects of unionization.

With thirty years of additional information that allows for more sophisticated summaries of many studies, we conclude that unions have a positive effect in some industries and no effect in others, which compares with Freeman and Medoff's (1984) conclusion from the very limited evidence then available that unions had a positive productivity effect. Still, with the exception of the United Kingdom, our findings reject the neoclassical economics view that unions are invariably harmful to productivity.

Notes

1 For example, unions lobby for minimum wage increases and they support regulations that reduce labor market flexibility. Critics argue that these interventions result in worsening macroeconomic outcomes. Others, however, argue that these interventions do not have adverse macroeconomic effects.
2 At the extreme, unions can accelerate the death of firms.
3 There is also the issue of the threat effect, where the threat of unionization might alter the behavior of the non-unionized firms.
4 These included EconLit, Proquest/ABI Inform, EBSCO, Google Scholar, and Scopus.
5 The impact of unions on productivity may be moderated by other factors. However, we are unable to perform a separate meta-analysis on the interactions because most studies do not report sufficient information. Interactions are potentially an important area of investigation and perhaps this can be the subject of a future meta-analysis once sufficient data and information becomes available. Our data contains 71 of the 73 studies included in Doucouliagos and Laroche (2003a). We exclude Bemmels (1987) and Meador and Walters (1994) because we exclude interaction terms from our meta-analysis.
6 Four of these come from the study by Anwar and Sun (2015), one from Freeman (1988), one from Hirsch (1991a), and two from Morikawa (2010). These four studies report several estimates so they are all retained in the data even after removing these outliers.
7 Restricting the meta-analysis only to estimates from studies published in 'good journals' will almost certainly lead to a biased and unrepresentative sample of the evidence base.
8 There are several interesting dimensions which cannot be explored due to insufficient information. For example, studies do not provide enough information on factors such as closed shop arrangements, multi-unionism, and the political orientation of unions.
9 The specification used here differs somewhat from Doucouliagos and Laroche (2003a).
10 A continuous measure of time is more informative than using dummy variables for various decades.
11 The labor index differs from most Fraser measures of economic freedom by being negatively related to GDP per capita, as advanced countries regulate labor more (have lower freedom) than developing countries, and by having little association with economic growth (Freeman, 2003).
12 Given the early view that unions reduced productivity, positive findings would arguably attract greater attention and be easier to publish. Once it became clear that there was evidence on both sides, such publication bias would likely fall.

4 Unions and productivity growth

> In sum, current empirical evidence offers little support for the assertion that unionization is associated with lower (or higher) productivity advance.
>
> (Freeman and Medoff, 1984: 170)

Many of the hypothesized benefits and costs associated with unions have implications for productivity growth. For example, in the CV/IR framework, unions can be associated with higher growth of productivity as well as a higher level of productivity through various channels. One channel arises through higher wages for unionized workers inducing substitution of capital for labor. This can affect total factor productivity growth if, as a response to rising labor costs, firms adopt new vintages of more productive capital or if they invest in research and development that leads to technological change.[1] Unions may foster training and skill formation, and by reducing labor turnover, they can help retain firm-specific skills that could contribute to future economic growth (Freeman, 1976; Addison and Barnett, 1982). By improving communications between workers and management, unions can improve workers' motivation and willingness to speak up about problems at their workplace or firm, which could facilitate productivity growth (Dworkin and Ahlburg, 1985).

But, as Hirsch and Link (1984: 32) note, it is possible for unions to increase productivity levels *and* decrease productivity growth: "One possible interpretation is that it is initial unionization that increases the level of productivity, presumably by providing an effective voice and reducing X-inefficiency. However, productivity growth in unionized industries is slowed, possibly due to the effects of monopoly unionism in restricting management flexibility and entrepreneurial activities or from decreased long-run profit expectations". Betts et al. (2001) point out that union wage increases act as a tax on labor which may increase or decrease investment, while union rent-seeking behavior can be a disincentive to investment. Restrictive work practices (MacKersie and Klein, 1983), strike activity (Flaherty, 1987), and inefficient personnel practices (Lawler and Mohrman, 1987) can all adversely affect productivity growth. The role of unions in supporting or resisting organizational change at the workplace has been the subject of much debate (Verma and MacKersie, 1987; Eaton and Voos, 1992; Kizilos and Reshef, 1997).

Some scholars see unions as inhibiting the introduction of alternative forms of control and ownership (Guest, 1995), while others see unions as playing a positive role in the successful adoption of such innovative practices (Eaton and Voos, 1992; Kochan and Osterman, 1994). Finally, unions can depress R&D spending and investment in intangible capital (Hirsch and Link, 1987), an issue we examine in Chapter 5.

Given that theory suggests channels of effects in different directions, the net impact of unions on productivity growth is, like most else in economics, an empirical matter. Many empirical studies have explored the link between unions and productivity growth with the majority finding a negative association between unions and productivity growth but with a substantial number reporting a positive association. This chapter updates and re-estimates Doucouliagos and Laroche (2003b) to assess estimates of the effects of unions on productivity *growth* over time. How does meta-regression analysis summarize the evidence?

Unions and productivity growth: new data for an old issue

Studies on unionization and productivity growth

We searched for studies in English or French on the impact of unionism on productivity growth in several databases, including EconLit and Scopus, as well as references in the literature, between January 2015 and June 2015. The inclusion criteria were similar to those for productivity levels laid out in Chapter 3 and excluded all unpublished studies and published studies that included unionization in their analysis of productivity growth but did not report the relevant regression output.

Our search identified 42 published studies that provide 272 estimates of the association between unions and productivity growth from multivariate regression analysis. From these studies we calculated the partial correlation coefficients as the measure of the association between unionization and productivity growth, other factors fixed. As in our analysis of productivity levels in Chapter 3, we used standardized residuals from the *FAT-PET* model to identify outliers and removed three outliers. We further eliminated one study from the MRA for not reporting the standard error, leaving us with a sample of 268 observations.

The studies differed in the measurement of the dependent productivity growth variable and of the independent union variable, in the covariates included (though there is much less variation here than in the case of productivity levels) and in the industry, country, and year of data. The dependent variable was measured either as the growth of labor productivity, total factor productivity, or sales growth. The majority of studies (36) report estimates of the level of unionization or union presence on productivity growth, while six studies report estimates for the *change* in union status/coverage and productivity growth. While the latter can be important if the degree of unionization is changing over time, data limitations can create sizeable measurement error in changes (see Bronars et al., 1994). The level of aggregation of the data ranges from firm data, industry data to provincial/state-level data and national, cross-country comparisons.

Table 4.1 lists the studies, the country to which they relate, sample size (N), the median *t*-statistic, and the median partial correlation coefficient (*r*).[2] The 42 studies represent a total of 39,786 observations across several countries and spanning several decades. Table 4.2 reports some of the salient features of the data. Most estimates are for US manufacturing and, as noted, the majority report a negative correlation between unionization and productivity growth.

The first ever meta-analysis of unions and productivity, Doucouliagos and Laroche (2003b) had a much smaller sample: 29 estimates from 26 studies and ignored the issue of publication selection in assessing those studies. The inference from this meta-analysis was that US unions had an adverse effect on growth. Following the path-breaking work by T.D. Stanley, our analysis here takes account of the dangers selection bias poses for statistical inference. Since productivity growth studies focus on many variables, with unionism being of modest interest in most cases, there is reasonable possibility that the published evidence suffers from publication bias. Researchers who included unions in a productivity growth regression, found that it was not statistically significant, and did not pursue the issue of unionization any further may have decided to report statistically significant results and not publish statistically insignificant results. Referees or journal editors might have recommended that tables or lines of a table with an insignificant union effect be dropped. While Table 4.2 reports that a large proportion of the studies find no relationship between unions and productivity growth, the possibility that other statistically insignificant results lie in file-drawers cannot be blithely dismissed.

In contrast to Doucouliagos and Laroche (2003b), which relied on the author's best estimate, or an average of reported estimates when the author expressed no preference, our meta-analysis uses all reported comparable estimates. Using all estimates does not eliminate publication selection bias due to authors' choosing which estimates to report (Stanley and Doucouliagos, 2012), but comes closer to representing what the data say than using only the authors' preferred estimate. Like any statistical analysis, meta-analysis is only as good as the raw data it uses. If the data is truncated or artificially truncated in some fashion, inferences from meta-analysis can be misleading. Hence, it is critical to test and correct for bias in the research record.

To do this we begin with the funnel plot of the partial correlations. Figure 4.1 presents the funnel plot of the 42 studies that estimate the impact of unionization or the change in unionization on productivity growth, taking an average of all estimates per study. Figure 4.2 presents the funnel plot of all estimates of the 36 studies that use the level of unionization as the independent variable. The data in these figures show that most estimates report adverse productivity growth effects. The simple unweighted and uncorrected estimate is –0.07 for the Average-set and –0.09 for the All-set. Many of the estimates are, however, reported with relatively low precision. The most precise estimates are at the top of the funnel. The two most precise estimates report a very small negative correlation and the next three most precise estimates report a small positive correlation. Compared to Figures 3.1 and 3.2 for productivity levels in Chapter 3, Figures 4.1 and 4.2 for productivity growth

Table 4.1 Econometric studies of unions and productivity growth

Author(s)	*Country*	*N*	*Median t-statistic*	*Median r*	*Author(s)*	*Country*	*N*	*Median t-statistic*	*Median r*
					North America				
Allen (1988b)	US	155	–1.15	–0.13	Bartel (1994)	US	155	–0.10	–0.01
Bronars et al. (1994)	US	510	–0.93	–0.07	Clark (1984)	US	4681	–0.32	–0.01
Clark & Griliches (1984)	US	4146	1.00	0.02	Freeman (1988)	US	650	–1.25	–0.05
Freeman & Medoff (1984)	US	676	1.04	0.08	Hirsch (1990a)	US	1932	–5.39	–0.12
Hirsch (1991a)	US	4258	–0.61	–0.04	Hirsch & Link (1984)	US	19	–2.27	–0.50
Kaufman (1992)	US	81	1.55	0.18	Kendrick (1973)	US	21	–2.32	–0.48
Kendrick & Grossman (1980)	US	20	–0.61	–0.17	Kruse (1993)	US	5652	–0.16	–0.01
Link (1981)	US	51	–1.83	–0.26	Link (1982)	US	97	–1.94	–0.20
Maki (1983)	Canada	53	–1.25	–0.18	Mansfield (1980)	US	20	–5.95	–0.84
Mitchell et al. (1990)	US	886	2.08	0.10	Pantuosco et al. (2001)	US	768	–2.80	–0.10

(*continued*)

Table 4.1 Econometric studies of unions and productivity growth (*continued*)

Author(s)	*Country*	*N*	*Median t-statistic*	*Median r*	*Author(s)*	*Country*	*N*	*Median t-statistic*	*Median r*
Pantuosco et al. (2002)	US	672	0.89	0.04	Schuster (1983)	US	474	0.65	0.08
Sveikauskas & Sveikauskas (1982)	US	138	–0.43	–0.04	Terleckyj (1980)	US	20	–1.49	–0.38
Terleckyj (1984)	US	192	–1.16	–0.08	Williams & Moomaw (1989)	US	49	–2.13	–0.33
Wilson (1995)	US	30	0.53	0.11					
				United Kingdom					
Davies & Caves (1987)	UK/US	61	–1.73	–0.23	Denny (1997)	UK	702	–1.28	–0.05
Gregg et al. (1993)	UK	1772	0.36	0.01	Haskel (1991)	UK	324	–0.46	–0.03
Monastiriotis (2007)	UK	180	0.49	0.04	Nickell et al. (1992)	UK	1342	–1.90	–0.05
				Other					
Asteriou & Monastiriotis (2004)	OECD	576	1.96	0.08	Cassoni et al. (2005)	Uruguay	3073	1.04	0.02
Kleiner & Ay (1996)	OECD	406	–2.40	–0.12	Menezes-Filho et al. (2005)	Brazil	255	0.07	0.00

Author(s)	*Country*	*N*	*Median t-statistic*	*Median r*	*Author(s)*	*Country*	*N*	*Median t-statistic*	*Median r*
Moriwaka (2010)	Japan	3508	1.69	0.03	Phipps & Sheen (1994)	Australia	812	3.54	0.12
Vernon & Rogers (2013)	OECD	83	0.01	0	Yu & Park (2006)	Korea	258	–1.04	–0.07
Zagler (2000)	Austria	28	1.30	0.27					

Notes: Calculated by the authors from the primary studies. The table reports medians for all comparable estimates, combining estimates from various measures of unionization and productivity growth. N denotes total sample size used in the study. *r* denotes partial correlation.

Table 4.2 Basic characteristics of the unions and productivity growth literature

	All studies (1)	*US studies (2)*	*UK studies (3)*
Number of studies	42	26	6
Number of estimates	269	165	52
Total sample size	39786	26353	4381
% reporting adverse effects	63%	67%	67%
% US	61%	100%	0
% manufacturing	64%	62%	85%
Average partial correlation	–0.076	–0.112	–0.037

Note: Average partial correlation is an unweighted average. Table includes estimates that use either the level or change in unionization.
Source: Authors' calculations.

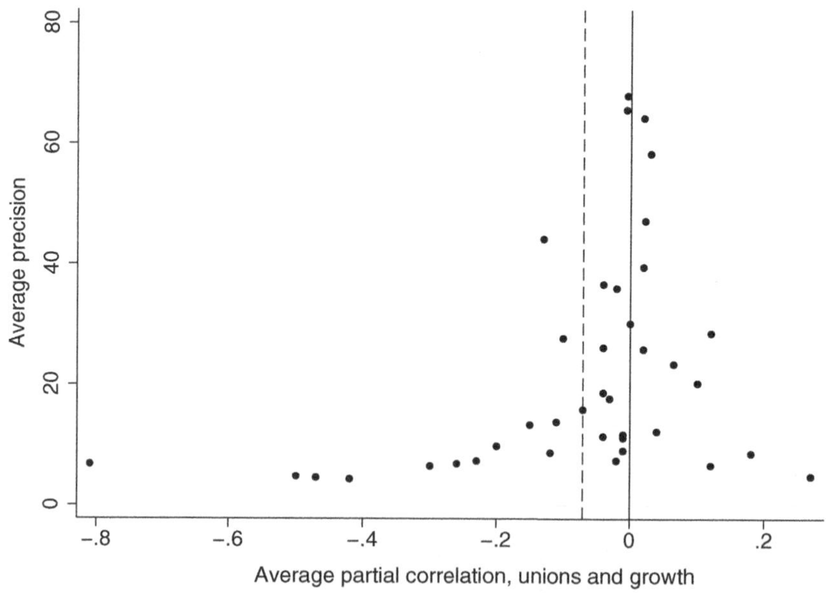

Figure 4.1 Funnel plot of unions and productivity growth, average estimate

Notes: Solid and dashed vertical lines denote zero and the unweighted average correlation (–0.07), respectively.

are fairly asymmetrical. The negative skew of the distribution of the correlations suggests preferential reporting of adverse productivity growth effects.

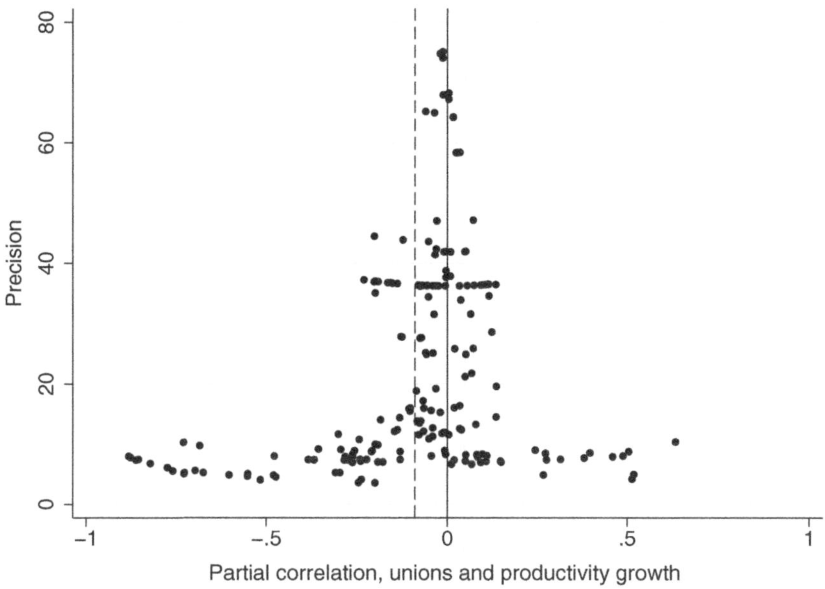

Figure 4.2 Funnel plot of unions and productivity growth, all estimates

Notes: Solid and dashed vertical lines denote zero and the unweighted average partial correlation (−0.09), respectively.

The unconditional average correlation between unions and productivity growth

Table 4.3 reports five meta-averages from the evidence base. Column (1) reports the OLS unweighted average, with each estimate assigned equal weight in the overall average. These estimates suggest that unions reduce productivity growth. Column (2) reports the weighted average using inverse variance weights by WLS – the fixed-effect unrestricted WLS estimate, *FEE-WLS*. It suggests no correlation between unions and productivity growth: a small effect with very low level of statistical significance when all estimates are used.

By contrast, the random-effects WLS (*REE-WLS*), estimated using REML, in Column (3) suggest an adverse effect on productivity growth in the United States. But these estimates are potentially distorted by publication selection bias (Stanley and Doucouliagos, 2015). Accordingly, in Column (4) we report weighted averages corrected for publication selection bias, using the *FAT-PET* model, and find evidence of such bias: these estimates show no significant adverse union effect on productivity growth. The Column (5) estimates of publication bias (the *FAT*) pin down the preferential reporting as being due to negative productivity growth effects among studies using United States data. Finally, Column (6) gives weighted averages corrected for publication selection bias, using the *PEESE* model that allows for non-linearities in publication selection, and again we find no correlation between unions and productivity growth.

Table 4.3 Unconditional meta-average partial correlation, unions and productivity growth

	Unweighted average (1)	*FEE-WLS weighted average (2)*	*REE-WLS weighted average (3)*	*FAT-PET, selection bias corrected weighted average (PET) (4)*	*FAT-PET, publication selection bias (FAT) (5)*	*PEESE corrected weighted average (6)*
All estimates (n = 210, k = 36) (1)	–0.089** (–2.56)	–0.019* (–1.89)	–0.070** (–2.67)	0.012 (0.84)	–1.170** (–2.47)	–0.010 (–0.98)
US estimates (n = 131, k = 25) (2)	–0.119** (–2.26)	–0.022 (–1.65)	–0.091** (–2.23)	0.011 (0.63)	–1.275** (–2.18)	–0.011 (–0.94)
Non-US estimates (n = 79, k = 11) (3)	–0.039* (–1.84)	–0.015 (–0.81)	–0.035** (–2.15)	0.010 (0.39)	–0.897 (–1.35)	–0.010 (–0.51)

Notes: Only level of unionization estimates used to estimate the meta-averages. The columns report the unweighted average, fixed-effect, random-effects, the *PET*, the *FAT*, and *PEESE* unconditional meta-averages, respectively. Figures in round brackets are *t*-statistics using standard errors corrected for clustering of estimates within studies. n is the number of observations. k is the number of studies. Note that All studies and US studies estimates in Column (1) use one more observation than all other columns, as the standard error for one estimated productivity growth effect is not defined. Column (4) reports the *PET* coefficient; publication bias corrected average. Column (5) reports the *FAT* coefficient; degree of publication bias. Columns (2) to (6) estimated using unrestricted weighted least squares, using inverse variance weights. ** and * denote statistically significant at the 5% and 10% levels, respectively.

In short, when either *FAT-PET* or *PEESE* corrects for the effects of publication selection bias, the empirical evidence suggests that there is no correlation between unionization and productivity growth: the unconditional meta-averages indicate that unionized and non-unionized entities experience similar rates of productivity growth.

We investigated the data further to test our mode of identifying selection bias by conducting our own selection bias with the sample. We first remove all estimates with a positive productivity growth effect, which reduced the sample size to 127 observations from 28 studies (compared to 210 observations from 36 studies) with negative estimated effects. This increased the estimated coefficient on publication selection bias in the *FAT-PET* model from –1.17 to –2.24, showing that the *FAT-PET* model indeed picked up this selection bias. The meta-average becomes –0.009, but this is still statistically insignificant (p-value = 0.68).

We then further truncated the data by removing more observations until we attained a p-value less than 0.05. This required the removal of any estimate that was greater than –0.036. This results in a final sample of 103 observations from 24 studies. The estimated meta-average (the *PET* coefficient) in this case is –0.05 (p-value = 0.023) and the publication bias term (the *FAT* coefficient) is now –1.95 (p-value = 0.005). By deliberately ignoring nearly half of the evidence base, we artificially generated a small adverse statistically significant productivity growth effect. But our statistics for selection bias alerts the reader to what we have done. This demonstrates the importance of testing for selection bias.

Analysis of heterogeneity: unions and productivity growth

Now we use the MRA model to analyze heterogeneity and identify potential moderator variables in the union-productivity growth association, estimating Eqn. (2.4), the multiple MRA version of the *FAT-PET* model. Table 4.4 presents these results. The first column reports descriptive statistics of the variables in the multiple MRA: the average year of the data used by primary studies (*AveYear*) and the average degree of labor market regulation (*LabReg*) at the time the samples were taken; three binary variables to reflect country: the *UK*, all other individual countries (*Other*), and estimates for the OECD (*MultipleCountries*), with the United States as the base; industry differences measured by the *NotManuf* variable for estimates that do not relate exclusively to manufacturing (the base); and a *NotFirm* dummy to explore differences between studies that use firm-level data (the base) and those that do not.[3] For the multiple MRA we also include the estimates relating to change in unionization. The variable *ChangeUnion* measures differences between studies that use change in unionism as the key union variable relative to those that use the level of unionization (the base). Additionally, we consider differences between studies that use a productivity growth measure (the base) and those that consider output growth (*Output*). Finally, we include measures for whether the original study included variables reflecting *R&D* and *Concentration*. Unions can affect productivity growth indirectly through R&D (see Chapter 5), so inclusion of R&D in a growth model may affect the reported coefficient on unionization. Concentration in a sector can affect productivity and may also contaminate the estimated union effect.

Table 4.4 Unions and productivity growth, multiple MRA

	Mean (SD)	*General FEE-WLS (1)*	*Specific FEE-WLS (2)*	*Specific N weights FEE-WLS (3)*	*Specific REE-WLS (4)*
SE	0.089 (0.062)	–0.834** (–2.20)	–1.038** (–2.83) [0.015]	–0.815*** (–3.33)	–1.141** (–2.21)
AveYear	0.00 (9.928)	0.001 (0.32)	–	–	–
LabReg	0 (1.103)	0.009 (0.51)	–	–	–
UK	0.191 (0.394)	–0.022 (–0.77)	–	–	–
Other	0.077 (0.267)	0.026 (0.79)	0.047*** (3.96) [0.000]	0.045*** (4.02)	0.079* (1.88)
MultipleCountries	0.099 (0.300)	0.096* (1.85)	0.087*** (3.79) [0.000]	0.083*** (4.19)	0.104*** (2.90)
NotManuf	0.360 (0.481)	–0.003 (–0.10)	–	–	–
NotFirm	0.482 (0.501)	–0.039 (–1.30)	–	–	–
ChangeUnion	0.213 (0.410)	0.043 (1.54)	–	–	–
Output	0.320 (0.467)	0.016 (0.87)	–	–	–
RD	0.371 (0.484)	–0.016 (–0.53)	–	–	–
Concentration	0.390 (0.489)	–0.013 (–0.50)	–	–	–
Constant		0.008 (0.22)	0.005 (0.39) [0.780]	0.001 (0.06)	0.009 (0.44)

	Mean (SD)	*General FEE-WLS (1)*	*Specific FEE-WLS (2)*	*Specific N weights FEE-WLS (3)*	*Specific REE-WLS (4)*
Studies/ Observations		42/268	42/268	42/268	42/268
Adjusted R^2		0.07	0.08	0.06	0.16

Notes: Dependent variable is partial correlation of unions and productivity growth. Columns (1) and (2) estimated with unrestricted WLS, using inverse variance weights. Column (1) reports results of the general model with all moderator variables included. Column (2) reports the specific model after removing any variable with a *p*-value greater than 0.1 in Column (1); Wald-test for redundant variables is 1.12 with *p*-value of 0.37. Column (3) uses unrestricted WLS with sample size weights. Column (4) uses random-effects weights. Figures in round brackets are absolute *t*-statistics using standard errors adjusted for clustering of observations within studies. Figures in square brackets reported in Columns (2) are *p*-values derived from applying the wild bootstrap to correct for uneven number of observations within studies and within study dependence. ***, **, and * denote statistical significance at the 1%, 5%, and 10% levels, respectively.

Column (1) reports our baseline general unrestricted *FEE-WLS* model that includes all the moderator variables. Only two variables are statistically significant: *SE* and *MultipleCountries*. Following Stanley and Doucouliagos (2012), we pruned the model with a general-to-specific modeling strategy by sequentially removing any variable that was not statistically significant, at least at the 10 percent level of significance. These results are presented in Column (2). For the purposes of robustness we re-estimate the specific model using the wild bootstrap. This confirms the same set of statistically significant variables. We also explored robustness by using alternate weights: Column (3) re-estimates the specific MRA model using sample size weights, while Column (4) reports results using the random-effects weights.[4] As was the case for productivity levels, we prefer the unrestricted *FEE-WLS* estimates that are reported in Column (2).

While the MRA for productivity growth explains a much smaller fraction of the variation in partial correlations than does the MRA for productivity levels, it identifies publication selection in these studies with preferential reporting for adverse productivity growth effects reflected in the statistical significance of *SE* in all columns. The bias is not extreme, with an estimated coefficient of about 1, which Stanley and Doucouliagos's (2013) guidelines view as modest. Still, this bias was enough to give the appearance of an adverse productivity growth effect when there in fact appears to be none.

Turning to the estimates on other moderator variables, *UK* is not statistically significant, suggesting no difference in the impact of unions between the United States and the United Kingdom. The only consistently statistically significant variables are on the *Other* and *MultipleCountries* dummies. Both of these moderator variables have positive coefficients suggesting that unions have a positive productivity growth effect in these sub-samples compared to the United States base group. The effect for *Other* is 0.05 with a *t*-statistic of 3.96 while the effect of the

MultipleCountries (essentially the OECD) is a positive and statistically significant 0.09 with a *t*-statistic of 3.79. But these findings are based on the results from only five studies with 19 estimates and three studies with 27 estimates, respectively.

The two specification variables are not statistically significant. Studies that include R&D or some measure of concentration find essentially the same union-productivity growth effect as those that do not. *ChangeUnion* has a positive coefficient in the general model, indicating that studies that use the change in unionization are less likely to report an adverse productivity growth effect. However, this variable is not statistically significant. Some authors find that the impact of unions varies over time (e.g., Nickell et al., 1992 and Gregg et al., 1993). However, our MRA detects no time variation, as measured by the average year of the data used by authors (*AveYear*). Finally, in contrast to the findings for productivity levels in manufacturing (recall Table 3.5, Chapter 3), we find that labor regulation does not moderate the union-productivity growth effect; this is not surprising given that there is no effect to moderate.

In short, corrected for selection bias, the meta-analysis suggests that unions have no effect on productivity growth in the United States and the United Kingdom. This is consistent with the view that productivity growth differentials between union and non-union firms arise from idiosyncratic industry or firm differences rather than from unionization. We need more studies to conclude that unions have a positive effect in other countries, though that is the way the evidence points.

Summary

As is the case with union-productivity effects, economic theory provides little guidance to whether unionism should have positive or negative effects on economic growth. To see whether the positive or negative effects dominate the relation of union growth, we applied meta-regression analysis to estimates of the effects of unions on productivity growth from studies that focused on the union impact and from the more numerous growth studies that included unionism as a secondary covariate. Taken as a whole, the estimates show little or no association between unions and productivity growth.

We conclude from these findings and those from Chapter 3 that the evidence base rejects the neoclassical economics view that unions are invariably harmful to productivity or its growth.

Notes

1 Total factor productivity refers to the change in outputs for a given set of inputs. Typically, estimates consider only labor and capital and hence this is more accurately referred to as multifactor productivity.

2 Table 4.1 reports the median for all estimates. As was the case for the analysis of productivity, in the meta-regression analysis of productivity growth we use all observations, and not the median value.

3 We also disaggregated this into three dummies for industry level data, regional level data, and nation level data. None of these dummies was statistically significant in the MRA. Here we report the more parsimonious models.

4 In addition, we tried various combinations of data, e.g., removing industry, regional, national, or non-US data. All these combinations produce similar results.

5 Unions and productivity

Investment channels

The generally insignificant relation between unionism and productivity and between unionism and productivity growth found in the Chapter 3 and 4 meta-regression analyses could result from weak relations between unionism and the various channels through which analysts expect unionism to increase or decrease those outcomes, or from the counterbalancing effect of strong positive and negative associations along specified channels. This chapter presents a meta-analysis of studies of the relation between unions and investment, which is invariably positively related to productivity as part of the stock of capital in production functions and to productivity growth as determined by the growth of capital. The first section treats studies of the association of unionism with physical/tangible capital investment. The second section does the same for studies of the association of unionism with intangible capital investment. In each section, we estimate whether unionism is associated with more or less investment and quantify the magnitude of the association. Then we test whether there are observable differences in this association between countries and over time and whether any differences depend on differences in country labor market regulations. Finally, we identify differences in reported effects among studies coming from differences in econometric specification, in the measurement of investment behavior, and/or in the measurement of unionism.

Our main result is that unionism has a modest negative association with investment in physical capital; and a large negative association with investment in intangible capital. Given that both tangible and intangible investment raise productivity, unionism likely reduces productivity modestly through the investment channel. If this was the only way in which unionism affected productivity, the reduced form association between unionism and productivity in Chapter 3 would be negative. The succeeding chapter examines the possible offsetting positive effects of unionism on productivity through its impact on employee behavior.

Unions and physical capital investment[1]

Physical capital is indispensable to the production process, as reflected in its entering the widely used Cobb-Douglas production function multiplicatively with labor and the treatment of the capital-to-labor ratio as the fundamental determinant of labor productivity. Increases in knowledge embedded in new plant and equipment also makes investment in physical capital critical for innovation. Most new products and processes of production require capital. So, what is the association of unionism with physical capital investment?

Theory review

Many studies develop or review the theory behind the association between unionization and capital investment, including Baldwin (1983), Grout (1984), Hirsch (1991a), Hirsch and Prasad (1995), and Addison and Chilton (1998). In the traditional neoclassical model of the firm, unions raise wages above the market-determined level, which act as a tax on labor. This induces substitution effects between capital and labor that can stimulate investment in unionized firms: with a greater increase in capital, the higher the elasticity of substitution. Estimates of the elasticity of capital for labor are typically far from the zero in fixed coefficient production models but generally less than one (Chirinko, 2008). At the same time, the higher cost of labor has a scale effect on the amount produced. By making production more expensive, the higher wage lowers the scale of production and reduces investment (Johnson and Mieszkowski, 1970). While the higher wage may reduce investment through the scale effect or increase investment through the substitution effect, it invariably increases the capital-to-labor ratio.

In a union rent-seeking model, the union wage premium captures some of the firm's quasi-rents from capital investments, and thus acts like a tax on capital. Long-lived assets are vulnerable to rent expropriation by unions and workers.[2] Machin and Wadhwani (1991) point out the time dimension of the relation between investment and likely rent-seeking behavior, as higher levels of investment in one period are likely to raise wage demands in the future, thereby increasing the cost of investing. Van der Ploeg (1987) argues that unions that announce low future wage demands to induce firms to invest may subsequently renege on this promise. Cavanaugh (1998: 36) argues that "the bargaining problem exists only in the presence of both high union density and asset-specific investment". Whatever its cause, union ability to capture quasi-rents should reduce employer investment in capital.

In contrast to predictions of adverse investment effects, Freeman and Medoff (1984) stress that unionized firms may have a more productive working environment, with the retention of higher skilled workers, mechanisms for voicing worker grievances, and improved communication channels that could induce additional investment. Hirsch and Link (1987) note that these positive effects on productivity would have to be large to offset the union tax on investment. Marxist and radical economists argue that if unionization shifts power within a firm, managers will have an incentive to replace labor with capital, independent of wage movements (Hyman, 2006), which could increase total investment. Whether industrial relations is cooperative or confrontational may also affect investment. Cooperative management and union relations may generate a favorable investment climate.

Confrontational relations may generate a poor investment climate. In efficient bargaining models, firms move off their demand for labor curves (McDonald and Solow, 1981). If firm-level bargaining includes wages and employment, this will moderate capital for labor substitution. It is possible that unions and the firm will collaborate to maximize the present value of the firm, though this will require a union with a long time horizon (Hirsch and Link, 1987). Hirsch and Prasad (1995) argue that even with efficient bargains, union activity remains a tax on capital that will depress investment.[3]

Given the conflicting theoretical considerations, the *net* effect of unions on investment in physical capital is an empirical issue.

Studies on unionization and physical capital investment

Doucouliagos and Laroche (2003c) gave the first meta-analysis on the association of unionism with physical capital investment based on 11 econometric studies. In this chapter, we update this study adding nine newer studies to create a sample of 20 econometric studies for meta-analysis.[4] The number of studies on union-investment associations is much smaller than the number on union-productivity effects, and to obtain our 20 studies we had to widen sample selection criteria, compared to Chapter 3's meta-analysis of productivity. We included six estimates relating to works councils from Addison et al. (1993) and Addison et al. (2007), and ten estimates from two studies that had a nonlinear quadratic specification (Odgers and Betts, 1997; Monastiriotis, 2007) from which we derived a linearized estimate of the correlation coefficients.[5] The widening of the inclusion criterion increases the number of observations and the statistical power of the meta-analysis.

All the estimates in this data set come from econometric models in which the dependent variable was a measure of physical capital investment and unionism was one of the independent variables. The construction of the data and the subsequent meta-analysis conform closely with the meta-analysis guidelines of Stanley et al. (2013).

Table 5.1 lists the studies in the meta-analysis in alphabetical order along with country investigated, total sample size, median *t*-statistic, and median partial correlation (the correlation between unions and investment in tangible assets, after controlling for other factors that may impact on investment). In their analysis of 11 studies Doucouliagos and Laroche (2003c) used one estimate from each study. Here we use several estimates from each study and adjust standard errors for the clustering of estimates within studies. From the 20 studies, we obtain 343 comparable estimates for the meta-regression analysis. Table 5.2 reports some of the salient features of the data for all studies combined (Column 1) and for the United States (Column 2) and the United Kingdom (Column 3), respectively. The table shows that most estimates relate to US manufacturing and most report adverse union effects on capital investment.

Table 5.1 Econometric studies of unions and physical capital investment

Author(s)	*Country*	*N*	*Median t-statistic*	*Median r*
		North America		
Bronars & Deere (1993)	US	666	−3.78	−0.15
Bronars et al. (1994)	US	850	1.39	0.10
Cavanaugh (1998)	US	722	−4.57	−0.17
Clark (1984)	US	4,681	−0.01	−0.01
DiNardo & Lee (2004)	US	20,346	−0.43	−0.01
Fallick & Hassett (1999)	US	2,102	−2.15	−0.05
Hirsch (1990a)	US	3,142	−4.06	−0.07
Hirsch (1991a)	US	6,232	−1.68	−0.09
Hirsch (1992)	US	5,841	−2.15	−0.10
Odgers & Betts (1997)	Canada	360	−1.31	−0.07
		All other		
Addison et al. (1993)	Germany	54	−1.15	−0.16
Addison et al. (2007)	Germany	1,780	1.12	0.03
Cassoni et al. (2005)	Uruguay	4,849	0.99	0.01
Coutrot (1996)	France	1,135	1.80	0.05
Denny & Nickell (1991)	UK	648	−1.70	−0.08
Doucouliagos & Laroche (2003c)	France	1,003	−0.03	−0.01
Kleiner & Ay (1996)	OECD & Sweden	406	−3.74	−0.40
Mefford (1986)	Various	126	5.32	0.44
Menezes-Filho et al. (2005)	Brazil	2,529	−0.48	−0.01
Monastiriotis (2007)	UK	180	−4.60	−0.37

Notes: Calculated by the authors from the primary studies. The table reports medians for all comparable estimates, combining estimates from various measures of unionization and investment in physical capital. *N* denotes total sample size used in the primary econometric study; *r* denotes partial correlation.

Figures 5.1 and 5.2 present the funnel plots using the average estimate per study and all 343 estimates, respectively. The figures show a range of results, though most estimated partial correlations are negative. There is no

Table 5.2 Basic characteristics of the unions and physical capital investment literature

	All studies (1)	*US studies (2)*	*UK studies (3)*
Number of studies	20	10	2
Number of estimates	343	211	31
Total sample size	57,652	44,582	828
% reporting adverse union effects	65%	68%	77%
% USA	62%	100%	0%
% manufacturing	76%	86%	97%
Average partial correlation	–0.036	–0.047	–0.059

Note: Average partial correlation is an unweighted average.
Source: Authors' calculations.

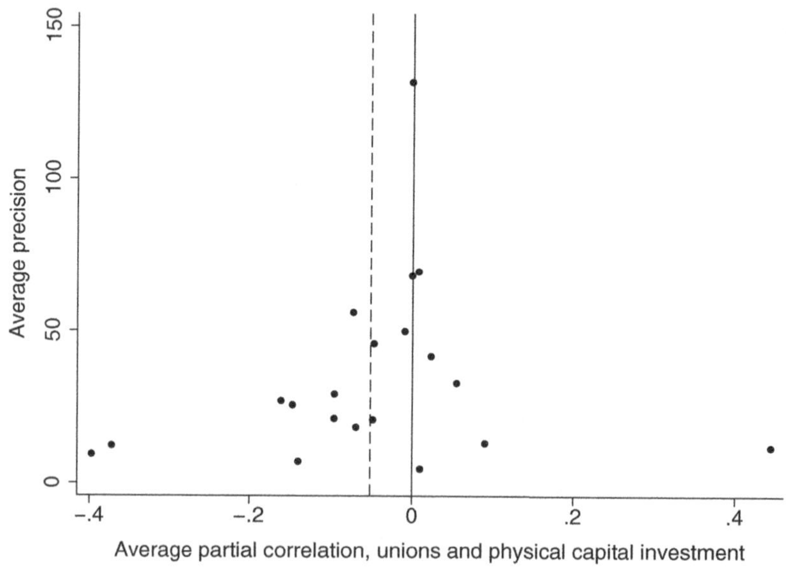

Figure 5.1 Funnel plot of unions and physical capital investment, average estimate

Note: Solid and dashed vertical lines denote zero and the uncorrected and unweighted average partial correlation (–0.051), respectively.

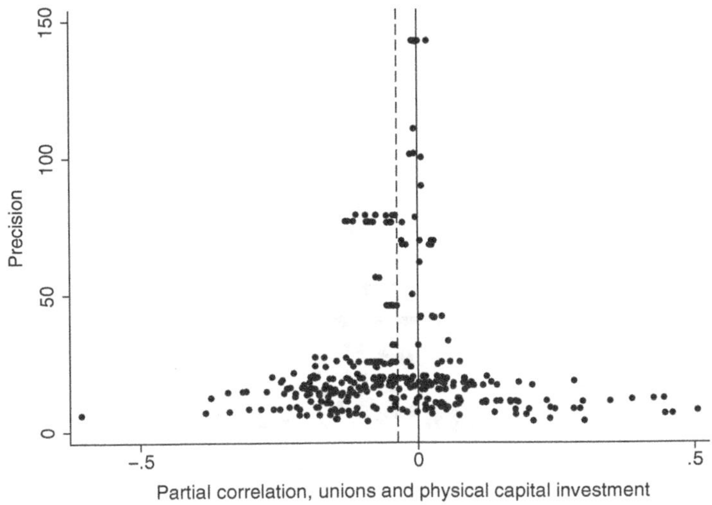

Figure 5.2 Funnel plot of unions and physical capital investment, all estimates

Note: Solid and dashed vertical lines denote zero and the uncorrected and unweighted average partial correlation (–0.036), respectively.

indication of publication selection bias – a result confirmed by the *FAT-PET* model. Figure 5.3 compares estimates for the United States and estimates for non-US countries, where there is also little indication of publication bias. Figure 5.4 examines the time series pattern in the reported estimates; it appears that over time, the partial correlations are, on average, becoming less negative, but as we will see shortly this pattern is not robust when other moderating variables are considered.

Unconditional meta-average correlations of unionization and physical capital investment

Table 5.3 reports the estimated unconditional meta-averages for all studies, US studies and non-US studies, in the same manner as we reported estimated unconditional meta-averages for productivity in Chapter 3. The first column gives unweighted averages that treat all estimates equally irrespective of the variation in estimated precision between estimates. The second column reports the fixed-effect weighted average (*FEE-WLS*), using inverse variance weights. The third column gives the random-effects weighted average (*REE-WLS*). The fourth column reports weighted averages derived from the *FAT-PET* model, where the average is corrected for publication selection bias, the *PET* coefficient, weighted by inverse variance and also corrected for publication selection bias. The fifth column reports the estimated degree of publication selection bias (the *FAT* coefficient). The final column gives weighted averages using inverse

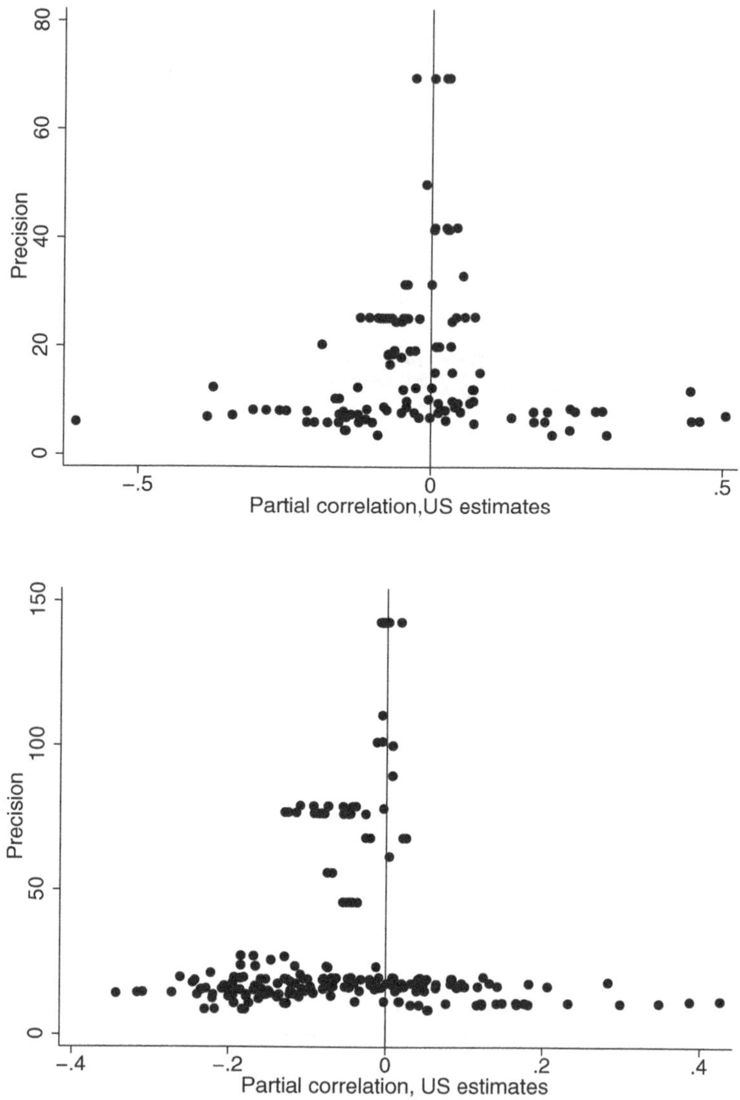

Figure 5.3 Funnel plots of unions and physical capital investment, comparison of non-US and US estimates

Note: The vertical solid lines show a zero effect size.

variance weights in the *PEESE* model (Eqn. (2.3), from Chapter 2).The *FAT* coefficients indicate no publication bias in the studies of the relation of unionism to physical capital investment. The unconditional meta-averages are all negative but not statistically significantly different from zero, suggesting no association or a small negative association between unionization and capital investment.

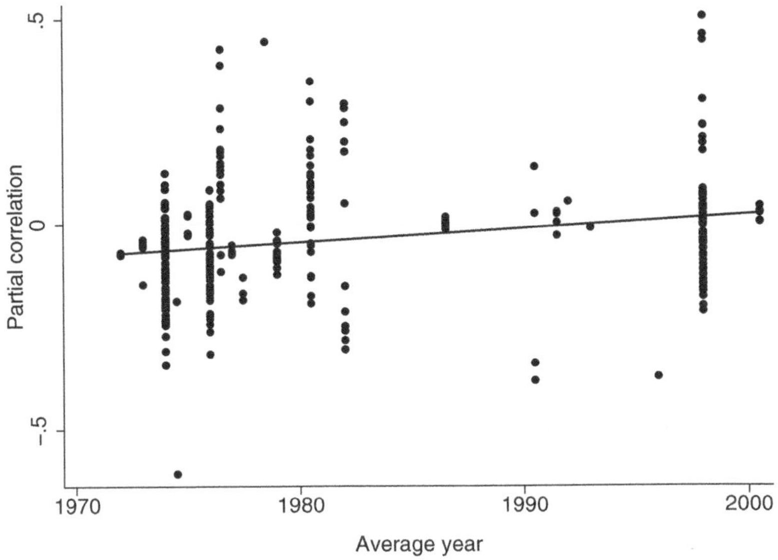

Figure 5.4 Unions and physical capital investment partial correlations, chronological order

Table 5.3 Unconditional meta-average partial correlation, unions and physical capital investment

	Unweighted Average (1)	*FEE-WLS weighted average (2)*	*REE-WLS weighted average (3)*	*FAT-PET, selection bias corrected weighted average (PET) (4)*	*FAT-PET, publication selection bias (FAT) (5)*	*PEESE corrected weighted average (6)*
All estimates (n = 343, k = 20)	−0.036 (−1.38)	−0.028 (−1.60)	−0.041* (−1.73)	−0.021 (−1.06)	−0.430 (−0.78)	−0.027 (−1.53)
US estimates (n = 211, k = 9)	−0.047 (−1.21)	−0.031 (−1.44)	−0.050 (−1.50)	−0.019 (−0.81)	−0.779 (−0.87)	−0.028 (−1.35)
Non-US estimates (n = 132, k = 11)	−0.019 (−0.94)	−0.011 (−0.75)	−0.029 (−1.30)	0.001 (0.09)	−0.336 (−0.88)	−0.009 (−0.61)

Notes: Column 1 reports the unweighted average. The other columns report the fixed-effect, random-effects, *FAT-PET*, and *PEESE* meta-averages, respectively. Columns (2) to (6) are estimated by WLS, using inverse variance weights; column (3) uses random-effects inverse variance weights. Column 4 reports the *PET* coefficient; publication bias corrected average. Column 5 reports the *FAT* coefficient; degree of publication bias. Figures in brackets are *t*-statistics using standard errors adjusted for clustering of observations within studies. n and k denote number of observations and studies, respectively. *denotes statistical significance at the 10% level.

Meta-regression analysis of heterogeneity, unionization and physical capital investment

Given the data set, our analysis of heterogeneity examines a smaller number of moderator variables than the MRA for productivity in Chapter 3. We use the standard MRA model, Eqn. (2.4), to identify sources of heterogeneity and to derive conditional MRA estimates and meta-averages:

$$r_{ij} = \mathbf{x}'_{ij}\,\beta + u_{ij}. \tag{2.4}$$

As potential moderator variables, we include *SE* to test for publication selection bias, and *Firm size*, *Growth*, and *Competition* to test for the effect of econometric specification differences on the estimated association. As there are strong reasons for including these variables in primary studies, exclusion is a potential source of specification bias.

Measurement differences are captured by *UnionDummy* for studies that use a binary measure of unionization, *WorksCouncil* for estimates relating to works councils, and *CapitalLabor* for studies that measure investment as the ratio of capital to labor rather than investment per se. Data differences are captured by *NotManuf* for estimates that do not relate to manufacturing and *NotFirm* for estimates that relate to a higher aggregation than firm or establishment-level data. Country differences are captured by *Developing* and *Europe*, for estimates relating to developing countries and Europe (including the United Kingdom), respectively, and separately by the variable *NonUSA*, for all non-US estimates.

Finally, we consider time variation and the impact of regulations through the variables *AveYear* (the average year of the data used by primary studies) and *LabReg* (the average degree of labor market regulation matched to the time period of the data used by primary studies).

Table 5.4 summarizes the results from the multiple MRA. Column (1) reports the general model with all moderator variables estimated using unrestricted WLS. Column (2) reports the specific MRA model after removing four variables that had a p-value greater than 0.3 in the general MRA. The Wald-test for these redundant variables is 1.68, with a p-value of 0.20. Columns (3) and (4) report robustness checks using sample size as weights and random-effects weights, respectively. Column (5) presents results using the variable *NonUSA* instead of the two country dummies.

The lack of statistical significance of *SE* confirms the absence of publication selection bias in studies of unionism and physical capital in the multiple MRA model that we saw in the Table 5.3 *FAT-PET* estimate and visual inspection of the funnel plots. *LabReg* is not statistically significant, suggesting that labor regulations do not moderate the impact of unions on capital investment. *AveYear* has a positive coefficient, suggesting that over time, the adverse relation between unionism and physical capital investment may be shrinking, though the result is not always statistically significant.

Table 5.4 Unions and physical capital investment, multiple MRA

	Mean (standard deviation)	*General FEE-WLS (1)*	*Specific FEE-WLS (2)*	*N weights FEE-WLS (3)*	*REE-WLS (4)*	*General FEE-WLS (5)*
SE	0.07 (0.05)	−0.106 (−0.66)	–	–	–	−0.078 (−0.47)
AveYear	−0.10 (9.54)	0.002** (2.34)	0.002 (1.64) [0.18]	0.002 (1.71)	0.002 (0.32)	0.003** (2.15)
LabReg	−0.02 (1.31)	−0.001 (−0.04)	–	–	–	−0.002 (−0.08)
Developing	0.01 (0.12)	0.045 (1.46)	0.051** (2.83) [0]	0.050** (2.83)	0.060 (1.36)	–
Europe	0.34 (0.47)	0.074** (2.21)	0.092** (2.67) [0.12]	−0.011 (−0.79)	0.043 (1.10)	–
NonUSA	0.38 (0.49)	–	–	–	–	0.050 (1.20)
CapitalLabor	0.20 (0.40)	0.034 (1.15)	0.022 (1.57) [0.19]	0.021 (1.56)	0.039 (1.45)	0.030 (1.03)
UnionDummy	0.51 (0.50)	−0.020* (−1.90)	−0.019 (−1.39) [0.36]	−0.019 (−1.44)	−0.041** (−2.40)	−0.018 (−1.66)
WorksCouncil	(0.02) (0.13)	−0.007 (−0.38)	–	–		−0.008 (−0.40)
Firm size	0.67 (0.47)	−0.129*** (−4.19)	−0.122*** (−6.35) [0]	−0.123*** (−6.91)	−0.119*** (−3.94)	−0.119*** (−4.26)
Growth	0.87 (0.34)	0.032 (1.73)	0.025 (1.64) [0.20]	0.026 (1.71)	0.055* (1.75)	0.037* (1.85)
Competition	0.49 (0.50)	0.078*** (6.02)	0.059*** (3.37) [0]	0.059*** (3.39)	0.014 (0.38)	0.059*** (3.48)
NotManuf	0.24 (0.43)	0.031 (0.87)	–	–		0.030 (0.91)

(*continued*)

Table 5.4 Unions and physical capital investment, multiple MRA (*continued*)

	Mean (standard deviation)	*General FEE-WLS (1)*	*Specific FEE-WLS (2)*	*N weights FEE-WLS (3)*	*REE-WLS (4)*	*General FEE-WLS (5)*
NotFirm	0.13 (0.33)	−0.136*** (−4.71)	−0.158*** (−5.16) [0]	−0.157*** (−5.29)	−0.158*** (−4.53)	−0.136*** (−3.63)
Constant		−0.024 (−0.51)	−0.012 (−0.84) [0.49]	−0.011 (−0.79)	0.006 (0.32)	−0.021 (−0.44)
Studies/ Observations		19/342	20/343	20/343	20/343	19/342
Adjusted R^2		0.48	0.46	0.45	0.36	0.48

Notes: The dependent variable is the partial correlation between unions and physical capital investment. Figures in brackets are *t*-statistics using standard errors corrected for clustering of estimates within studies. Figures in square brackets in Column (2) are *p*-values derived from applying the wild bootstrap. All estimates use weighted least squares using inverse variance weights; these are slightly different when *REE-WLS* is applied. One estimate is lost when the general model is estimated due to missing data on labor market regulation.

***, **, and * denote statistically significant at the 1%, 5% and 10% levels, respectively.

Both country dummies, *Europe* and *Developing*, have positive coefficients but with limited statistical significance, and the statistical significance of *Developing* in Column (2) is based on only two studies so it should be treated cautiously. When the two country dummies are replaced by a *NonUSA* binary variable pooling all non-US studies, the variable is not statistically significant. The evidence seems insufficient to identify country differences in the impact of unions on physical capital investment.

The measurement variables (*UnionDummy*, *WorksCouncil*, and *CapitalLabor*) are not individually or collectively statistically significant. What does matter is the specification of other variables. Inclusion of firm size results in correlations moving in the negative direction, whereas inclusion of competition or market share moves correlations in a positive direction. Estimates with data aggregated beyond the firm level find larger negative/smaller positive correlations *(NotFirm)*.

Conditional meta-average

We use the multiple MRA coefficients to derive conditional meta-averages in an econometric model that controls for firm size and competition or market share. Evaluating the meta-average for the United States and for firm-level data, we derive an estimated partial correlation of –0.075 with a *t*-statistic of –5.13. Using the wild bootstrap to correct standard errors for data dependence reduces the t-statistic to –1.58. In contrast, evaluating the meta-average for the impact of unions on investment at the industry level, we derive an estimated partial correlation of –0.233 with a t-statistic of –6.72. When the wild bootstrap is applied, the associated t-statistic is –3.22. Following the guidelines of Doucouliagos (2011), we view the partial correlation of –0.23 to represent a moderate to large adverse effect on capital investment.

Updating the data and re-calculating the meta-averages alters the Doucouliagos and Laroche (2003c) conclusion that unions had a negative effect on physical capital investment except in France. The larger data base shows that unions have a negative correlation with physical capital investment that is statistically significant when data beyond the firm level are used. This might reflect the spillover of small negative effects at the firm level that become detectable only when data are aggregated beyond the firm level. Or, it could reflect measurement issues relating to firm-level investment data. The safest conclusion is that unionization has a modest negative effect at the industry level.

Unions and investment in intangible capital[6]

Intangible forms of capital, associated with stocks of useful knowledge that show up in innovations, are essential drivers of economic growth and cross-country differences in incomes. Understanding the factors that obstruct or facilitate investment in intangible capital is important for firms and policy makers. Absent direct measures of innovation, defined in the Oslo Convention as the introduction of new products or processes to the market, almost all studies of innovation focus on investments in R&D or on indicators of innovation in the form of patents. Limited availability of data on unionization, R&D, and patents or other indicators of innovation has necessarily led to a limited supply of studies. In this section we seek to draw as much information as possible from the extant evidence.

Theory review

Much of the theory about union effects on physical capital applies to intangible capital as well. Unions can affect investment in intangible capital and innovation and technological change in various ways (Booth, 1995; Menezes-Filho and Van Reenen, 2003; Hirsch, 2007). They can induce firms to *invest in R&D* to improve technology to offset the higher cost of union labor. They can reduce the firm's ability to *gain fully* the benefits of new technology by appropriating some of the economic rents from those investments (Grout, 1984; Hirsch and Link, 1984; Fitzroy and Kraft, 1990; Denny and Nickell, 1991, 1992; Hirsch, 1991a). If projects vary in their vulnerability to quasi–rent appropriation, unions can affect the *type* of investment project firms make (Schnabel and Wagner, 1992b). Unions can also impact the *adoption* of technological change by influencing physical capital formation with technology embedded in new plant and equipment.

On the other side, unions receptive to organizational change and helping the firm retain trained staff can speed the diffusion of technology (Freeman and Medoff, 1984), which could produce a positive *net* effect on the incentives to invest in intangible assets (Menezes-Filho et al., 1998b). Bargaining models offer a wide range of theoretical possibilities (Tauman and Weiss, 1987; Ulph and Ulph, 1988, 1994, 1998; Menezes-Filho et al., 1998b) that vary with union attitudes to technological change that depend on organization and bargaining strength, members' preferences between wages and employment, product market competition, and the direction of technological change itself.

Consistent with this wide range of possibilities, econometric studies report a heterogeneity of results that is difficult to summarize save through meta-analysis. Doucouliagos and Laroche (2013) presented the first meta-analysis of extant studies, an analysis too recent to merit an effort to update, so in this section we reproduce the main results from it.

Studies of unionization and intangible capital investment

Our focus is on investments in intangible capital or proxies for innovation intended to produce innovation (Hornstein et al., 2007). Our sample excludes studies of new technologies imbedded in physical capital dealt with in the section on unions and physical capital investment and nine studies of the effects of unions on the *adoption* of technology. We also excluded several studies where key data, such as a *t*-statistic or a coefficient and its standard error were not reported. Studies that involve the same author(s) with the same data were combined together (e.g., Acs and Audretsch, 1987, 1988). Our literature search and selection produced 25 studies with 208 comparable estimates of the partial correlation of the association between unions and investments in intangible capital. The construction of the data and the subsequent meta-analysis conforms to the meta-analysis guidelines of Stanley et al. (2013).

The studies included in the MRA are listed in Table 5.5, with the country investigated, sample size, the median *t*-statistic and the median partial correlation. Table 5.6 lists some of the key features of this data, for all studies and also separately for US and UK studies. Most US studies report adverse innovation effects and just over half of the UK studies also report adverse associations. The simple unweighted average suggests a modest negative effect on intangible investment in the United States and a small adverse effect in the United Kingdom.

The funnel plot showing the association between partial correlations and their estimated precision in Figure 5.5 shows that the majority of estimates are negative. The dashed vertical line positions the unweighted average partial correlation at –0.09. The funnel plot appears to be roughly symmetrically distributed around the unweighted average, suggesting the relative absence of publication bias. Figure 5.6, which compares the funnel plots for estimates using US data to those for the rest of the world, shows a predominance of negative estimates in the United States and a more varied set of estimates for non-US studies. The time series pattern in the reported estimates displayed in Figure 5.7, shows that the partial correlations are, on average, becoming less negative. As we shall see, this finding is robust to the inclusion of other moderating variables in meta-regressions.

Table 5.5 Econometric studies of unions and investment in intangible capital

Author(s)	*Country*	*N*	*Median t-statistic*	*Median r*
		North America		
Acs & Audretsch (1987 & 1988)	US	247	−2.99	−0.19
Allen (1988b)	US	74	−3.42	−0.38
Audrecht & Schulenburg (1990)	US	246	−2.92	−0.19
Betcherman (1991)	Canada	455	−0.79	−0.04
Betts et al. (2001)	Canada	247	−3.82	−0.24
Bronars & Deere (1993)	US	660	−3.78	−0.15
Bronars et al. (1994)	US	320	−1.09	−0.08
Connolly et al. (1986)	US	367	−2.66	−0.14
Hirsch (1990a)	US	3,001	−3.30	−0.06
Hirsch (1991a)	US	4,327	−8.69	−0.13

(continued)

Table 5.5 Econometric studies of unions and investment in intangible capital (*continued*)

Author(s)	*Country*	*N*	*Median t-statistic*	*Median r*
Hirsch (1992)	US	4,176	−3.70	−0.15
Koeller (1996)	US	246	−0.77	−0.05
Nair-Reichert & Pomery (1999)	US	419	−2.51	−0.13
Taymaz (1991)	US	42	−0.71	−0.12
		All other		
Addison & Wagner (1994a & 1994b)	UK	33	0.03	0.01
Blundell et al. (1999)	UK	4,125	3.12	0.05
Fitzroy & Kraft (1990)	Germany	57	−2.44	−0.34
Geroski (1990)	UK	73	−1.00	−0.13
Kraft et al. (2011)	Germany	2,062	3.24	0.07
Menezes-Filho et al. (1998a & 1998b)	UK	3,611	−0.23	−0.01
Schnabel & Wagner (1992a & 1992b)	Germany	29	0.12	0.03
Schnabel & Wagner (1994)	Germany	31	0.15	0.04
Schulenburg & Wagner (1990)	Germany & US	247	−1.22	−0.21
Ulph & Ulph (1989)	UK	33	−2.86	−0.48

Notes: Calculated by the authors from the primary econometric studies. The table reports medians for all comparable estimates, combining estimates from various measures of unionization and innovation. *N* denotes total sample size used in the study; *r* denotes partial correlation.

Table 5.6 Basic characteristics of the unions and intangible capital investment literature

	All studies (1)	*US studies* (2)	*UK studies* (3)
Number of studies	25	15	5
Number of estimates	208	120	54
Total sample size	25,884	18,334	4,669
% reporting adverse union effects	75%	86%	56%
% US	58%	100%	0%
% manufacturing	64%	85%	20%
Average partial correlation	−0.094	−0.120	−0.021

Note: Average partial correlation is an unweighted average.
Source: Authors' calculations.

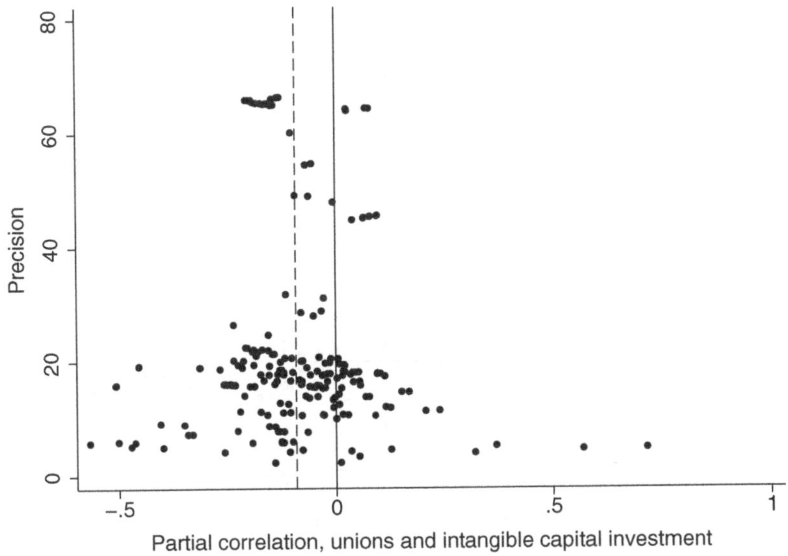

Figure 5.5 Funnel plot of unions and intangible capital investment, all estimates

Note: Solid and dashed vertical lines denote zero and the uncorrected and unweighted average correlation (−0.09), respectively.

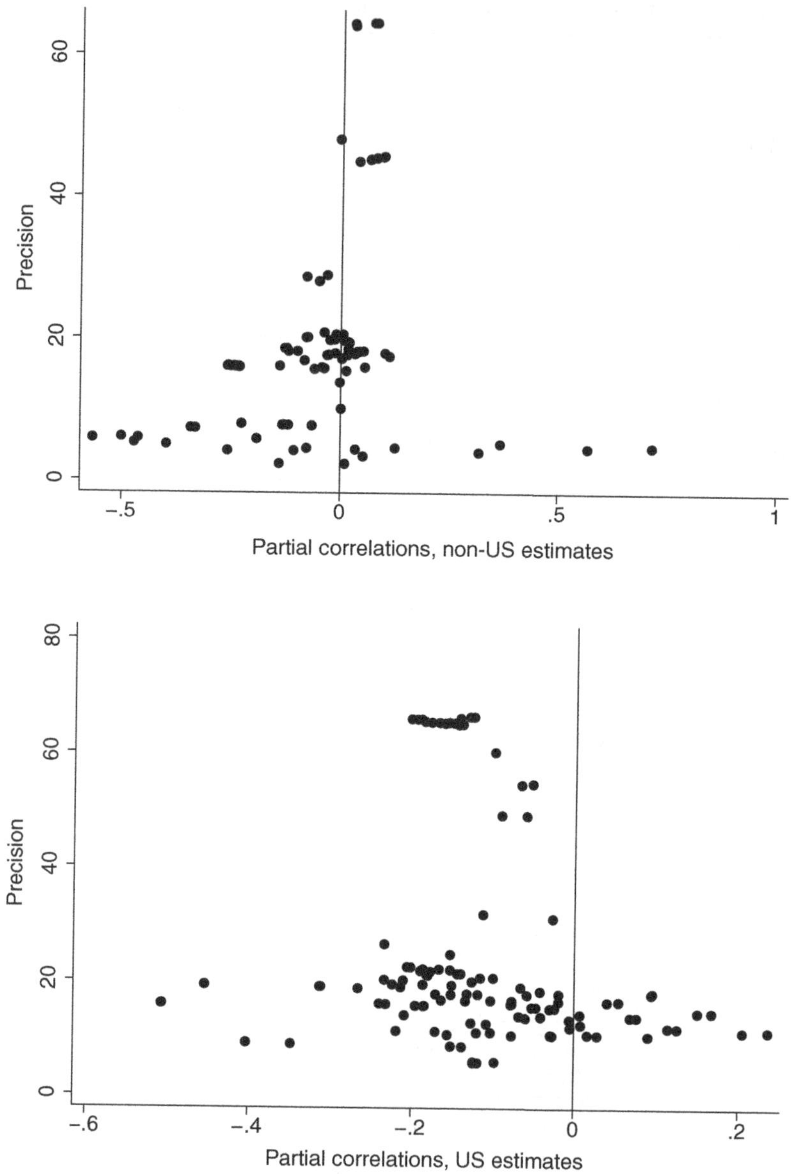

Figure 5.6 Funnel plots of unions and intangible capital investment, comparison of non-US and US estimates

Note: The vertical solid lines show a zero effect size.

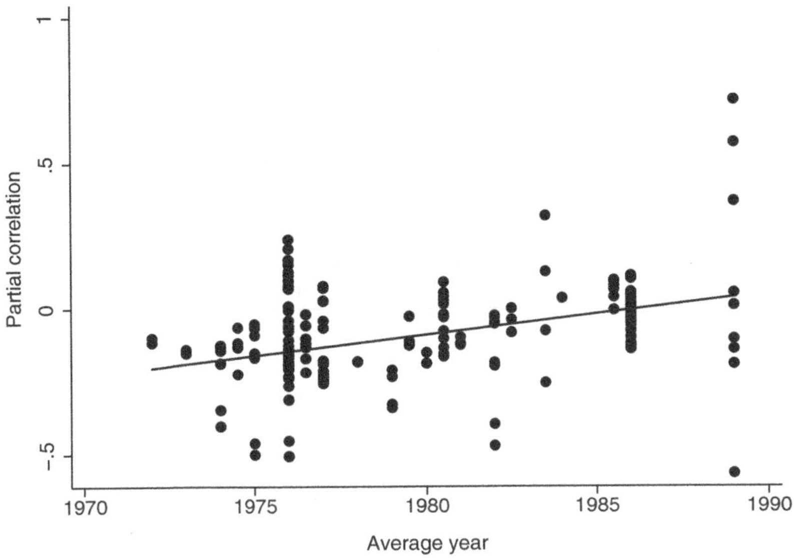

Figure 5.7 Unions and intangible capital investment, partial correlations, chronological order

The unconditional meta-average correlation, unionization and investment in intangible capital

Table 5.7 reports the unconditional averages for all studies, US studies and non-US studies. Column (1) reports unweighted averages. Columns (2) and (3) report the *FEE-WLS* and *REE-WLS* weighted meta-averages, respectively. Columns (4) and (5) report the *PET* and *FAT* coefficient estimates, respectively. Column (6) reports the *PEESE* model estimates. On balance, the unconditional meta-averages show the negative correlation between unions and investment in intangible capital found in the visual reading of the funnel plots and show that this is driven mainly by the United States. But the *FAT* coefficient suggests preferential reporting bias in favor of positive investment in intangible capital correlations in the United States and in favor of negative investment in intangible capital correlations in non-US studies.

Meta-regression analysis of heterogeneity, unionization and investment in intangible capital

The unconditional averages ignore the heterogeneity displayed in Figures 5.5 and 5.6. Several moderating factors might explain the variation in findings. One potential contextual factor is the environment in which unions operate. Union effects may vary according to industry and time period, and to country differences in industrial relations and regulatory regimes. Measurement differences among the indicators of intangible capital, which range from R&D relative to sales to the number of patents, might moderate the unions and investment in intangible capital findings.

Table 5.7 Unconditional meta-average partial correlation, unions and intangible capital

	Unweighted average (1)	*FEE-WLS, weighted average (2)*	*REE-WLS, weighted average (3)*	*FAT-PET, selection bias corrected weighted average (PET) (4)*	*FAT-PET, publication selection bias (FAT) (5)*	*PEESE corrected weighted average (6)*
All studies (n = 208, k = 25) (1)	−0.094*** (−3.91)	−0.095** (−2.39)	−0.096*** (−3.70)	−0.096 (−1.66)	0.031 (0.04)	−0.095** (−2.19)
US studies (n = 120, k = 15) (2)	−0.120*** (−8.88)	−0.143*** (−8.62)	−0.125*** (−8.45)	−0.159*** (−7.44)	0.638** (2.06)	−0.150*** (−7.61)
Non-US studies (n = 88, k = 12) (3)	−0.059 (−1.46)	0.014 (0.48)	−0.051 (−1.25)	0.078*** (3.50)	−1.961** (−2.50)	0.022 (0.88)

Notes: Column 1 reports the unweighted average. The other columns report the fixed-effect (*FEE-WLS*), random-effects (*REE-WLS*), *FAT-PET*, and *PEESE* meta-averages, respectively. Columns (2) to (6) are estimated using WLS, using inverse variance weights; column (3) uses random-effects inverse variance weights. Column 4 reports the *PET* coefficient; publication bias corrected average. Column 5 reports the *FAT* coefficient; degree of publication bias. Figures in brackets are *t*-statistics using standard errors adjusted for clustering of observations within studies. n and k denote number of observations and studies, respectively.

*** and ** denote statistical significance at the 1% and 5% levels, respectively.

Differences in labor market regulations and the centralization or decentralization of industrial relations may also affect the association between unions and investment in intangibles. Less regulated labor markets could stimulate innovation by increasing flexibility, reducing production cost and increasing incentives to innovate, especially where technological change requires labor adjustment, and could limit the extent to which unions can capture rents arising from technology. This would reduce the negative correlation between unionism and investment in intangibles. Alternatively, labor market regulation might stimulate innovation. Tighter labor market regulations strengthen the position and bargaining power of insiders, increasing their wages and increasing incentives to invest in R&D and process innovations that save on labor. In the Freeman and Medoff tradition, Storm and Naastepad (2009) argue that regulations might increase innovation if they increase worker motivation and commitment to the firm, making it easier to introduce labor-saving technical change. Indeed, they find that for OECD countries, labor market regulation increased productivity growth. Francois and Roberts (2003) argue that the more regulated European labor markets might enable firms to extract work effort at a lower cost, compared to US-type labor markets; while

Acharya et al. (2013) note that labor market flexibility might reduce innovation if employees fear that they will be punished for 'short-run failures' in innovative activities.

Moderator variables

We include 26 potential explanatory variables in our meta-regression analysis of heterogeneity, from *SE* to control for publication bias to industry and country dummy variables, measures of unionization, measures of investment in intangible capital, and labor market regulations. Doucouliagos and Laroche (2013) provide details on the construction of the data variables and full results.

The general MRA includes eight data variables. Three are binary variables relating to country differences: *UK*, *Germany*, and *Canada*, with the United States used as the base. *Industry level* is a binary variable taking the value of 1 if the estimates relate to industry-level innovation data and 0 if they relate to firm/establishment-level data. *Services* and *Various* are binary variables taking the value of 1 if the estimates relate purely to services industries or several industries, respectively, with manufacturing as the base, to examine the Hirsch (1990a, 1991a, 1992) view that the association of unionism with investment in intangible capital varies by sector. *Panel* is a binary variable with the value of 1 if panel data are used (with cross-sectional data as the base). *AveYear* represents the average year of the sample.

The MRA includes four variables for differences in measures. *Industry union* taking the value of 1 if industry-level union density is used (with firm-level unionization as the base). *UnionDummy* takes the value of 1 if a union dummy is used (with a firm-level union density as the base). *RD Level* and *Innovation* are binary variables taking the value of 1 if the dependent variable is measured as the dollar value of R&D and the number of patents, respectively, with R&D-to-sales ratio as the base.

We also consider twelve covariates likely to impact investment in intangible capital: *Firm size*, *Profitability*, *Concentration*, *Market share*, *Firm age*, *Wages*, *Advertising*, *Skills*, *Industry dummies*, *Growth*, *High-tech firm*, and *Time trend*. These are all binary variables taking the value of 1 if these variables are part of the econometric specification. The human capital (*Skills*) measure may affect the union intangible investment association because unions in high-skilled firms are likely to view technological change more favorably if, as seems plausible, their skill protects them from possible job loss. Likewise, profits (*Profitability*) are important, as they finance investments.

Finally, the MRA includes *Non-OLS* to capture the effect of different estimators, with OLS as the base.

The association between unions and innovation can depend on the institutional structure of collective bargaining and the nature of the industrial relations system in ways that our *LabReg* indicator will only imperfectly measure. In countries such as Germany, unions and employers are more likely to regard each other as partners. Such cooperative industrial relations can facilitate technological progress and innovation (Schnabel and Wagner, 1992a). Our *LabReg* variable is constructed by taking into account the existence and size of the minimum wage, the degree of hiring and firing regulation, the degree of centralization of collective bargaining, and the mandated cost of hiring and firing. It is a proxy to which labor markets deviate from the competitive labor market model that we constructed from information outside the primary studies. As discussed in Chapter 3, one benefit of MRA is that it can consider factors that were not considered by the original econometric studies. Pooling the estimates from different studies and collecting data on labor market regulation, we can explore the links between these two series.

What do the MRA results show?

The baseline multiple MRA results are reported in Table 5.8. The constant in the MRA is negative, suggesting an inverse association between unions and investment in intangible capital when all other binary variables take a value of zero. However, the coefficient on *AveYear* is positive which indicates that this adverse association is *declining* over time. The three non-US dummies (*Canada*, *Germany*, and the *UK*) were not statistically significant and were removed in the general-to-specific modeling. The similarity of the partial correlation in these countries with that for the United States suggests that the negative association of unionism with investment in intangible capital applies to *all* countries in the data set.

While the country dummies are not statistically significant, the MRA indicates that regulatory differences matter and that the *negative* partial correlation of unionism with investments in intangible capital is higher with weaker regulations. These results contrast to the view that regulations are harmful to innovation (e.g., Alesina et al. 2015) and supportive of Schnabel and Wagner's (1994) view that adversarial industrial relations (such as those found in the United States and the United Kingdom) are more likely to result in adverse effects on innovation, than cooperative ones (countries such as Germany), reflecting their general point that "Efficient bargaining and the cooperative behavior it entails depend on the legal framework, the institutional structure of collective bargaining, the design of negotiated contracts, and the style of industrial relations" (p. 493). The variable *LabReg*, however also includes the minimum wage and regulations over hiring and firing. Doucouliagos and Laroche (2013) examined a variable that focused purely on collective bargaining and found the expected negative coefficient but with lower statistical significance.

Data differences are a prime determinant of heterogeneity in reported union-investment in intangible capital correlations. The use of industry-level data produces larger negative correlations, compared to firm-level data. In contrast, the use of industry-level unionization data results in smaller negative correlations compared to firm-level union data. Measuring unionization as a binary variable instead of the more informative union density also results in smaller adverse union-innovation effects. More important, studies that use number of patents and number of innovations (*Innovation*) find a much smaller adverse effect than studies that make R&D the dependent variable. This indicates that while unions depress investment in R&D, they may not affect actual innovation as much.

Table 5.8 Unions and investment in intangible capital, multiple MRA

Explanatory variable	*Specific FEE-WLS*
	(1)
Constant (USA)	−17.095*** (−5.45)
Industry level	−0.190*** (7.14)
Industry union	0.06*** (2.89)
UnionDummy	0.046*** (5.14)
Innovation	0.139*** (6.99)
Profitability	0.013** (2.51)
Skills	0.074** (2.69)
Advertising	−0.109*** (3.99)
Market share	0.041* (1.91)
Wages	−0.036* (1.74)
Firm age	−0.058*** (3.09)
Industry dummies	0.014** (2.55)
Time trend	0.022*** (2.87)
AveYear	0.009*** (5.44)
LabReg	−0.010** (2.38)
SE	0.795** (2.41)
Studies/Observations	208 (25)
Adjusted R^2	0.68

Notes: The dependent variable is the partial correlation between unions and intangible capital investment. Estimated by unrestricted weighted least squares, using inverse variance weights. Figures in brackets are *absolute* values of *t*-statistics, using cluster data analysis to adjust standard errors.
***, **, and * denote statistically significant at the 1%, 5% and 10% levels, respectively.
Source: Doucouliagos and Laroche (2013).

The MRA shows that econometric specification differences affect the results. Controlling for the firm's age, advertising and wages produces larger negative unionization and investment in intangible capital correlations. In contrast, inclusion of industry dummies, a time trend (or time fixed effects), market share, human capital (skills), and profitability in the econometric specification produce smaller adverse effects.

Several variables did not appear to be important in explaining the differences between estimates. Controlling for industry concentration, firm size, the firm's growth, and whether a firm is a high-tech firm all make no difference to the partial correlations. The MRA also suggests no difference in the estimates of union-intangible capital association between cross-sectional and panel data nor between estimates derived from OLS and those derived from other estimators, with one exception: use of time fixed effects in panel estimations results in slightly less adverse innovation effects.

Conditional meta-average correlation, unionization and intangible capital

How strong is the correlation between unionization and intangible capital? According to Cohen (1988), a correlation of 0.2 is a 'small' effect, 0.50 is a 'medium' effect, and anything larger than 0.8 is 'large'. However, partial correlations can be larger or smaller than zero order correlations. Following Doucouliagos's (2011) guidelines for partial correlations, we label a partial correlation less than 0.048 as 'small', 0.112 as 'medium', and greater than 0.234 as 'large'.

When firm-level data are used and intangible capital measured as R&D, the partial correlation for the United States is estimated to be –0.22, rising to –0.34 when industry-level data are used – moderate to large. If the measure is patents and innovation counts the partial correlation for the United States is estimated to be –0.08, rising to –0.20 when industry-level data are used – small to medium.

For a sub-set of 128 estimates we calculated the percentage change in intangible capital resulting from a one percentage change in unionization. Evaluated at sample means, this suggests that unionization is associated with a 7 percent reduction in investment in intangible capital, which if causal is of practical economic significance.

We draw four conclusions from the meta-analysis of unions and intangible capital. First, the available evidence indicates that unions are associated with lower investment in intangible capital – a result consistent with the tax on capital and union rent-seeking monopoly face of union behavior. But the evidence also indicates that unions have larger negative correlations with R&D than with counts of patents and innovations. Second, country differences in the association are driven largely by the degree of labor market regulation, with more regulated labor markets seeming to experience less union resistance to technology. Third, the unionization and investment in intangible capital association has been declining over time. Fourth, MRA shows that most of the variation in reported estimates can be explained by differences in the data used (firm versus industry), the measurement of technology (R&D versus patents), and the econometric specification.

Summary

Our meta-regression analysis points to a modest negative association between unions on physical capital formation when data is aggregated beyond the firm level, and a larger negative association of unionism with investments in intangible capital, consistent with the tax on capital and union rent-sharing predictions. The meta-regressions showed heterogeneity in reported estimates and identified several factors that can explain heterogeneity. Some of these factors relate to specification of the econometric models and others relate to genuine economic effects. While we found no evidence of selection bias in estimates of the association of unionism and physical capital investment, we found some modest selection bias in estimates of the impact of unions on investments in intangible capital investment. We also uncovered a pattern in which the negative union effect on intangible capital investment is greater in less regulated labor markets. Perhaps the most important finding that deserves further analysis is the weakened negative association between unionism and investment over time: Does it reflect differential success of unions more favorable to investment? Changes in union attitudes over time? Or increased ability of firms to protect the rents from investments for the firm? Given that policy is forward-looking, it is important to pin down the trend and determine if it is likely to eliminate the negative association, and if so, why.

The association of unionism with less investment in physical capital and intangible capital suggests that unions have an adverse association with productivity and productivity growth through the channel of investment behavior of firms. To what extent, if at all, does the effect of unions on the behavior of workers counteract this impact to produce the negligible net effects on productivity and productivity growth discussed in Chapters 3 and 4? We address this question in Chapter 6.

Notes

1 This section builds upon Doucouliagos, C.(H.) and Laroche, P. (2003c) Unions and tangible investments: A review and new evidence in France, *Relations Industrielles/ Industrial Relations*, 58: 14–37. Here we update the data and meta-regression analysis.

2 Landlords and governments can behave in a similar fashion. Thus, even non-unionized industries may face these threats.

3 Underinvestment can also occur in non-unionized firms faced with efficiency wages (Shapiro and Stiglitz, 1984; Machin and Wadhwani, 1991).

4 As was the case in Chapter 3, we estimate a *FAT-PET* and then identify any observation with a standardized residual greater than 3.5 as an outlier. As a result we eliminated the study of Chen and Chen (2013) as being an outlier. We also exclude studies that present probit estimations and, hence, are not comparable with the rest of the literature (e.g. Machin and Wadhwani, 1991).

5 The combined coefficient, β, was calculated as $\beta = \beta_1 + 2\beta_2\overline{X}$, where β_1 and β_2 are the coefficients on the linear and quadratic terms, respectively, and $\overline{X}$ is the mean value of union density. This was then converted into a partial correlation. The standard error was calculated as $SE(\beta) = \sqrt{SE(\beta_1)^2 + 4SE(\beta_2)^2\overline{X}^2}$. In deriving this standard error we assume, out of necessity, that the covariance between the two density terms is zero.

6 This section draws very heavily from Doucouliagos, C.(H.) and Laroche, P. (2013) Unions and innovation: New insights from the cross-country evidence, *Industrial Relations: A Journal of Economy and Society*, 52: 467–91.

6 Unions and productivity

Employee behavior channels

This chapter synthesizes research on estimates of union effects on three types of employee behavior and attitudes that are potential channels through which unionization impacts productivity: voluntary turnover, job satisfaction, and commitment to the organization for whom they work. In contrast to the investment decisions analyzed in Chapter 5, which firms determine, the behaviors and attitudes investigated in this chapter are set by workers.

Our review of the meta-statistics evidence finds: (1) that unions are associated with reduced employee turnover, per Freeman and Medoff's (1984) analysis; (2) that the magnitude of the union job satisfaction effect has varied over time, trending toward zero over time, but does not appear to be causal; and (3) that commitment to unions is positively associated with workers' commitment to the firm. Since reduced turnover cuts labor costs and increases worker and firm incentives to invest in firm-specific skills, and since increased organizational commitment is associated with performance, these seem to be the strongest channels of worker behavior through which unions improve productivity.

The results in this chapter and those in Chapter 5 together help explain the negligible union productivity effects found in the reduced-form production function estimates in Chapter 3, as the positive effects on productivity through the worker channels counterbalance the negative effects of unions on productivity on capital investment. The results also fit well with studies of union wage effects and Chapter 7's analysis of union effects on the firm's finances that show unions shifting factor incomes from capital to labor.

Unions and employee turnover

Voluntary labor turnover is essential to re-allocating labor among establishments and sectors and allowing workers and firms to obtain better matches over time, but turnover above some basic level raises the cost of production and lowers productivity and profitability, especially if it results in a loss of firm-specific skills (Freeman, 1976; Brown and Medoff, 1978; Addison and Barnett, 1982). When experienced employees leave the organization, they take with them their accumulated human capital (Osterman, 1987) and add to the human resource management costs of recruitment, selection, and training expenses associated with their replacement. If unions reduce voluntary employee turnover, by raising wages and benefits that keep them with an employer longer than otherwise, by providing greater employment security and better conditions at work, and by establishing a means of expressing discontent in the workplace, unions can raise productivity and profitability (Hammer and Avgar, 2005).

There is a sufficiently large body of research documenting that low turnover improves company performance and a smaller but still substantial number of studies that report that unionization is associated with low turnover to make the union–turnover–productivity relation a real rather than a theoretical channel from unionism to productivity.

Turnover and performance

There are two ways to study the relation between turnover and performance: by examining the effect of turnover at establishments or firms on the establishment or firm output and/or labor productivity, conducted primarily by economists or business specialists; and by examining studies of the job performance of workers who leave a firm, conducted primarily by psychologists. Both sets of studies tend to find that turnover is negatively correlated with output, but they have very different causal meanings. As noted above, economics studies of firm turnover focus on the costs that high turnover brings to a firm: loss of output before the worker is replaced, which can be especially high when workers with firm-specific skills leave; and the resources needed to recruit and train a replacement. Psychology studies of turnover typically contrast the performance of a worker who leaves a firm to that of workers who remain at the firm.[1] A negative correlation implies that below average performers were more likely to leave, presumably because they had a bad employer-employee match. It is silent on the effects of turnover on the firm or organization. To the extent that lower performers leave a firm and the costs of replacement and disruption are modest,[2] a negative effect suggests a positive effect on firms.

The three meta-studies that examine turnover and performance of a work unit – Hancock et al. (2013), Heavey et al. (2013), and Park and Shaw (2013) – find a negative association between employee turnover and performance with diverse measures of productivity or other factors that contribute to profitability, with the magnitude of the correlations varying across industries and with measures of productivity. On the low side, Hancock et al. (2013) apply meta-analysis to 134 estimates from 48 studies and find a correlation of –0.03 when all estimates are assessed – a correlation of –0.07 for manufacturing and transportation industries – but stronger associations when productivity is measured by quality of output in terms of customer service (–0.10) or quality and safety (–0.12).

Heavey et al. (2013) give a meta-analysis of the relation between turnover and its determinants and turnover and indicators of productivity from 82 studies with 694 estimated effects. But the number of primary studies included in the meta-analysis and estimated effects varies with the measure of productivity and turnover. There are just four studies which relate voluntary turnover to measures of productivity at the work unit. They give an average correlation of –0.25 for productive efficiency, –0.29 for customer satisfaction, and 0.14 for error rates, with the sign reversal reflecting the positive value of the first two variables and the cost of error rates. Heavey et al. also report on 10 studies that link sales efficiency to involuntary turnover, with an average correlation of –0.11. Results for total turnover are qualitatively similar, with larger samples.[3]

Park and Shaw (2013) use 61 studies that collectively draw upon 56,761 observations for their analysis of turnover and productivity. They report an average corrected correlation of –0.13 between turnover and productivity and an average correlation of –0.15 between *voluntary* turnover and workforce productivity. They also use 53 samples for turnover and financial performance and obtain a correlation of –0.11.

In sum, the evidence from the extant meta-studies confirms an overall negative association between turnover and productivity that by Cohen's (1988) guidelines for zero-order correlations, range between small to medium, depending on the measure of productivity, turnover, and organizational unit.

Unionization and turnover

In their review of nine studies, Freeman and Medoff (1984: 101) conclude that "independent of raising wages, unionism substantially reduces quits". Following their work on the United States, studies for the United Kingdom (e.g., Wilson and Peel, 1991) and Australia (e.g., Miller and Mulvey, 1991) also reported negative relations between unionism and voluntary separations. In the 2000s Martin (2003) examined unionization and labor turnover in UK establishments and also reported a substantial negative relation. Without providing a meta-analysis of preceding work, he summarized the existing literature of studies of individuals and industries as giving a "well established" negative effect, with debates focused on the pathway for the effect (p. 398). Many industrial relations researchers treat the unionization and turnover issue as settled.

We have identified two meta-analyses that study the impact of union presence on employee turnover. Cotton and Tuttle (1986, Table 4) conducted a meta-analysis of 10 studies that included a union variable and found that employee turnover declines with union presence with higher statistical significance than any other variable "external" to the person and work. Heavey et al.'s (2013) meta-analysis examined 13 studies that linked union density to turnover and 18 studies that linked a 0–1 dichotomous union presence variable to turnover. This analysis reported negative correlations of –0.21 and –0.13 between turnover and union density and union presence, respectively.

These meta-studies have weaknesses that make their estimates not fully comparable with the meta-analysis in Chapters 3, 4, and 5. They do not address issues of publication and specification bias nor report the research designs in a sufficiently clear way to easily assess potential bias introduced by research design.

The biggest weakness in extant studies, however, is in determining the extent to which turnover is lower in unionized than in non-unionized firms through greater voice mechanisms such as grievance and discipline arbitration as opposed to the union wage premium. Since most union workplaces have both greater voice mechanisms, including collective bargaining, and higher wages, it is hard to differentiate the two. Analysis of turnover among individuals conditional on wages shows a union effect independent of wages (Freeman, 1980), which suggests that unions do something more to reduce worker quits than raising wages, but it is hard to determine exactly what that something is, absent detailed data on the full set of work conditions facing an employee.

Studies of the channel by which unions reduce turnover vary by industry. Rees (1991) reported that turnover was lower in schools with stronger grievance procedures. Delery et al. (2000) show that in trucking, the union wage premium accounts for most of the union effect on turnover, with union grievance systems and other voice mechanisms contributing little to the union turnover effect. Martin (2003) attributed most of the reduction in UK establishments to unions improving working conditions. By contrast, in telecommunications, Batt et al. (2002) found that union representation was associated with lower quit rates independent of compensation and other human resource practices likely to be affected by collective bargaining. Voice mechanisms such as self-directed teams and problem-solving groups also lowered quits but found no link between quit rates and non-union dispute resolution procedures. As teaching, trucking, and telecommunications have different work environments, the heterogeneity in the channel for the reduction in turnover associated with unions meshes with the differences in union effects presented throughout this book.

Finally, since some voluntary separation is almost certainly optimal for the firm as well as for the employee who chose to leave, and possibly for other employees (if the departing worker performed poorly), reductions in labor turnover need not invariably raise productivity. Still, the desire of most firms to reduce turnover suggests that turnover is likely to be excessive. From this perspective, the findings from meta-studies and referenced articles in this section are consistent with the CV/IR model in which union reductions in turnover is a major channel through which unions contribute to productivity.

Unions and job satisfaction[4]

The literature on job satisfaction and productivity is enormous, with studies beginning in the 1930s "coinciding with (and as a result of) the Hawthorne studies and the ensuing human relations movement" (Judge et al. 2001: 376) that examine the linkage between employee attitudes and performance from what seems to be every possible angle. There are two requisites for job satisfaction to be a channel by which unions affect productivity: satisfaction must link to performance, and unions must affect satisfaction. We examine the evidence for these two requisites in turn.

Job satisfaction and performance

Several researchers have used meta-analysis to review studies of the association between job satisfaction and job performance from the 1980s to the present, uniformly finding a positive association. The implication is either that more satisfied workers are more productive, or that more productive workers are more satisfied, or both. In an early review of 16 studies Petty et al. (1984) report a correlation of 0.31 between satisfaction and performance. Using a larger database of 74 studies, Iaffaldano and Muchinsky (1985) found a lower correlation of 0.17, which they viewed as showing relatively little association between the variables. A larger meta-analysis by Judge et al. (2001) found a correlation of 0.30 between job satisfaction and job performance, based on 312 estimates. Bowling's (2007) meta-analysis found that the satisfaction–performance correlation drops substantially after controlling for general personality traits or work locus of control and was almost completely eliminated after controlling for organization-based self-esteem. This result highlights the problem of differentiating the widely used satisfaction variable from other self-reported measures of personality/self-esteem. But at the *workplace level*, the raw link between the job satisfaction measure of subjective attitudes and performance remains at high, statistically significant levels. Whitman et al.'s (2010) meta-analysis reported a correlation of 0.35 between collective job satisfaction and work unit performance.

Overall, we view the evidence for the positive association of satisfaction with performance as strong, though subject to the proviso that all the meta-analysis studies summarize studies with simple correlations, compared to the partial correlations that we used in Chapters 3, 4, and 5. Still, even modest correlations can be potentially meaningful from a practical perspective, depending on the size of the regression coefficients that link performance to satisfaction.

Unionization and job satisfaction

There is a considerable literature exploring the relationship between unionization and job satisfaction (see Hammer and Avgar, 2005, for a review). Freeman (1978) notes the paradox in the 1970s data that showed unionized workers reported themselves less satisfied than non-union workers but also as less inclined to leave their jobs, and attributed it to the greater willingness of union members to express discontent with working conditions, particularly when their union was entering into bargaining. By expressing dissatisfaction with current terms and conditions, this voice mechanism could identify working conditions that the firm should improve. Other analysts grounded the greater job dissatisfaction under unionism with the characteristics of the jobs union workers held and/or the attributes of workers that led them to unionize. Pfeffer and Davis-Blake (1990) argue that unionized jobs are less attractive than comparable non-union jobs in the nature of tasks or working conditions, producing greater dissatisfaction. In this case the lower quit rate would presumably be due to the higher union wages and benefits. For example, unpleasant jobs (e.g., in the mining and chemical industries) are more likely to lead workers to unionize, which may produce higher wages and benefits without doing much to change the work conditions that underlie the job dissatisfaction (Pfeffer and Davis-Blake, 1990; Gordon and Denisi, 1995; Bender and Sloane, 1998). In addition, jobs may also become less attractive after unionization if management reacts to higher labor costs by decreasing allocations to the physical work environment or putting pressure on employees (see Hammer and Avgar, 2005).

Bryson et al. (2010) argue that dissatisfied workers have greater incentives to join a union, so that job dissatisfaction influences union membership.

Other research challenges the view that unionized workers are less satisfied with their jobs than non-unionized workers. Pfeffer and Davis-Blake (1990) stress three channels by which unions might make workers more satisfied with their jobs: (1) by improving job outcomes that benefit most workers, such as reducing wage inequality and creating more open managerial procedures in the workplace; (2) by giving workers greater power over their work (Kanter, 1977); and (3) by creating stronger organizational commitment, which should raise job satisfaction, especially in workplaces where union members are more often involved in union activities.

What does meta-analysis of research tell us about how union membership affects job satisfaction?

Premack (1984) provides the only meta-analysis of unions and overall satisfaction for the earlier period. Synthesizing the results of 10 studies published between 1976 and 1981, he found a negative correlation of –0.38.[5] With data covering a much longer period, Laroche (2016) examines the relationship between unionization and job satisfaction with a meta-analysis of 235 estimates from 59 studies published between 1975 and 2015.[6] These studies are listed in Table 6.1, with Table 6.2 giving some of the salient features of the meta-data. The studies, which are nearly evenly split between the United States and the United Kingdom, show considerable difference between the associations by country. Eighty percent of the UK estimates give a negative union-satisfaction relation compared to 58 percent of the US estimates. The uncorrected and unweighted average is negative in both samples and is twice as large for the United Kingdom, but the unweighted average partial correlation is small, suggesting that unions have little impact on satisfaction.

Table 6.1 Econometric studies of unions and job satisfaction

Author(s)	*Country*	*N*	*Median t-statistic*	*Median r*
	North America			
Artz (2010)	US	70,523	–1.39	–0.01
Artz (2012)	US	40,937	–0.26	–0.01
Artz & Kaya (2014)	US	2,133	1.52	0.03
Bartel (1981)	US	2,728	–0.97	–0.02
Bender et al. (2005)	US	1,819	–1.42	–0.04
Bender & Sloane (1998)	UK	346	–0.97	–0.07
Berg (1999)	US	1,355	1.10	0.03

(*continued*)

Table 6.1 Econometric studies of unions and job satisfaction (*continued*)

Author(s)	*Country*	*N*	*Median t-statistic*	*Median r*
Blanchflower & Oswald (2000)	US/ Various	14,571	–2.36	–0.05
Borjas (1979)	US	1,873	–2.56	–0.06
Cotti et al. (2014)	US	1,636	2.33	0.06
Donohue & Heywood (2004)	US	6,017	1.04	0.02
Evans & Ondrack (1990)	Canada	1,193	0.19	0.01
Freeman (1978)	US	3,730	–2.60	–0.06
Gius (2012)	US	32,050	–1.08	–0.01
Gordon & Denisi (1995)	US	1,513	–0.01	–0.01
Hersch & Stone (1990)	US	380	–1.95	–0.10
Heywood & Wei (2006)	US	8,859	1.36	0.02
Idson (1990)	US	1,455	–0.47	–0.01
Kalleberg & Loscocco (1983)	US	1,303	1.81	0.05
Kosteas (2011)	US	18,364	–0.92	–0.01
Lillydahl & Singell (1993)	US	918	–2.00	–0.08
Lincoln & Boothe (1993)	US/Japan	2,788	–3.39	–0.08
Meng (1990)	Canada	2,000	–0.92	–0.02
Mohr & Zoghi (2008)	Canada	23,211	–0.39	–0.01
Pfeffer & Davis-Blake (1990)	US	978	1.77	0.06
Pohler & Luchak (2014)	Canada	8,300	–0.50	–0.01
Renaud (2002)	Canada	3,352	–0.50	–0.01
Smerek & Peterson (2007)	US	1,132	–0.64	–0.02
Uppal (2005)	Canada	4,474	0.00	0
	United Kingdom			
Artz (2008)	UK	1,627	–0.70	–0.06
Belfield & Harris (2002)	UK	3,223	–1.73	–0.04
Bryson et al. (2004)	UK	18,012	–3.93	–0.03

Author(s)	*Country*	*N*	*Median t-statistic*	*Median r*
Clark (1997)	UK	4,743	–2.85	–0.04
Clark et al. (1996)	UK	4,478	–2.25	–0.03
Drakopoulos & Theodossiou (1997)	UK	1,183	1.89	0.06
Green & Heywood (2008)	UK	43,215	–5.86	–0.03
Green & Heywood (2015)	UK	79,472	–3.27	–0.02
Guest & Conway (2004)	UK	28,147	–1.96	–0.01
Heywood et al. (2002)	UK	9,604	–3.80	–0.05
Jones & Sloane (2009)	UK	15,916	–6.69	–0.05
Pouliakas & Theodossiou (2009)	UK	43,540	–2.14	–0.03
Powdthavee (2011)	UK	23,259	–0.21	–0.01
Rose (2003)	UK	7,292	–2.58	–0.03
Sloane & Williams (2000)	UK	2,128	1.71	0.04
Sousa-Poza & Sousa-Poza (2003)	UK	43,231	–6.47	–0.04
Theodossiou & Zangelidis (2007, 2009)	UK	16,809	–0.90	–0.01
	All others			
Bockerman & Ilmakuna (2006)	Finland	2,745	–0.07	–0.01
Drago et al. (1993)	Australia	565	0.00	0
Fiorillo & Nappo (2014)	Italy	68,325	–3.06	–0.01
Fleming & Kler (2008)	Australia	3,006	–0.20	–0.01
Garcia-Serrano (2009)	Spain	12,241	0.06	0.01
Garcia-Serrano (2011)	Spain	12,183	0.35	0.01
Holland et al. (2011)	Australia	1,022	0.47	0.02
Kim & Kim (2004)	Korea	857	4.69	0.16
Long (2005)	Australia	3,499	–2.64	–0.05

(*continued*)

Table 6.1 Econometric studies of unions and job satisfaction (*continued*)

Author(s)	*Country*	*N*	*Median t-statistic*	*Median r*
Miller (1990)	Australia	1,903	–3.17	–0.07
Theodossiou & Vasileiou (2007)	Europe	5,778	–2.76	–0.04
Wooden & Warren (2004)	Australia	3,401	–2.23	–0.04
Zeytinoglu et al. (2013)	Turkey	305	0.95	0.06

Notes: Calculated by the authors from the primary studies. The table reports medians for all comparable estimates. N denotes total sample size used in the primary econometric study; *r* denotes partial correlation.

Table 6.2 Basic characteristics of the unions and job satisfaction literature

	All studies (1)	*US studies (2)*	*UK studies (3)*
Number of studies	59	22	17
Number of estimates	235	90	84
Total sample size	721,647	259,938	345,879
% reporting adverse union effects	68%	58%	80%
% US	38%	100	–
Average partial correlation	–0.016	–0.010	–0.024

Note: Average partial correlation is an unweighted and uncorrected average.
Source: Authors' calculations.

Figure 6.1 presents a funnel plot of partial correlations of unionization and satisfaction. Given the division of the sample between the United States and United Kingdom, Figure 6.2 presents the funnel plots for only UK and only US estimates, respectively. The funnel plot for US studies is symmetrically centered on a zero partial correlation, while the funnel for the United Kingdom displays some asymmetry, centered on a negative value.

Table 6.3 reports unconditional meta-averages using a format similar to those in Chapters 3, 4, and 5. The meta-averages are small and statistically significant only for the United Kingdom.

Laroche's (2016) meta-analysis finds that when primary studies control for the endogeneity of union membership through instrumental variables or fixed effects models, the difference in job satisfaction between unionized and non-unionized workers disappears. This suggests that the relationship between unionization and overall job satisfaction is not truly due to unionism but is more related to the type of individuals or jobs that get unionized. The next two tables from Laroche (2016) probe the statistical evidence behind this claim. Table 6.4 gives descriptive statistics of the moderator variables for the satisfaction-union relation. Table 6.5 gives the characteristics of meta-regressions that analyze heterogeneity.

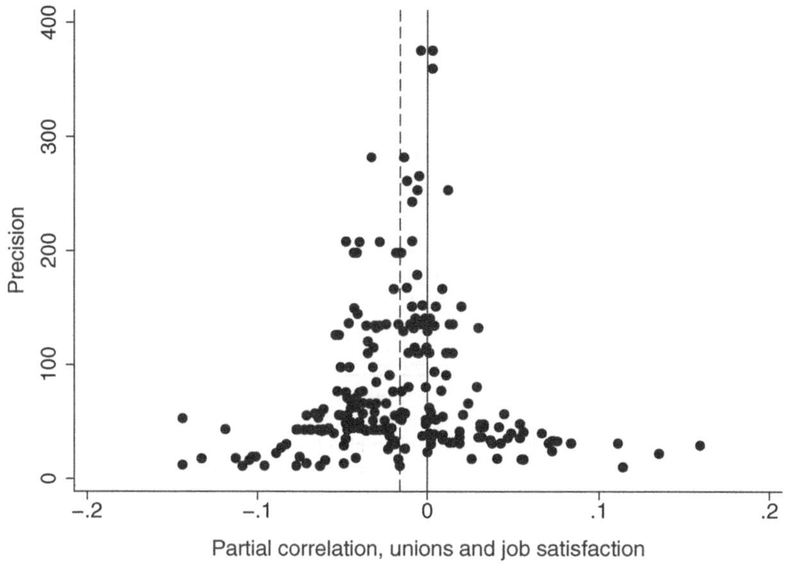

Figure 6.1 Funnel plot of unions and job satisfaction

Notes: Solid and dashed vertical lines denote zero and the uncorrected and unweighted average partial correlation ($r = -0.016$), respectively.

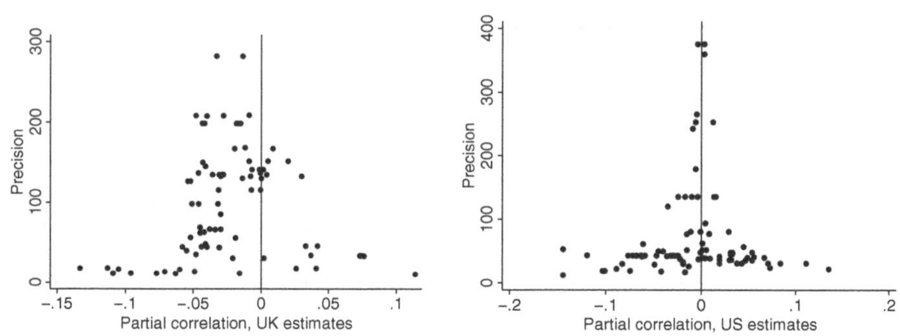

Figure 6.2 Funnel plots of unions and job satisfaction, UK and US

Note: The vertical solid lines show a zero effect size.

Table 6.3 Unconditional meta-average partial correlation, unions and job satisfaction

	Unweighted average (1)	*FEE-WLS weighted average (2)*	*REE-WLS weighted average (3)*	*FAT-PET, selection bias corrected weighted average (PET) (4)*	*FAT-PET, publication selection bias (FAT) (5)*	*PEESE corrected weighted average (6)*
All estimates (n = 235, k = 59)	–0.016*** (–2.90)	–0.013*** (–3.59)	–0.016*** (–2.64)	–0.010* (–1.80)	–0.431 (–0.97)	–0.012*** (–3.29)
US estimates (n = 90, k = 22)	–0.010 (–0.91)	–0.003 (–1.41)	–0.008 (–0.82)	–0.001 (–0.14)	–0.443 (–0.73)	–0.002 (–1.65)
UK estimates (n = 84, k = 17)	–0.024*** (–2.90)	–0.021*** (–6.44)	–0.021*** (–4.64)	–0.021*** (–4.60)	–0.006 (–0.01)	–0.021*** (–6.30)

Notes: Column 1 reports the unweighted average. The other columns report the fixed-effect, random-effects, *FAT-PET*, and *PEESE* meta-averages, respectively. Columns (2) to (6) are estimated by WLS, using inverse variance weights; column (3) uses random-effects inverse variance weights. Column 4 reports the *PET* coefficient; publication bias corrected average. Column 5 reports the *FAT* coefficient; degree of publication bias. Figures in brackets are *t*-statistics using standard errors adjusted for clustering of observations within studies. n and k denote number of observations and studies, respectively. *** and * denote statistical significance at the 1% and 10% levels, respectively.

Table 6.4 Variable definitions and summary measures

Moderator variables		*Mean*	*SD*
SE	Standard error of the partial correlation	0.022	0.018
Coverage	= 1 if study takes into account whether workers are covered by a union or collective bargaining at the workplace level	0.217	0.413
Group 1: Measures of job satisfaction (JS)			
JS 1–4	= 1 if JS measured using a 4-point Likert scale	0.268	0.444
JS 1–5	= 1 if JS measured using a 5-point Likert scale	0.119	0.325
JS 1–7	= 1 if JS measured using a 7-point Likert scale	0.255	0.437
JS 1–10	= 1 if JS measured using a 10-point Likert scale	0.119	0.325
JS DUMMY	= 1 if JS measured as a binary outcome variable (used as the base)	0.179	0.384

Moderator variables		*Mean*	*SD*
Group 2: Data characteristics			
Service	=1 if estimate for the service industry	0.064	0.245
Various	=1 if estimate for various industries (used as the base)	0.898	0.253
Fixed effects	=1 if estimate relates to panel data (fixed effects models)	0.149	0.357
Pooled	=1 if estimate relates to pooled cross-sectional data	0.077	0.267
Cross	=1 if estimate relates to cross-sectional data (used as the base)	0.774	0.419
Df	=1 if degrees of freedom < 2,788 (median)	0.500	0.501
Group 3: Spatial, temporal, and econometric issues			
1970	= 1 if the study used observations prior 1980	0.187	0.391
1980	= 1 if the study used observations between 1980 and 1989	0.260	0.439
1990	= 1 if the study used observations between 1990 and 1999 (used as the base)	0.357	0.480
2000	= 1 if the study used observations after 2000	0.302	0.460
USA	= 1 if the study used US data	0.383	0.487
UK	= 1 if the study used UK data (used as the base)	0.357	0.480
Others	= 1 if the study used data from other countries	0.119	0.325
Ecojourn	= 1 if the estimates come from a publication in an economics journal	0.391	0.489
Irjourn	= 1 if the estimates come from a publication in an industrial relations journal	0.430	0.496
Manag	= 1 if the estimates come from a publication in a management journal (used as the base)	0.115	0.320
OLS	= 1 if used ordinary least square (used as the base)	0.306	0.462
Instrument	= 1 if used 2SLS or IV Probit estimations	0.081	0.273
Probit	= 1 if used Logit or Probit estimations	0.570	0.496

(continued)

Table 6.4 Variable definitions and summary measures (*continued*)

Moderator variables		*Mean*	*SD*
Group 4: Control variables in primary studies			
Firm size	= 1 if the study used firm/organization size as a control variable	0.630	0.484
Promotion	= 1 if the study used promotion opportunities as a control variable	0.221	0.416
Wages	= 1 if the study used wage or pay level as a control variable	0.838	0.369
Gender	= 1 if the study used gender as a control variable	0.591	0.492
Malesubgroup	= 1 if estimate relates to a male subgroup	0.234	0.424
Femalesubgroup	= 1 if estimate relates to a female subgroup	0.119	0.325
Race	= 1 if the study used race as a control variable	0.438	0.497
Hours	= 1 if the study used working hours as a control variable	0.630	0.484
Age	= 1 if the study used age as a control variable	0.817	0.387
Education	= 1 if the study used education as a control variable	0.919	0.273
Married	= 1 if the study used marital status as a control variable	0.664	0.473
Training	= 1 if the study used training opportunities as a control variable	0.821	0.383
Irclimate	= 1 if the study used good industrial relations climate as a control variable	0.754	0.431
Occupation	= 1 if the study used occupation as a control variable	0.838	0.370

Source: Laroche (2016).

Table 6.5 Unions and job satisfaction, multiple MRA

	General FEE-WLS	*Specific FEE-WLS*	*REE-WLS*	*Multi-level*
	(1)	(2)	(3)	(4)
SE	0.439 (0.84)	–	–0.035 (–0.10)	–0.263 (–1.05)

	General FEE-WLS	*Specific FEE-WLS*	*REE-WLS*	*Multi-level*
JS 1–4	0.004 (0.82)	–	0.013* (1.84)	0.021** (2.05)
JS 1–5	–0.003 (–0.27)	–	–0.001 (–0.14)	0.006 (0.42)
JS 1–7	0.002 (0.18)	–	0.009 (0.74)	0.009 (0.56)
JS 1–10	0.010 (0.70)	–	0.013 (1.21)	0.016 (1.11)
Coverage	0.006 (0.80)	–	0.005 (0.95)	–0.003 (–0.37)
Services	0.017 (1.17)	0.013** (2.40)	0.022* (1.70)	0.038*** (2.79)
Fixed effects	0.021*** (3.52)	0.024*** (9.15)	0.022*** (2.81)	0.015 (1.22)
Pooled	0.014** (2.43)	0.016*** (5.28)	0.008 (1.11)	0.004 (0.35)
Df	0.015 (1.38)	–	0.025*** (3.19)	0.018** (2.04)
1970	–0.009 (–0.73)	–	–0.000 (–0.02)	0.028 (1.59)
1980	–0.026** (–2.31)	–0.022*** (–2.73)	–0.024*** (–3.07)	–0.022* (–1.81)
2000	–0.009* (–1.88)	–0.005** (–2.42)	–0.000 (–0.04)	0.016 (1.35)
UK	–0.019* (–1.78)	–0.023*** (–18.17)	–0.016* (–1.72)	0.005 (0.31)
Others	0.014* (1.77)	0.016*** (3.21)	0.007 (0.62)	0.011 (0.75)
Ecojourn	–0.009 (–1.01)	–	–0.020** (–2.07)	–0.031** (–2.14)
Irjourn	0.014 (1.20)	0.020*** (6.34)	0.001 (0.01)	–0.007 (–0.43)
Instrument	0.014 (0.94)	–	0.008 (0.63)	0.039*** (3.21)
Probit	0.002 (0.36)	–	0.007 (1.22)	0.015* (1.83)
Firm size	0.001 (0.02)	–	0.001 (0.18)	–0.002 (–0.17)
Promotion	0.016*** (2.73)	0.012*** (6.50)	0.010 (1.55)	0.007 (0.64)

(continued)

Table 6.5 Unions and job satisfaction, multiple MRA (*continued*)

	General FEE-WLS	*Specific FEE-WLS*	*REE-WLS*	*Multi-level*
Wages	0.017 (1.43)	0.025*** (4.15)	0.001 (0.09)	0.004 (0.26)
Gender	–0.031*** (–4.06)	–0.024*** (–5.28)	–0.043*** (–3.87)	–0.038** (–2.29)
Msubgroup	–0.032*** (–4.03)	–0.022*** (–4.15)	–0.041*** (–3.45)	0.030 (–1.62)
Fsubgroup	–0.043*** (–5.26)	–0.033*** (–4.96)	–0.057*** (–4.36)	–0.048*** (–2.57)
Race	0.006 (0.90)	–	0.004 (0.64)	–0.003 (–0.28)
Hours	–0.007 (–0.69)	–	0.001 (0.07)	0.007 (0.55)
Age	0.024* (1.94)	0.022*** (3.22)	0.029*** (2.93)	0.015 (1.09)
Education	0.005 (0.39)	–	–0.001 (–0.07)	–0.007 (–0.46)
Married	–0.019** (–2.38)	–0.023*** (–5.00)	–0.012* (–1.91)	–0.001 (–0.04)
Training	0.003 (0.46)	–	0.001 (0.02)	0.008 (0.75)
Irclimate	0.017 (1.56)	0.025*** (3.45)	0.037*** (3.79)	0.021* (1.95)
Occupation	0.003 (0.27)	–	–0.006 (–0.77)	–0.038*** (–3.05)
Constant	–0.034 (–1.04)	–0.043*** (–3.49)	–0.006 (–0.23)	0.013 (0.39)
Studies/ Observations	235 (59)	235 (59)	235 (59)	235 (59)
Adjusted R^2	0.49	0.46	0.53	–

Notes: See Table 6.4 for variable definitions and summary statistics. The dependent variable is partial correlation of unions and overall job satisfaction. Figures in brackets are *t*-statistics using standard errors adjusted for clustering. Columns 1 and 2 use weighted least squares using inverse variance weights. Column 1 is the general WLS model, including the full set of controls. Column 2 reports the specific WLS MRA after removing all statistically insignificant variables. Column 3 is the random-effects weighted least squares. Column 4 reports the multi-level (REML) estimates.
***, **, and * denote statistical significance at the 1%, 5%, and 10% levels, respectively.
Source: Laroche (2016).

The meta-regressions show that specification of the econometric model is important. Promotion, wages, age, and industrial relations climate (*Irclimate*) have positive and statistically significant coefficients on the estimated union-satisfaction effect. Studies that control for these variables find that unionization has a smaller negative impact on job satisfaction. The union relation to them can be interpreted as a pathway, explaining the negative impact. In contrast, the inclusion of a control for gender and marriage in the econometric specification produces a larger adverse effect of unionization on job satisfaction.

More important, the multiple MRA finds differences in estimates between studies that use cross-sectional data that compare one worker with another worker who may differ in some unobservable characteristic that affects job satisfaction, and studies that use panel data with fixed effects to control for unobservable heterogeneity (*Fixed effects*). Table 6.6 shows that the fixed effects estimator in panel studies obtains smaller negative effects of unions on job satisfaction than the OLS estimator. The implication is that much of unionized workers' lower job satisfaction is due to unobservable worker and/or job characteristics associated with unionization.

Looking deeper, there is variation within the panel studies, depending on the nature of the change the researcher identifies in the panel. With data that follow a worker who moves between a union and non-union job, researchers use a person-fixed effect, which identifies the union effect by the difference in satisfaction between union and non-union jobs for the same person. With data that has information on the change in union status of a workplace, researches use an employer-fixed effect, which identifies the union effect by the difference in satisfaction between union and non-union status for the same workplace, which can be further refined to limit the comparison to workers who were in the workplace

Table 6.6 Estimated effect of unionization on job satisfaction

	US (1)	*UK (2)*	*Australia (3)*	*Canada (4)*	*Europe (excluding UK) (5)*
Cross-sectional design	–0.03* (–1.70)	–0.04** (–2.29)	–0.06** (–2.48)	–0.03 (–1.26)	–0.04* (–1.78)
Panel design	–0.02 (–0.71)	–0.02 (–1.03)	–0.04 (–1.55)	–0.01 (–0.42)	–0.02 (–0.70)

Notes: Figures in brackets are *t*-statistics using cluster adjusted standard error. ** and * denote statistically significant at the 5% and 10% level, respectively.
Source: Laroche (2016).

before and after the change in status. Changes in the satisfaction of workers who joined the newly unionized or de-unionized workplace from their previous workplace and those who left it and report satisfaction at their new workplace provide further contrasts from which to draw inferences. Finally, workplace conflicts such as strikes or lockouts will impact satisfaction, possibly in time-varying ways. Laroche (2016, Appendix Table A4) summarizes the extent to which different panel treatments reduce the negative relation between unions and satisfaction.

Laroche's (2016) meta-analysis also confirms the funnel figures that studies from the United Kingdom report larger negative effects than studies for the United States. One plausible explanation for this is that in the United Kingdom, trade unions expand in struggle, with shop stewards playing a critical role in a number of important disputes. One could argue that the negative relationship between unionization and job satisfaction in the United Kingdom is due to a shop stewards' movement which has become synonymous with the idea of trade union militancy, especially after the severe weakening of union organizations in the 1980s in Britain. Thus, joining a union in Britain may be a more militant act related to job dissatisfaction than in other countries (Cappellari et al., 2004). The negative effect of unionization on job satisfaction cannot in any case be generalized to all industrialized countries, particularly in countries where workers do not join unions but act militantly when unions lead disputes with workers (Garcia-Serrano, 2009; Powdthavee, 2011). In France, for example, distinguishing between members and non-members is not sufficient. As in many European countries, French workers may be covered by a workplace collective agreement without joining the union, so that any distinction must treat collective bargaining as well as unionism. In the United States, by contrast, almost all workers covered by an agreement are union members, even in states with "right to work laws" that allow for free riding.

The conclusion from this meta-analysis is that the evidence for a negative impact of union membership on job satisfaction weakens as the research design moves closer to a random assignment controlled experiment. Differences in estimation methods, model specification, and sample coverage affect the magnitude of the estimated effect of union membership on overall job satisfaction. Studies that account for endogeneity through instrumental variables and those that adopt a fixed effects model find no significant effect of union membership on overall job satisfaction. The most likely reason for the stronger negative results in the cross-section union-satisfaction studies is selection of workers and workplaces into unionism. On the basis of this result, we conclude that association between unionization and satisfaction is weak and that unionism is likely to exert little effect on productivity through the job satisfaction channel.

Unions and organizational commitment

Employee behavior can also affect productivity through the organizational commitment of workers to their firm. In the Hirschman (1970) *Exit, Voice, and Loyalty* analysis, this is the loyalty channel that Freeman and Medoff ignored in their book. Organizational commitment is the relative degree to which an employee identifies with a particular organization. Meta-studies conducted by Mathieu and Zajac (1990), Riketta (2002), and Jaramillo et al. (2005) report a positive correlation between organizational commitment and measures of job performance. Harter et al.'s (2002) meta-analysis of the relationships among employee engagement and productivity, profitability, and employee turnover shows that organizational commitment is positively correlated with productivity (0.15) and profits (0.10) but negatively correlated with turnover (–0.13), which makes it a natural intermediary between turnover and productivity and profitability.

Several meta-studies have explored the relation between commitment of workers to unions and their commitment to organizations. Mathieu and Zajac (1990) report a positive correlation of 0.22 between union commitment and organizational commitment based on a sample of five studies. In a larger meta-analysis of 76 samples, Reed et al. (1994) find a larger 0.42 positive correlation between union commitment and organizational commitment and find that this was moderated by country, presumably because of differences in industrial relations regime. They contrast a 0.20 correlation in Canada and the United States with 0.62 in Japan and Sweden. In their meta-analysis of 41 studies, Bamberger et al. (1999) find a correlation of 0.31 between union commitment and organizational commitment, which, however, drops to 0.11 if one Japanese outlier study is removed from the sample. Johnson et al.'s (1999) meta-analysis of 31 studies spanning seven countries finds a positive association between union commitment and organizational commitment. Finally, Cooper-Harim and Viswesvaran (2005) report a positive correlation of 0.15, based on a meta-analysis of 22 samples. These studies, however, have a particular theoretical focus that may miss important aspects of labor-management issues. They assess 'dual commitment' of workers to unions and employer on the notion that workers have simultaneous commitment to both without considering the direct relationship between union membership and organizational commitment. Gordon and Ladd (1990) argue that dual commitment implies industrial harmony and obscures fundamental differences in the goals of labor and management.

Studies of organizational commitment pay little attention to the role of unionization in either increasing or decreasing workers' commitment to the employer and conversely on the role of employers in increasing or decreasing workers' commitment to the union. By confining analysis to union members, nearly all studies of dual commitment do not compare unionized and non-unionized labor. Lincoln and Booth (1993) is one of the rare *primary* studies that examines the direct effect of unions on organizational commitment. They find a negative relationship between the existence of a union contract at the plant and company commitment. Kalleberg and Mastekaasa (1994), which is another of the rare studies looking at how union presence relates to organizational commitment in the United States context, find a positive relation in the United States and a negative relation in Japan. Thus, while the dual commitment studies show that unionized workers who are more committed to the union tend to be more committed to the firm as well, there are insufficient studies to determine whether workers in unionized workplaces have greater, lesser, or the same organizational commitment as workers in non-union workplaces.

Summary

Social science research provides fewer estimates about the employee behavior channels through which unions may affect productivity – turnover, satisfaction, and commitment – than the direct productivity estimates literature. As a result, many of the meta-studies on which we rely are based on a relatively small number of studies. There is need for further primary studies, especially those using panel studies to help distinguish the effects of selectivity from the effects on unionism on attitudes and behavior. The prior meta-analyses on which we rely to assess turnover and organizational commitment sometimes correct correlations for reliability, but they do not deal with publication bias, which can inflate reported correlations. As our meta-analyses do not find a great deal of publication bias in the firm performance effects literature, perhaps this is not such a major issue.

While our methodology follows worker channels through three variables, the correlations among them (Kinicki et al., 2002) make it difficult to disentangle those effects. Several meta-studies show that primary studies find that job satisfaction is negatively correlated with turnover, as more satisfied workers are less likely to leave (Cotton and Tuttle, 1986; Griffeth et al., 2000; Heavey et al., 2013), while organizational commitment is also negatively correlated with turnover (Cotton and Tuttle, 1986; Griffeth et al., 2000; Heavey et al., 2013). Satisfaction is also correlated with organizational commitment (Mathieu and Zajac 1990; Whitman et al., 2010).

Taken as an exogenous factor, unionism will thus have indirect effects on the three variables in this chapter. To the extent that unions affect job satisfaction and organizational commitment, they may also impact turnover indirectly through these channels. If unions increase organizational commitment, then this will reduce turnover; that is, organizational commitment is one channel through which unions reduce turnover.

In any case, taking the available meta-studies on each of the variables as separate indicators suggests that unionization reduces turnover and that union commitment is positively related to organizational commitment, which should contribute to productivity, while having little direct effect on job satisfaction, and thus little impact on productivity through this channel. The one exception is for the United Kingdom, where unions are negatively correlated with satisfaction; this may be one contributing factor to the negative union impact on productivity given in Chapter 3.

Combining the results from this chapter with those from Chapter 5, we can conclude that employee turnover is a channel through which unions improve firm performance that would balance in part the effect of unions on intangible and tangible capital investments through which unions harm firm performance. Perhaps this conclusion will not come as a surprise; unions benefit labor at cost to capital, albeit with great heterogeneity.

Nevertheless, while we try to infer causality from unionization to productivity via employee and investment behavior channels, it needs to be borne in mind that most of the estimated effects on which we rely are based on correlations that do not necessarily reflect causation. In some cases panel data and/or instrumental variables allow for a stronger causal interpretation of results, but most of the evidence does not do much to probe for causal links.

If unions have in general little effect on net productivity, raising productivity through the labor behavior channels discussed in this chapter but reducing productivity through the investment channels discussed in Chapter 5, then union increases in wages and benefits for workers must come at the expense of the return to capital, to which we turn next.

Notes

1 McEvoy and Cascio (1987) and Bycio et al. (1990) found moderate negative correlations between turnover and job performance, ranging from –0.28 for McEvoy and Cascio to –0.17 for voluntary turnover in Bycio et al. Williams and Livingstone's (1994) meta-analysis of 55 studies shows an inverse association between employee turnover and job performance, with estimates of the average correlation ranging from –0.14 to –0.30.
2 The leavers can reduce some components of compensation, e.g., vacation, sick leave, and insurance charges.
3 Heavey et al. (2013) Table 6, p. 425.
4 This section draws heavily from Laroche, P. (2016) A meta-analysis of the union-job satisfaction relationship, *British Journal of Industrial Relations*. doi: 10.1111/bjir.12193.
5 Premack's focus is on how employee dissatisfaction affects unionization, but he includes studies in his meta-analysis that report correlations between unionization and job satisfaction.
6 While Premack relies on bivariate correlations, Laroche uses partial correlations. See Laroche (2016) for details on the data construction and choice of studies.

7 Unions and financial performance of firms[1]

> Though exceptions can be found, unionization is more often than not associated with lower profitability.
>
> Freeman and Medoff (1984: 181)

The main channel through which unions adversely impact profitability is by increasing the costs of unionized labor. These higher costs arise from the wage premium and higher fringe benefits for unionized labor that virtually every union study of compensation finds. In their review, Freeman and Medoff (1984) conclude that unions have an adverse effect on profits primarily because union wage increases exceed productivity improvements. One of the first meta-regression analysis in economics was Jarrell and Stanley's (1990) study of the union-nonunion wage gap. Analyzing a meta-analysis of 152 estimates from 114 studies, Jarrell and Stanley (1990) found that the union-nonunion wage gap varied between 8.9 percent and 12.4 percent. While this is lower than Lewis's (1986) estimate of 10 percent to 16 percent, it is a significant cost differential. Differentials of these magnitudes combined with our Chapter 3 meta-analysis of union effects on productivity indicate that most unionized firms experience higher production costs that should translate into lower financial rewards to firms. If unionized firms pay 10 percent higher labor costs and do not gain any productivity advantage, gross profits will be lower by approximately the share of labor in cost times 10 percent. In situations where unionization increases productivity, the increases in output per worker would have to exceed wage increases per worker to produce higher profits, and those cases would be far outnumbered by cases in which the productivity effect is negligible or negative and the wage effect is positive.

A meta-analysis directs attention at the heterogeneity of research findings in an area as well as at the central tendency of results. Independently of variation in estimates that arises from differences in the details of studies, union effects on profitability will almost certainly vary across industries, unions, and countries at a point in time and over time, as they do for productivity and the channels by which unions impact productivity and wages. If, as seems likely, union wage effects are positively related to productivity effects, the variation in profitability should be smaller than the variation in wages or productivity. Union effects in productivity and wages that move together will generally produce a smaller range of effects in profits, since the profit effect depends on the difference between productivity and wages.

The market in which the firm operates should also influence the union effect on profits. Firms in concentrated markets should have smaller negative union-profit effects, because they can raise prices to meet higher labor costs; see Turnbull (2003) and Hirsch (2007). If the major firms in a sector have collective agreements with a union, the wage agreement could trigger joint increases in prices that raise profits for the group.

Since Menezes-Filho (1997) suggested that the negative effect of unions on profits declined in the 1980s and 1990s compared to the 1960s and 1970s and became insignificant in the United Kingdom, the change in the profit effect over time has been in the forefront of researcher concerns. Batt and Welbourne (2002, p. 169) confirm Menezes-Filho's findings for the United States and conclude that "unionization does not inevitably reduce financial performance". Guest et al. (2003) and Laroche (2004) report negative but statistically insignificant union-profitability effects, while Gittell et al. (2004) find a positive significant effect. Doucouliagos and Laroche (2009) gave the first meta-regression analysis of the evidence base, which we update here. Our major finding is that unionization has a statistically significant negative correlation with profits that is larger for market-based measures of profitability, and has indeed declined over time. The section "Theory review" is a brief review of theoretical arguments over the union profits effect. The section "The unionization and financial performance data" describes the studies that provide the data for the meta-analysis. The section "The unconditional meta-average correlation, unionization and profitability" reports unconditional meta-averages of the estimated association between unions and profitability while the section "Meta-regression analysis of heterogeneity, unionization and profitability" reports the analysis of heterogeneity and conditional averages. The section "Summary" concludes the chapter.

Unions and profits

Theory review

The monopoly face of unions predicts that profits will fall because unions extract rents principally in the form of higher wages and other benefits (Booth, 1995). In bargaining models, the firm's profits fall with increased union bargaining power. Since one of the most well-established empirical effects of unions is their ability to increase wages above competitive levels (see Lewis, 1963, 1986; Jarrell and Stanley, 1990; and Blanchflower and Bryson, 2004, for reviews), there is a presumption that unions lower profits. Higher wages reduce profits, unless union activities offset higher labor costs through higher productivity or by passing the higher costs on to consumers (Hirsch, 1991b). It is possible that "unions increase the surplus available to the firm through any union-productivity enhancing effects (…) and if this effect more than offsets the higher wages paid to union workers, then unions might have a positive effect on profitability" (Booth, 1995: 212). But Freeman and Medoff (1984) viewed this as unlikely in most cases.

Estimates of the effect of unions on wages are subject to two main problems. First, standard cross-section OLS estimates are potentially biased due to sorting of workers into unionization by unobservable characteristics. To treat this problem, analysts have two possible strategies. They can simultaneously estimate union status and earnings equations if they can find exogenous factors that affect them, which is usually hard to do. Alternatively, they can estimate the union effects on wages through longitudinal comparisons of the same worker in a union and non-union job or of the same establishment before and after the establishment changed union status. The second problem relates to the institutional context across countries, which requires different modes of estimation for different labor relations systems. In the United States, wage differences between union members and non-members in the private sector provide a reasonable first approximation estimate of union wage differentials, because almost all union members are covered by collective bargaining contracts and almost all non-members are not covered.[2] As a result, many US studies take the difference between wages of union members and of non-members as the starting point for analysis of union wage effects. The widely used Current Population Survey does not ask workers who report being a union member whether or not they are covered by collective bargaining, in the belief that the question is redundant.

But in other countries, membership is not a good indicator of whose wages unions raise. The reason is that extension of a national or sectoral collective agreement to non-unionized workers (*erga omnes* principle) means that many workers are covered by a collective agreement without being union members. In this context, it makes more sense to analyze the impact of different collective bargaining agreements on the wages of all covered workers compared to some group of non-covered workers. In France, for example, where union membership is at similar low levels to the United States, collective coverage is on the order of 95 percent. Comparisons of wages between union and non-union members give a misleading comparison of the effect of unions on wages.

Table 7.1 illustrates the problem. The table shows that the pay of union workers to non-union workers differs from one country to another. For example, it is about 17 percent in the United States compared to 3 percent for France. This is because extension of contracts allows unions to set wage outcomes in the non-union sector in France, which does not occur in the United States (Blanchflower and Bryson, 2004). It is also important to distinguish between countries where industry-level bargaining can be combined with workplace-level bargaining and countries where industry-level and workplace-level bargaining tend to be substitutes (Schnabel et al., 2006).

In sum, research on the union wage effects needs an analytic framework appropriate to the institutional context of the countries under investigation. In countries where bargaining coverage is widespread, studies need to focus on the level

Table 7.1 Union membership wage premium in different countries

Country	*Union % wage increase*
Australia	12
Austria	15
Brazil	34
Canada	8
Chile	16
Cyprus	14
Denmark	16
France	3 (ns)
Germany	4 (ns)
Italy	0
Japan	26
Netherlands	0
New Zealand	10
Norway	7
Portugal	18
Spain	7
Sweden	0
UK	10
US	17

Note: ns denotes not statistically significant.
Source: Bryson (2007: 38)

of bargaining (national, sectoral, firm) and the degree of coordination among these levels and must consider carefully the counterfactual in estimating a union wage effect. In countries where workplace-level bargaining can supplement a sectoral or regional agreement, union density is a valuable indicator for local union bargaining power. In the United Kingdom, it is useful to take into consideration both union coverage and union membership, since collective bargaining is fragmented and the ability of recognized unions to raise pay may depend on density. These differing situations suggest different union impacts on wages and by extension on firm profits as well.

Within a country, Hirsch and Addison (1986) point out that the impact of unions on profits is likely to depend on the magnitude of potential rents related to the market structure facing the firm, the production technology, and union bargaining power. For example, firms dealing with a firm with a competitive advantage in technology or those operating in less competitive markets have greater opportunities to earn monopoly profits. In such cases, unions might find it easier to extract higher wages for their members than in other firms (Hirsch and Addison, 1986). Freeman (1983), Salinger (1984), and Karier (1985) argue that unions capture monopoly rents associated with industry concentration. But Hirsch and Connolly (1987) find that the union wage premium is not larger in highly concentrated industries and that concentration is not necessarily linked to a higher rate of profit. However, Hirsch (2007: 213) believes these findings "do not reject the conclusion that union bargaining power and wage gains derive in part from firm market power … (but rather) … reject the thesis that *concentration*-related profits provide a major source for union gains". The missing element in the concentration argument is that it ignores the fact that "unions can and do capture rents stemming from sources of limited competition other than concentration, such as limited trade penetration or firm special advantages".

Unions may also capture quasi-rents from long-lived investments, such as investment in equipment and buildings, R&D, and advertising. The appropriation of quasi-rents has the potential to reduce investment in tangible and intangible assets, with the risk that it reduces long-run growth (Baldwin, 1983). This could create a long-term feedback, with unions reducing profits, which decreases the capacity and incentive to invest, which then reduces future profits. The impact of unions on R&D in particular has thus received considerable attention from researchers; recall Chapter 5. As in many areas of economics, there are competing views. In the traditional approach where union wage demands are viewed as a tax on labor, the effect on investment depends on the impact of higher wages on production costs and the optimal level of output, which reduces capital requirements and the incentive to substitute capital for relatively more expensive labor (Denny and Nickell, 1991). There are also non-wage effects. For example, unions can resist and obstruct the introduction of new technology, with restrictive work practices that increase the cost of investment in tangible and intangible assets.

In contrast, the CV/IR perspective sees several avenues that may increase profits, or at least limit deterioration in profits, arising from unionization. Improved communication between workers and management, a more cooperative and productive workforce, the retention of highly trained staff, and a 'shock effect' induced by unionization may all improve financial performance. Hence, as was the case with the other outcome variables reviewed in earlier chapters, it is theoretically difficult to predict the impact of unions on firm financial performance.

The only way to get answers is with direct empirical analysis and with meta-regression analysis to summarize the answers across studies.

Studies on unionization and financial performance[3]

Doucouliagos and Laroche's (2009) meta-analysis of the effects of unionization on financial performance of firms included 45 comparable published studies. The update in this chapter follows a similar search strategy to that in the previous chapters: finding published studies through an extensive search and limiting studies to those that reported the necessary test statistics to measure union effects.[4] Our new meta-analysis differs from Doucouliagos and Laroche (2009) in two ways. First, we focus only on direct estimates of union effects on profitability, and we do not explore the sources of union-profit effects. Second, we include several new studies not included in Doucouliagos and Laroche (2009). Even though we include several new studies, the focus on direct reduced-form estimates means that the new data set consists of 44 comparable published econometric studies, one less than the original meta-analysis.

Studies that estimate the impact of unions on financial performance have different forms. The studies in our meta-analysis relate an objective measure of profitability, measured as a continuous variable, to unionism. There are two other kinds of studies that provide information on the effect of unions on profitability that do not enter our meta-analysis. First are a relatively small group of studies that also uses a multivariate framework with binary and ordered probit analysis of subjective financial performance data rather than objective measures of performance.[5] Second are event studies[6] that do not readily fit into our meta-regression framework, because they study profits surrounding an event and do not consider moderators on the notion that the event dominates all other factors. Hence, for reasons of comparability, we exclude the probit and event studies from our meta-analysis.[7] Viewing them as orthogonal pieces of evidence, we note that they generally find a negative association between unions and profits as well.

Table 7.2 lists the 44 studies included in the meta-analysis. They have a combined sample size of 89,827 and have produced 492 estimated union-financial performance effects. We discarded 17 of the estimates to obtain a usable sample of 475 in the multiple MRA analyses: of the 17, four were extreme outliers from Hirsch (1991a); ten did not provide estimates of the standard error; and three were missing information on some of the moderator variables. We measure the union effect as the partial correlation between unionization and profitability, holding all other factors constant. Because many studies do not offer sufficient information from which to calculate accurately our second measure of union effects, the percentage impact of unions on profits, we do not report the effect of unionism on percentage changes in profitability attributable to unions.

Table 7.3 gives some of the features of these studies. Most of the estimates relate to US manufacturing. Most find that profitability is negatively correlated with unionism.

Table 7.2 Econometric studies of unions and profitability

Author(s)	*Country*	*N*	*Median t-statistic*	*Median r*
		North America		
Batt & Welbourne (2002)	US	444	2.59	0.13
Becker & Olson (1992)	US	297	–2.66	–0.15
Bronars et al. (1994)	US	940	–0.96	–0.06
Caves et al. (1980)	Canada	83	–2.09	–0.24
Chappell et al. (1991)	US	327	–4.07	–0.22
Chiles & Stewart (1993)	US	106	0.68	0.07
Clark (1984)	US	4,681	–4.21	–0.07
Connolly et al. (1986)	US	367	–2.00	–0.11
Gittell et al. (2004)	US	489	2.17	0.10
Hirsch (1990b)	US	247	–1.01	–0.07
Hirsch (1991a)	US	5,824	–1.63	–0.15
Hirsch (1991b)	US	6,248	–3.52	–0.17
Hirsch & Connolly (1987)	US	367	–1.28	–0.07
Huselid (1995)	US	826	0	0
Karahasan (1995)	US	204	–3.47	–0.31
Karier (1985)	US	341	–2.81	–0.15
Laporta & Jenkins (1996)	Canada	62	1.05	0.14
Maki & Meredith (1986)	Canada	220	–3.29	–0.08
Volpe (2014)	US	1,052	0.93	0.04
Voos & Mishel (1986a)	US	139	–2.81	–0.25
Voos & Mishel (1986b)	US	71	–2.31	–0.28
		United Kingdom		
Cable & Machin (1991)	UK	208	0.62	0.05
Conyon & Machin (1991b)	UK	360	–2.16	–0.12
Cowling & Waterson (1975)	UK	94	1.19	0.15

Author(s)	*Country*	*N*	*Median t-statistic*	*Median r*
Dowrick (1990)	UK	103	–2.80	–0.29
Guest et al. (2003)	UK	366	1.04	0.06
Haskel & Martin (1992)	UK	567	0.28	0.01
Machin (1991)	UK	290	0.01	0.01
Menezes-Filho (1997)	UK	3,312	–2.61	–0.04
	All other			
Addison et al. (1993)	Germany	52	–0.07	–0.01
Bae & Lawler (2000)	Korea	136	–2.41	–0.30
Brunello (1992)	Japan	979	–2.63	–0.08
Cassoni et al. (2005)	Uruguay	4,849	1.36	0.02
Fitzroy & Kraft (1985)	Germany	123	4.93	0.58
Fitzroy & Kraft (1986)	Germany	123	1.81	0.24
Fitzroy & Kraft (1993)	Germany	112	–0.52	–0.05
Kleiner & Lee (1997)	Korea	188	–1.64	–0.12
Laroche (2004)	France	792	0.06	0.01
Lee (2012)	Korea	13,333	–2.58	–0.03
McDonald (1999)	Australia	4,786	–1.77	–0.04
McDonald & Bloch (1999)	Australia	4,590	–1.52	–0.03
Menezes-Filho et al. (2005)	Brazil	2,529	–1.97	–0.04
Morikawa (2010)	Japan	27,431	–5.73	–0.05
Morishima (1991)	Japan	97	–0.82	–0.10

Notes: Calculated by the authors from the primary studies. The table reports medians for all comparable estimates reported within studies. N denotes total sample size used in the primary econometric study; *r* denotes partial correlation.

Figures 7.1, 7.2, and 7.3 give estimates of the union effects on profitability for the entire sample, for the United States, and for all non-US countries, respectively. All three figures show wide variation in reported union-profit effects around an unweighted negative average.

Table 7.3 Basic characteristics of the unions and profitability literature

	All studies (1)	*US studies (2)*	*Non-US studies (3)*	*UK studies (4)*
Number of studies	44	18	26	9
Number of estimates	482	340	142	71
Total sample size	89,827	23,670	66,157	5,672
% reporting adverse union effects	78%	81%	72%	65%
% US	71%	100%	0%	0%
% manufacturing	75%	79%	65%	72%
Average partial correlation	–0.108	–0.128	–0.062	–0.077

Note: Average partial correlation is an unweighted average. All estimates including outliers. The MRA uses a smaller number of observations.
Source: Authors' calculations.

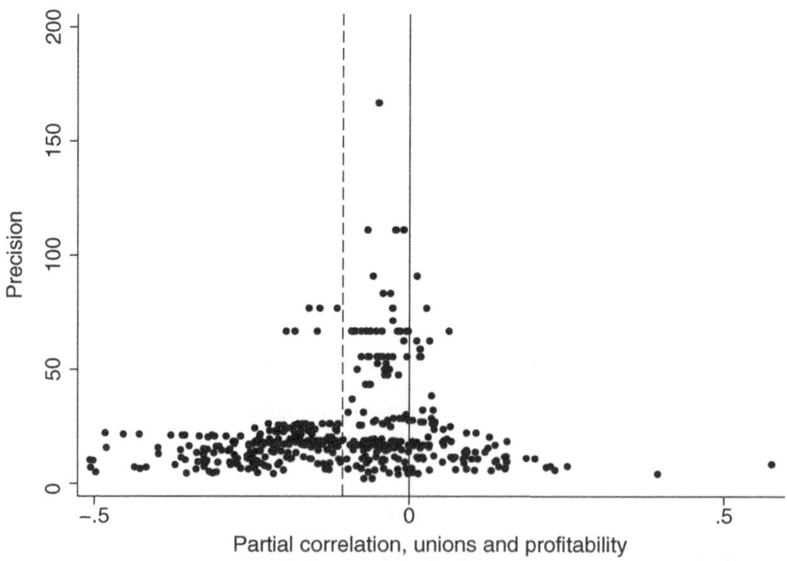

Figure 7.1 Funnel plot of unions and profitability, all estimates

Notes: Solid and dashed vertical lines denote zero and the uncorrected and unweighted average correlation (–0.108), respectively.

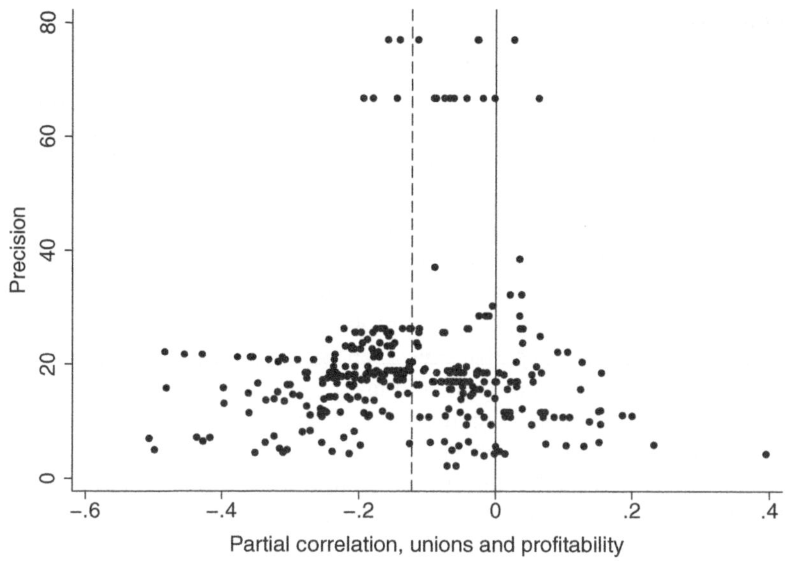

Figure 7.2 Funnel plot of unions and profitability, US estimates

Notes: Solid and dashed vertical lines denote zero and the uncorrected and unweighted average correlation (–0.127), respectively.

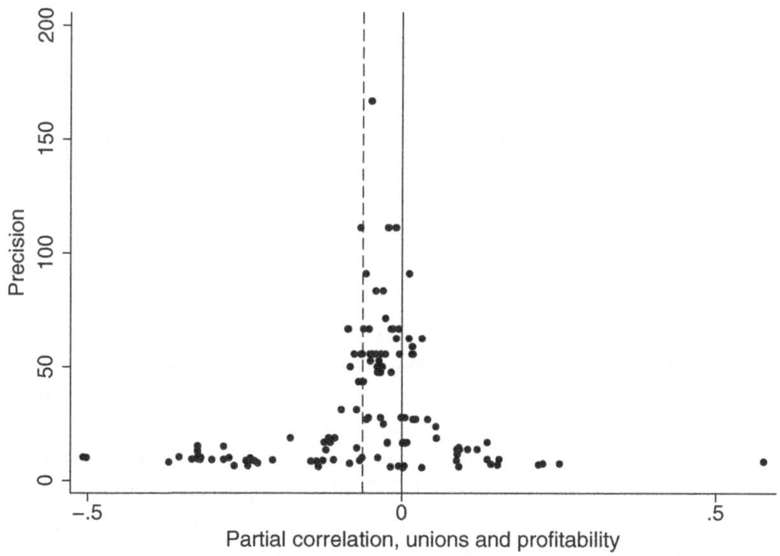

Figure 7.3 Funnel plot of unions and profitability, non-US estimates

Notes: Solid and dashed vertical lines denote zero and the uncorrected and unweighted average correlation (–0.062), respectively.

The unconditional meta-average correlation, unionization and profitability

Table 7.4 gives the estimated unconditional meta-averages for all studies, US and non-US studies, using the same six-column format of presenting the estimates as we have used in earlier chapters. The columns give in order the unweighted average, *FEE-WLS, REE-WLS*, the *FAT-PET*, and the *PEESE* model. All the meta-averages confirm the existence of a negative correlation between unionization and financial performance. The magnitude of the negative correlation in the United States is more than double the size elsewhere. Considering the accumulated evidence over the past 30 years, meta-analysis confirms that, on average, unions have a statistically significant negative effect on profits.

The *FAT* coefficient has a negative sign when all studies are combined, indicating that a publication selection process is in favor of negative union-profit effects. However, *FAT* is not statistically significant when the data are portioned into US and non-US samples. Moreover, we show below that the *FAT* is not statistically significant when we add moderating variables in the mete-regression, i.e., what appears as publication bias is actually heterogeneity in the data.

Meta-regression analysis of heterogeneity, unionization and profitability

In this section we apply meta-regression analysis to identify some of the sources of differences in union-profit estimates. Our MRA regresses estimates of the union-profit effect on a set of potential explanatory variables, including a correction for publication bias, using unrestricted weighted least squares. The standard errors are adjusted for clustering of observations within studies.[8]

We include the following potential explanatory variables in the meta-regression analysis: standard error (*SE*) to identify and correct publication selection bias; *AveYear* for the average year of the data used to generate the econometric estimates in primary studies; *LabReg* for the degree of labor market regulation when the samples were taken; and two regional dummies, *Developing* for estimates relating to developing countries and *NonUSA* for all other non-US estimates, with the United States being the base.[9] In addition, we examine moderators for whether a study included R&D spending (an *R&D* dummy), advertising expenditures (an *Advertising* dummy), the amount of capital (*Capital*), and wages (*Wages*). To the extent that unions reduce intangible capital in the form of R&D and advertising expenditures and/or total capital, they may also reduce profits. Including this in the primary profitability model thus helps control for this channel. Including wages in the primary model partials out the effects of wages in order to get more accurate measure of non-wage effects.

We also include several other covariates that are exogenous to union activity: the firm's age (*Firm age*) and size (*Firm size*), whether the primary study controls for demand (*Demand*), industry concentration (*Concentration*), import penetration (*Import*), market share (*Market share*), and a dummy for *NotManuf* if the estimates relate to non-manufacturing industries.

We also have a set of variables measuring the characteristics of the study. *NotFirm* is a binary variable for estimates that relate to industry- or state-level

Table 7.4 Unconditional meta-average partial correlation, unions and profitability

	Unweighted average (1)	*FEE-WLS weighted average (2)*	*REE-WLS weighted average (3)*	*FAT-PET, selection bias corrected weighted average (PET) (4)*	*FAT-PET, publication selection bias (FAT) (5)*	*PEESE corrected weighted average (6)*
All estimates (n = 478, k = 44)	–0.108*** (–6.07)	–0.062*** (–4.40)	–0.105*** (–5.60)	–0.032*** (–3.01)	–1.329*** (–3.25)	–0.055*** (–4.17)
US estimates (n = 336, k = 18)	–0.127*** (–6.57)	–0.105*** (–9.60)	–0.128*** (–6.48)	–0.074***(–4.00)	–0.919 (–1.53)	–0.098*** (–7.92)
Non-US estimates (n = 142, k = 26)	–0.062** (–2.29)	–0.035*** (–7.87)	–0.047*** (–3.21)	–0.027*** (–2.78)	–0.506 (–0.97)	–0.032*** (–7.10)

Notes: Column 1 reports the unweighted average. The other columns report the fixed-effect, random-effects, *FAT-PET*, and *PEESE* meta-averages, respectively. Columns (2) to (6) are estimated by WLS with inverse variance weights; column (3) uses random-effects inverse variance weights. Column 4 reports the *PET* coefficient; publication bias corrected average. Column 5 reports the *FAT* coefficient; degree of publication bias. Figures in brackets are *t*-statistics using standard errors adjusted for clustering of observations within studies. n and k denote number of observations and studies, respectively. Outliers removed.
*** and ** denote statistical significance at the 1% and 5% levels, respectively.

data; the base is firm-level estimates. *UnionDummy* is a binary variable taking the value of 1 if the study measures unionization using a dummy variable for union presence (with union density as the base). *Accounting* is a binary variable for accounting-based measures of profitability as opposed to market-based measures of profits. Market-based measures of profits are generally forward-looking, while accounting-based measures report what has happened in the past. Finally, *Panel* is a binary variable taking the value of 1 if panel data are used (with cross-sectional data as the base), and *Endogeneity* is a binary variable taking the value of 1 if the estimate treats unionization as endogenous.

Table 7.5 presents the MRA results. Column (1) reports the general model without the variables that may be influenced by unionization: *Wages*, *R&D*, *Advertising*, and *Capital*. Column (2) reports the general model with all moderator variables included. Our preferred specific *FEE-WLS* results are reported in Column (3).[10] Columns (4) and (5) report sensitivity analysis using sample-size weights and random-effects weights, respectively. Column (3) identifies nine variables as statistically significant determinants of the size of the union effect on profits: average year, labor regulation, advertising, firm size, non-manufacturing data, non-US, use of accounting measures of profits, panel data, and measuring unionization with a dummy variable.

The variable *AveYear* has a positive coefficient, indicating that the negative association between unions and profits is declining over time. This time variation is consistent with the evidence from Menezes-Filho (1997) and Batt and Welbourne (2002) that the adverse effect of unionism on profits has trended downward. It also fits with studies that show declines in the union wage effect, such as Blanchflower and Bryson (2004) for the union wage premium in Britain and the United States. The decline in the union wage premium can arise from increased opportunities for union employers to substitute non-union for union labor, especially through their ability to outsource production in less-developed countries (Stewart, 1995). *LagReg* is statistically significant with a negative coefficient, suggesting that unions have a more adverse effect on profitability when labor markets are less regulated.

The MRA controls for labor market flexibility (*LagReg*). Hence, the two country dummies need to be interpreted with this in mind. Holding labor market flexibility constant, *Developing* has a positive coefficient in the general specification, suggesting that unions have less of an adverse impact on profits in developing countries. However, this coefficient is estimated with poor precision and is not statistically significant. *NonUSA* (excluding developing countries) has a statistically significant negative coefficient, indicating that the union-profit effect is larger in this group of countries, compared to the United States, for the same level of labor market flexibility.

In addition, the evidence shows that the profit effect differs between manufacturing and non-manufacturing: unions have a more adverse effect on profitability in manufacturing. Controlling for advertising and firm size produces larger negative correlations, as does the use of a dummy variable to indicate union presence. We also find that accounting measures show smaller effects than market-based measures, i.e., forward-looking measures have stronger negative correlation/association with unionization. Finally, the positive coefficient on panel data indicates that studies that use panel data find smaller adverse profitability effects.

Table 7.5 Unions and profits, multiple MRA

	Mean (Standard deviation)	*General FEE-WLS (1)*	*General FEE-WLS (2)*	*Specific FEE-WLS (3)*	*N weights FEE-WLS (4)*	*REE-WLS (5)*
SE	0.07 (0.05)	–0.422 (–1.15)	–0.359 (0.90)	–	–	–
AveYear	0.15 (7.78)	0.003*** (4.14)	0.003*** (3.94)	0.004*** (6.63) [0]	0.003*** (6.16)	0.003* (1.71)
LabReg	–0.133 (1.03)	–0.007 (–1.28)	–0.008 (–1.47)	–0.018*** (–5.74) [0.005]	–0.019*** (–5.70)	–0.013 (–1.64)
Developing	0.01 (0.08)	0.061* (1.68)	0.034 (0.84)	–	–	–
NonUSA	0.29 (0.45)	–0.007 (–0.25)	–0.027 (–1.05)	–0.061*** (–3.71) [0.005]	–0.060*** (–3.87)	–0.021 (–0.65)
Wages	0.07 (0.26)	–	0.019 (1.11)	–	–	–
R&D	0.63 (0.48)	–	–0.027 (–0.70)	–	–	–
Advertising	0.48 (0.50)	–	–0.025** (–2.01)	–0.041*** (–4.69) [0.005]	–0.041*** (–4.51)	–0.035 (–1.67)
Capital	0.82 (0.39)	–	–0.005 (–0.25)	–	–	–
Firm size	0.60 (0.49)	–0.036** (–2.37)	–0.034** (–2.33)	–0.042*** (–5.42) [0.005]	–0.041*** (–5.68)	–0.034 (–1.64)
Firm age	0.03 (0.17)	–0.007 (–0.31)	–0.032 (–1.44)	–	–	–
Demand	0.77 (0.42)	0.040 (1.24)	0.057* (1.72)	–	–	–
Concentration	0.80 (0.40)	–0.001 (–0.04)	–0.012 (–0.33)	–	–	–

(*continued*)

Table 7.5 Unions and profits, multiple MRA (*continued*)

	Mean (Standard deviation)	*General FEE-WLS (1)*	*General FEE-WLS (2)*	*Specific FEE-WLS (3)*	*N weights FEE-WLS (4)*	*REE-WLS (5)*
Imports	0.35 (0.48)	–0.022 (–1.63)	–0.007 (–0.40)	–	–	–
Market share	0.22 (0.41)	0.016 (0.55)	0.003 (0.08)	–	–	–
NotManuf	0.24 (0.43)	0.059*** (2.80)	0.076*** (3.70)	0.081*** (4.40) [0]	0.078*** (4.48)	0.095*** (4.59)
NotFirm	0.14 (0.35)	–0.054 (–1.66)	–0.061 (–1.31)	–	–	–
UnionDummy	0.28 (0.45)	–0.046** (–2.51)	–0.042** (–2.16)	–0.051* (–2.55) [0.23]	–0.048** (–2.62)	–0.044** (–2.70)
Accounting	0.68 (0.47)	0.022** (2.27)	0.023*** (2.85)	0.024** (2.10) [0.25]	0.023** (2.15)	0.027** (2.16)
Panel	0.67 (0.47)	0.030* (1.83)	0.033** (2.23)	0.040** (2.10) [0.095]	0.039** (2.01)	0.039** (2.20)
Endogeneity	0.09 (0.29)	0.028* (1.76)	0.026 (1.60)	–	–	–
Constant		–0.119*** (–4.01)	–0.100*** (–3.48)	–0.092*** (–3.89) [0.010]	–0.091*** (–3.89)	–0.123*** (–4.31)
Studies/Observations		475 (44)	475 (44)	475 (44)	475 (44)	475 (44)
Adjusted R^2		0.32	0.33	0.33	0.31	0.52

Notes: The dependent variable is the partial correlation between unionization and financial performance. Figures in brackets are *t*-statistics using standard errors corrected for clustering of estimates within studies. Figures in square brackets in Column (3) are *p*-values derived from applying the wild bootstrap. All estimates use weighted least squares using inverse variance weights; these are slightly different when REE-WLS is applied. Three observations are lost because of missing values on labor regulations. ***, **, and * denote statistically significant at the 1%, 5%, and 10% levels, respectively.

Table 7.6 Unions and profits, conditional meta-average correlation, by degree of labor market regulation, manufacturing

	Labor market regulation at sample means (1)	*Most liberal labor markets (2)*
Specific model (1)	–0.133*** (–17.17)	–0.168*** (–14.50)
General model equivalent (2)	–0.129*** (–5.58)	–0.145*** (–4.86)
General model – only statistically significant (3)	–0.073* (–1.78)	–0.073* (–1.78)

Notes: Predictions based on coefficients from Column (3), Table 7.5, for Row (1) and Column (2), Table 7.5, for Row (2). Column (1) evaluates at the sample mean of labor market regulation. Column (2) evaluates at the most liberal labor market regime. Rows (1) and (2) control for advertising, firm size, panel data, market based measures of profitability, continuous measure of unionization, and sample mean for *AveYear*. Row (3) controls for advertising, firm size, panel data, demand, market based measures of profitability, continuous measure of unionization, sample mean for *AveYear*, and sets *LabReg* to zero. Standard errors adjusted for clustering.
*** and * denote statistical significance at the 1% and 10% levels, respectively.

Conditional meta-averages

Table 7.6 presents meta-averages conditional on various moderator variables based on the MRA estimates. Column (1) evaluates the estimates for the mean value of labor market regulation, while Column (2) evaluates for the most liberal labor market regime. In Row (1) we use the MRA coefficients from the preferred specific model: Column (3) of Table 7.5. In Row (2) we use the coefficients for the same specific model covariates from the equivalent general MRA model: Column (2) of Table 7.5. In order to explore the sensitivity of the meta-averages, in Row (3) we use only those estimates from the general model with statistically significant moderator variables, again from Column (2) of Table 7.5. All the conditional meta-averages indicate statistically significant negative associations between unionization and profitability.

Summary

We draw two conclusions from this chapter's meta-regression analysis of studies of the effect of unions on profitability. First, unions have a negative impact on financial performance. Second, much of the heterogeneity in the estimated union-profit effects in published papers reflects differences in data, measures used, specification of the econometric model, and sampling error. In particular, once these factors are taken into account, there is little disagreement that unions depress profits.

Combining the findings from studies of the union wage effect and studies of the effect of unions on profit, we see that by increasing wages that benefit workers, unions also reduce profits, which harms shareholders. At the heart of trade union effects on the economy is a shift in income from capital to labor. To the extent that reduction in profits comes in markets that are concentrated, this will have little adverse effect on long-term investments and growth (Hirsch and Connolly, 1987). To the extent that it comes by shifting quasi-rents from long-lived assets, as Doucouliagos and Laroche (2009) find, it can have such an effect. In this case the absence of any negative association of unions with productivity growth, as found in Chapter 3, would have to be explained by other channels – such as union policies that encourage public sector infrastructure investments, full employment policies, and other macro-economic factors[11] – that lie beyond the scope of this book.

Notes

1 This chapter draws from and builds upon Doucouliagos, C.(H.) and Laroche, P. (2009) Unions and profits: A meta-regression analysis, *Industrial Relations: A Journal of Economy and Society*, 48: 146–84.
2 The public sector is different, with states regulating municipal and state employees so that union members may not have a contract in many cases.
3 We use the terms 'financial performance' and 'profitability' interchangeably.
4 The search for studies was terminated in December 2015.
5 Examples of probit studies include Bryson et al. (2005), Benson (2006), and Laroche and Wechtler (2011). The probit studies inform on the *probability* of unions impacting financial performance. We are able to derive marginal effects for only a portion of these papers and, hence, are unable to combine these effectively with the main group of studies.
6 Examples of event studies include Ruback and Zimmerman (1984), Becker and Olson (1989), and Lee and Mas (2012).
7 We also excluded cost studies, as these show the effects of unions on production costs, but not on profits.
8 This differs from Doucouliagos and Laroche (2009), which did not correct for publication bias and where estimation was through a linear hierarchical model.
9 Introducing a dummy variable for the United Kingdom (or any other country) adds nothing to the explanatory power of the model; these non-US country-specific dummy variables are not statistically significant.
10 The Wald test for the exclusion of redundant variables (comparing Column 3 to 2) has a Chi-squared value of 0.98, with a p-value of 0.48.
11 In the case of the United States, Freeman (1985) stresses union pension funds that increase private savings and investments.

8 Summary and conclusions

Workers form unions to communicate their views about workplace issues to management and to bargain collectively over areas of disagreement. As labor and capital have joint interest in producing efficiently and antipodal goals about dividing the rewards, the relations between unions and management range between cooperation and conflict. Most managements prefer to run business themselves but will bargain with unions when necessary. Governments enact laws and regulations regarding the formation of unions, their rights and responsibilities and those of employers, and modes for resolving disputes. Some legal settings encourage unions. Others discourage union organization and limit the bargaining power of workers.

Economists and other social scientists have long debated the benefits and costs of unionism to the economy and society writ large. The result is a huge body of research papers and books on the effects of unions across many disciplines. In August 2016, as this book moved to completion, Google Scholar listed 1.22 million results on articles on unions, 2.14 million on labor-management relations, 2.54 million on labor relations, and 3.28 million on industrial relations. Figure 8.1 shows the growth pattern of articles in peer-reviewed scientific journals on unions, collective bargaining, and industrial relations in the Web of Science. The number increased nearly fourfold, from 65 in 1960 to 243 in 2015. But the union share of social science articles declined, as the study of unions matured and as the fall in union density in many OECD countries reduced union influence on economic outcomes and policies.

How can someone who wants to find out "what unions do" make sense of this large body of research? The standard modes of finding out about an area of knowledge through textbooks, articles in Wikipedia, or expert reviews in journals, rely on the judgment/tastes of the writer or reviewer in assessing research findings. The meta-statistical method in this book has used a more objective way by pooling estimated quantitative effects of unionism across studies into their central tendency and modelling the variation across all studies.

As we laid out in Chapter 2, meta-analysis is a statistically valid approach to research synthesis. It requires that analysts turn estimates presented in different ways in different studies into a consistent measure of union effects – in our case, largely the partial correlation coefficient conditioned on other factors that affect

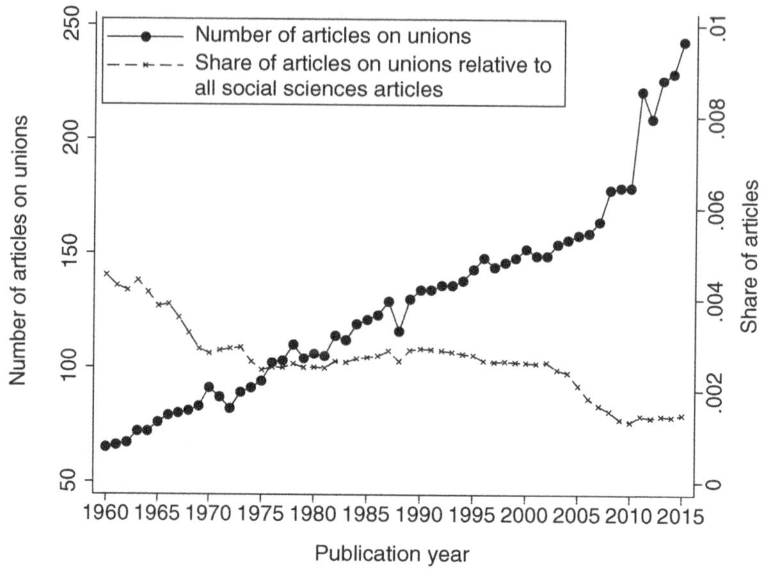

Figure 8.1 The rising number of articles on unions and the share of articles among all social sciences articles, Web of Science, 1960–2015

Source: Web of Science Core Collection, Articles in English, Social Sciences Research Area.

an outcome – and the precision of those estimates. Meta-analysis weighs more precisely estimated union effects more heavily in computing the average effect than less precisely estimated effects. By pooling estimates from many studies, it gives a valid picture of the findings of the studies as a group. It also helps detect moderator variables that account for differences among studies and offers ways to correct the evidence base for publication selection bias and other problems.

This chapter summarizes our findings on estimated union effects (section "Findings on union effects") and on the variation in research design that affects estimates (section "Measured and unmeasured artifacts in research of union effects"), and concludes with suggestions for future research to address open questions and policy issues (section "Challenges for future research and policy").

Findings on union effects

We posed our meta-analyses around Freeman and Medoff's *What Do Unions Do?* as the book that set the theoretical and empirical framework for three to four decades of ensuing union research. Chapter 1's scientometric analysis of the impact of *What Do Unions Do?* justifies our taking it as a starting point for our meta-analyses.

Table 8.1 compares the findings in Chapters 3–7 to those in Freeman and Medoff (1984) and in earlier meta-analyses of union effects. Column 1 reports the Freeman and Medoff findings and the number of estimates that underlay their conclusions. Column 2 gives the results of earlier meta-analyses. Column 3 summarizes our Chapters 3–7 findings. As we did not conduct new meta-analysis studies on wages and turnover, where results seem well established, we rely on the earlier meta-analyses in Column 2 for our assessments.

The bottom line of our investigation is simple. Hundreds of econometric studies and two thousand or so estimates after *What Do Unions Do?* the fundamental claims of the book stand up well, though not perfectly. We identify three areas where succeeding work has revised the picture of unions: (1) on productivity, where ensuing research replaces the generalization of a positive effect with a central tendency of negligible effects, and finds positive results in only some sectors; (2) on job satisfaction, where the causal route of the negative union association with satisfaction lies in selectivity of workplaces and members into unions rather than the collective voice stressed in Freeman and Medoff; and (3) on the variation in union effects with institutional settings, found by extending studies outside the United States.

Table 8.1 Summary of meta-analysis findings on the economic impact of trade unions

Dimension	*Freeman and Medoff (1984) (1)*	*Earlier meta-analysis (2)*	*New findings (3)*
		Broad economy	
Productivity	16 estimates from 8 studies. Positive correlation	Doucouliagos and Laroche (2003a): 73 estimates from 73 studies. Positive correlation for US, negative correlation for UK & Japan	Chapter 3: 710 estimates from 111 studies. Manufacturing: no association for US, negative correlation for UK and positive correlation for developing countries. Other sectors: positive correlation for construction and education
Productivity growth	5 estimates from 3 studies. No association	Doucouliagos and Laroche (2003b): 29 estimates from 26 studies. Negative correlation for US, no association elsewhere	Chapter 4: 268 estimates from 42 studies. No association

(*continued*)

Table 8.1 Summary of meta-analysis findings on the economic impact of trade unions (*continued*)

Dimension	*Freeman and Medoff (1984) (1)*	*Earlier meta-analysis (2)*	*New findings (3)*
		Firm channels of union impact	
Profitability	5 estimates from 4 studies. Negative correlation	Doucouliagos and Laroche (2009): 532 estimates from 45 studies. Negative correlation	Chapter 7: 478 estimates from 44 studies. Negative correlation
Physical capital investment	Negative correlation	Doucouliagos and Laroche (2003c): 11 estimates from 11 studies. Negative correlation	Chapter 5: 343 estimates from 20 studies. Negative correlation
Intangible capital investment	Negative correlation	Doucouliagos and Laroche (2013): 208 estimates from 25 studies. Negative correlation	nn
		Labor channels of union impact	
Turnover	18 estimates from 9 studies. Negative correlation	10 studies (Cotton and Tuttle, 1986) and 31 studies (Heavey et al., 2013). Negative correlation	nn
Wages	Positive correlation	152 estimates from 114 studies (Jarrell and Stanley, 1990). Positive correlation	nn
Job satisfaction	Negative correlation	10 studies (Premack, 1984). Negative correlation	Chapter 6: 235 estimates from 59 studies. No association

Note: nn denotes no new meta-analysis reported in this book.

On the productivity issue, Freeman and Medoff (1984) concluded from the small number of econometric studies then available that US unionism raised productivity while having no effect on its growth, contrary to critics of unionism who believed that it had adverse consequences on economic efficiency and growth. Our synthesis of ensuing empirical work in the first row of Table 8.1 suggests that unionism in the United States is associated with higher productivity in construction and education, but that in manufacturing the central tendency of union effects on productivity is near zero. Studies too late to be included in our meta-analysis find positive productivity effects for nursing as well (Sojourner et al., 2015; Dube et al., 2016), which suggests that the manufacturing/non-manufacturing division may be critical in understanding this industry source of variation.

In comparison to Freeman and Medoff (1984), who relied on 16 estimates for their 1984 book, and Doucouliagos and Laroche (2003a), who relied on 73 estimates in their 2003 assessment, our meta-average comes from 710 estimates – a sufficiently large number to allow us to delve into some of the reasons for difference in estimates. Freeman and Medoff's estimates were limited to the United States, and thus blind to cross-country differences in productivity effects identified in Chapter 3: negative in the United Kingdom and positive in the developing countries for which evidence exists. For productivity growth, the number of estimates in our meta-average also vastly exceeds the number in Freeman and Medoff, while confirming the conclusion of no union impact on productivity growth.

Companies are concerned with profitability rather than productivity or its growth. The 478 estimates of union effects on profitability shown in Chapter 7 support the Freeman and Medoff conclusion, from five estimates, that unionization is associated with lower profitability. The negative profits effect presumably explains the general business opposition to unionization, though, as Register (1988) notes, management may also oppose unions because they reduce managerial autonomy and force managers to find ways to restore profitability.

Estimates of the routes by which unions affect productivity differ markedly between the routes that relate to firms and those that relate to workers. Union effects on firm decisions to invest in physical and intangible capital are negative, presumably because union increases in wages and benefits lower the firm's retained earnings, which are a substantial source of funding for investment, and/or because the likelihood that unions will bargain for higher future wages and benefits lowers expected future profits.

Which of these channels or other channels accounts for the lower investments by firms is difficult to determine for two reasons. First, because there is limited data on the extent of unionization of firms to link to investment behavior. Second, because it is difficult to disentangle the effect of lower profits as a source of financing from its effect on expected *future* returns on capital. Expected profits will almost surely depend greatly on past profits. Using firm-level union data for the United States from his own survey, Hirsch (1992) regresses investment in physical capital on firm union density and diverse covariates, with and without inclusion of the profit rate (Hirsch, 1992, Table 5), and concludes that the finance effect accounts for about half of the total union effect for physical capital but for none of the effect for investment in R&D, albeit with substantial industry differences. A more definitive way to pin down the union effect on expected future profits independent of retained earnings/profits would be to take a firm with a given amount of retained earnings and that has both union and non-union plants in which it could invest its money, and see how much it allocates in the union and non-union plants. Presumably it would invest more of its retained earnings in the plants that would earn it more money.

At first blush, the finding that unionization is negatively correlated with investments in physical and intangible capital but uncorrelated with productivity and its growth appears paradoxical. How can unionism reduce two key inputs into production but not productivity itself? Assuming that both sets of findings are correct, Freeman and Medoff's (1984) collective-voice arguments proposed that part of the explanation lay in the offsetting benefits that unions bring to workers through reduced turnover, which lowers costs and improves returns to investments in firm-specific capital. Another possibility is that union wages and benefits increase the supply of workers seeking jobs at union firms, allowing management to select better workers along dimensions not captured in standard skill measures. Table 8.1's summary of meta-analyses of the effects of unions through worker channels supports the claimed reduction in turnover, though there is no consensus on how much of the lower turnover comes from voice channels versus other changes in the workplace.

Given that job satisfaction is positively related to productivity, the Freeman and Medoff (1984) finding that unionism was associated with lower job satisfaction suggested a workers' channel reducing productivity. Ensuing studies confirm the negative association between union membership and job satisfaction but find that the correlation has weakened over time and reject the central role of voice in the link in favor of a selectivity explanation for the negative correlation. In this reading of the evidence, a worker in a union job is neither more nor less satisfied with work than the same worker in a non-union job with comparable attributes to the union job, which forecloses the possible negative union–job satisfaction–productivity relation.

The largest literature on union effects are on what unions do to wages, where H. Gregg Lewis (1963) first organized diverse studies into a coherent picture and later updated this (Lewis, 1986). Rather than undertaking a new meta-analysis of wage effects, we rely on Lewis and Jarrell and Stanley (1990), who found modestly lower wage effects than Lewis. We note in addition that longitudinal analysis of union wage effects show smaller impacts than cross-section analysis with the same data (Freeman, 1984). This reflects positive selectivity for lower-paid workers for whom union wage effects tend to be large (Card, 1996), implying that the selectivity channel reduces union wage effects based on unobserved skills.

The biggest weakness in *What Do Unions Do?* is that, notwithstanding the broad title question, the book dealt almost exclusively with US evidence.[1] In succeeding years, analysis of the effects of union in countries outside the United States, with diverse levels of economic development, political institutions, and labor laws and regulations, provides a stronger basis for answering the title question. Since labor institutions are more idiosyncratic than most other economic institutions (Freeman, 2003), the growing body of studies outside the United States finds quantitatively different effects on economic outcomes and in some cases qualitatively different results as well: for example, the negative association of productivity and unionism in the United Kingdom compared to the positive association in developing countries reported in Chapter 3.

Country differences and labor regulations

Table 8.2 reports the meta-average partial correlations for unionism and outcomes for country units with enough estimated effects to be differentiated by the meta-regression analysis. Column (1) gives conditional meta-averages for the United States, which still has the largest number of studies. Column (2) gives comparable estimates for the United Kingdom, and Column (3) for developing countries.[2] Column (4) reports unconditional meta-averages for all countries and industries combined. With the exception of turnover, the meta-averages are constructed from our meta-regressions using partial correlations, unrestricted weighted least squares, and corrected for publication selection. The turnover results come from the summary meta-analyses of others.

The estimates for the United States display a small negative correlation of unionism with productivity in manufacturing and a moderate to large positive correlation with productivity in construction. They also show a moderate to large

Table 8.2 Meta-regression estimates of union effects on specified outcomes, by country group

	Conditional			*Unconditional*
Dimension	*US (1)*	*UK[3] (2)*	*Developing[3] (3)*	*All countries (4)*
Productivity – manufacturing	–0.02	–0.21*	0.08*	–0.01
Productivity – other[1]	0.20*	–	–	0.04*
Productivity growth	0.01	0.01	–	0.01
Physical capital investment[2]	–0.23*	–	–	–0.02
Intangible investment[2]	–0.34*	–0.34*	–	–0.10
Job satisfaction	–0.03	–0.04*	–	–0.01*
Profitability	–0.13*	–0.13*	–	–0.03*
Turnover†	–	–	–	–0.21*

Notes: Cells report our best estimates of the meta-average, using partial correlations corrected for publication bias, estimated using unrestricted WLS with inverse variance weights. Columns (1) to (3) report conditional meta-averages; for conditioning variables see individual chapters and Laroche (2016) for job satisfaction. Column (4) reports unconditional meta-averages for all estimates combined using the *PET* estimate from the *FAT-PET* model; see individual chapters for details.

[1]Conditional estimate is for construction.

[2]Estimates for physical capital investment and intangible capital investment relate to industry level.

†Simple correlation, uncorrected for publication bias.

*denotes statistical significance at least at the 10% level, using cluster adjusted standard errors (except for turnover where standard errors are unadjusted).

negative correlation with physical capital investment, a large negative correlation with investment in intangible capital, and a moderate negative correlation with profitability. For the United Kingdom, the correlations for investment in intangible capital and job satisfaction are also negative, and, as noted above, the correlation of unionism with productivity is moderate to large negative. For developing countries, by contrast, the meta-analysis shows a small to moderate positive correlation with productivity. Averaged across all countries, Column (4) shows that the empirical evidence supports the claim that unions reduce turnover and that they increase productivity in non-manufacturing industries while lowering profitability. Unionized workers report lower job satisfaction than non-unionized workers, but this is a selection rather than a causal effect. Unionism is largely associated with lower job satisfaction because unionized workers and jobs are intrinsically less satisfied than non-unionized workers, rather than because of what unions do to jobs/workers.

One of the critical results from our analysis is the wide variation of union effects around the meta-averages. The different estimated productivity effects by industry and country merit further investigation. Do the industry differences reflect technological characteristics of the sectors, where the skilled workers in construction and education have greater scope to affect productivity positively compared to machine-driven production workers in manufacturing? Do the country differences reflect levels of development? Legal settings? The history of union movements? Is the positive association of unions on productivity in developing countries due to their organizing large firms or multinationals with modern technology, or their concentration in particular industries?

The ideal way to address these questions would be to apply our meta-statistical methodology to meta-estimates of union effects for different firms, industries, or countries. Given a large number of estimates for firms in many industries in many countries, one could calculate meta-average effects for industries by country and use meta-regression analysis to find industry or country moderator variables in a meta-meta-analysis. But existing work reports on too few industries and too few countries for such an analysis.

We also explored whether the way unions operate across countries is a function of labor market regulations. We find that unions are more likely to have positive productivity effects in less regulated labor markets, at least in manufacturing. By contrast, less regulated labor markets are associated with greater negative union effects on investments in intangible capital and profitability. Given the crude nature of our labor market regulation measure, and potential differences in enforcement and the way regulations affect firms across countries, these results are best seen as suggesting the value of including analyses of regulations in new primary studies.

Time variation

The three to four decades post *What Do Unions Do?* allow us to examine time variation in the estimated partial correlations. Table 8.3 reports the time patterns in the various union effects. The correlation between unionization and productivity became more negative/less positive over time. The correlations between unionism and investment in physical and intangible capital and reduction in profits became less negative over time. The negative association of unionism with job satisfaction also decreased. Figure 8.2 illustrates the unconditional time effects in four union-effects: productivity effects in manufacturing, job satisfaction, investment in physical capital, and investment in intangible capital. While the coefficients for the conditional and unconditional estimates of the time trends are small, over time they amount to a significant difference in union effects, relative to the size of the meta-averages.

These trends may reflect genuine changes in how unions and firms interact over time. The decline in the union effect of productivity in manufacturing, from the positive effect in Brown and Medoff (1978) to the negligible effects in later studies, could reflect the spread of "good labor practices" over time as non-union firms copied attributes of union workplaces – seniority systems, job posting and bidding systems for filling vacancies rather than relying on supervisors to promote workers, establishing formal wage scales, grievance systems and mechanisms for employee voice, and so on. Many studies document the spread of "positive labor relations practices" pioneered by unions/unionized firms to non-union firms. To the extent that these practices gave union firms a productivity edge, their spread would reduce that advantage over time.[3]

The decline in the magnitudes of union-induced reductions in profitability and investments may also reflect learning what works by unions and firms. To the extent that reductions in profits and in capital investment harm the long-term prospects of workers, unions should adjust bargaining demands to offset those adverse effects. As union density has fallen in the United States and many other advanced

Table 8.3 Time variation in union effects

Dimension	*Time trend*
Productivity – manufacturing	More negative/less positive: –0.003 (–3.11)
Productivity – other industries	No effect
Productivity growth	No effect
Physical capital investment	Less negative: 0.002 (1.64)†
Intangible capital investment	Less negative: 0.009 (5.44)
Job satisfaction	Varies over the decades
Profitability	Less negative: 0.004 (6.63)
Turnover	Not investigated
Wages	Less positive

Note: Estimates from the conditional specific MRA models estimated using unrestricted weighted least squares. First number is the coefficient on *AveYear* and figure in brackets is *t*-statistic using cluster adjusted standard errors. † statistically significant in some of the estimated models. See individual chapters for details.

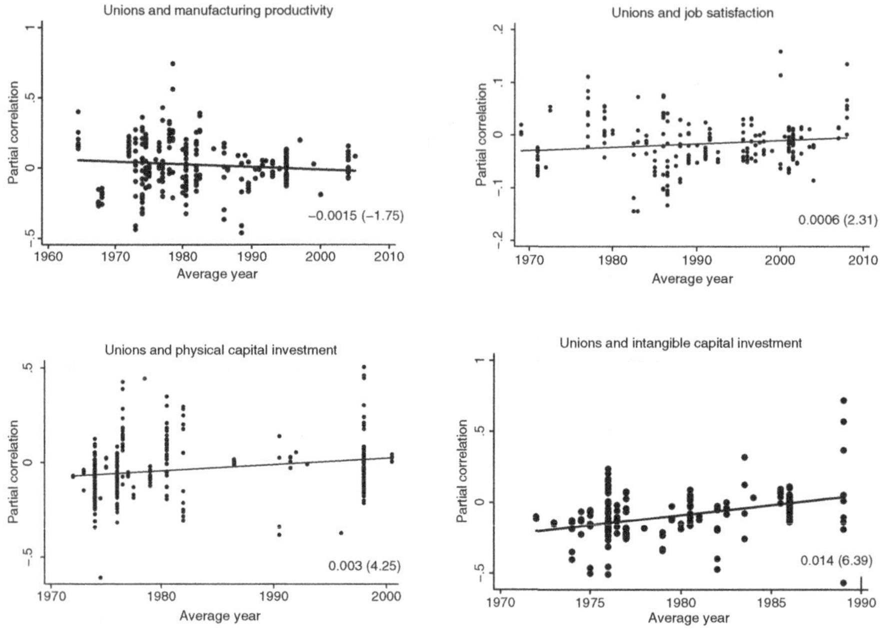

Figure 8.2 Union effects, chronological order

Note: Unconditional coefficient on time trend reported with *t*-statistic in brackets.

countries, it is also likely that surviving union firms had smaller loss of profits and higher investments than the firms that closed down.

But the trend factors may also be an *artifact* of improved research tools and data beyond those covered by our measures of methods and publication bias. Finding significant moderator effects on estimates suggests that the moderator variables we have, or others, may help explain part of the observed shrinkage of union effects.

Measured and unmeasured artifacts in research of union effects

Our analysis has examined data aggregation, endogeneity, and publication bias as moderators for the estimated union effects. The MRA regressions estimated coefficients on these effects on the assumption that the artifact effects are constant over time.

Improved data and statistical methodology

Column (1) of Table 8.4 examines the dependence of estimated union effects on the level of data aggregation. With establishment or firm as the base, the reported effects on productivity in manufacturing and investment in physical and intangible capital are more negative at higher levels of aggregation (e.g., industry or province/state). Since analyses tend to use less aggregate data over time, this relation cannot account for the estimated trend decline in union productivity but could help explain the declining estimate union effect on physical capital investment and investment in intangible capital.

Column (2) of the table considers the effects of measuring the union dependent variable with union density, used primarily in studies of industries or areas, and a binary union variable that contrasts a union worker or unionized establishment with a non-union worker or establishment in less aggregated data. The results show that the estimated union effect on investment in intangible capital became less negative with the 0/1 binary variable, while the estimated union effect became more negative for profitability. With an increase in studies using 0/1 binary measures, this could contribute to the falling union effect for investment in intangible capital.

Given that the statistical data and research techniques to analyze union effects have improved over the years, it is possible that further analysis of the effects of better data and econometric tools could help explain part of the time trends. Prior to the 1970s, most studies of union effects used aggregated area and industry data. The wage studies reviewed in Lewis (1963) compared wages by occupation or industry and areas with differing union rates. The most recent studies use individual workers or establishments, often in a before/after panel framework.

Table 8.4 Effects of data aggregation and measurement on estimated union effects

Dimension	*Data aggregation (1)*	*Measure of unionization (2)*
Productivity – manufacturing	More negative at state level	None
Productivity – other industries	None, all at establishment or firm level	None
Productivity growth	None†	None
Physical capital investment	More negative beyond firm level	None
Intangible capital investment	More negative beyond firm level	Less negative with binary 0/1
Job satisfaction	Not relevant, individual only	Not investigated
Profitability	None, all at establishment or firm level	More negative with binary 0/1

Notes: Columns (1) and (2) report whether data aggregation (with establishment and firm level as the base), and the measure of unionization (with union density as the base), affect the magnitude of reported partial correlations, controlling for other aspects of research design, respectively. See individual chapters for details.

† Some evidence of positive effects using national data but from a small sample.

Similarly, the Brown and Medoff (1978) estimates of productivity effects in US manufacturing come from production function data on industry and area, rather than from data on individual establishments or firms that offer a better research design. Our measures of moderators provide some control for this, but are still not as good as estimating changes in effects over time with studies done with the same type of data.

Thin or inconsistent meta-studies over time

The thousands of estimates from hundreds of studies that form the evidence base for this book appear impressive. They are large enough to distill an unwieldy literature into statistically valid summary statistics, with minimal role for personal judgment/tastes. But the evidence base is thin in several key areas. The number of studies for investment in physical capital and productivity growth is relatively modest. The number of studies for most countries beyond the United States is insufficient to estimate country dummies. Even in productivity equations where the number of primal studies is relatively large, there are few studies for industries in the service economy that dominates employment. The ideal data for a meta-analysis would be studies on many countries and industries to allow for an analysis of variance of the country and industry effects, followed with meta-regressions. It is hard to reach firm conclusions about trends when data is thin along some key dimensions.

But the potentially biggest problem in assessing the union effect over time is that while there are a substantial number of studies today for meta-analysis evaluation, the number of studies in the early period was fewer; vide the growing literature shown in Figure 8.1. In addition, the earlier meta-studies we used to determine association between unions and turnover and organizational commitment reported simple (zero order) correlations instead of the partial correlations, and none corrected the evidence base for publication bias. The earlier studies require updates for consistency with the partial correlations we used, but that would be a Herculean task, from the reported data. It is important that future studies give partial correlations comparable to those currently used to ease analysis of union effects over time. Similarly, historical studies that seek to assess union effects in the past should also try to produce statistics comparable to those in current data.[4]

Publication bias and timing of topic choice

As Stanley and Doucouliagos (2012) stress, it is important to use research synthesis methods that identify and correct the selection bias that may tilt the published literature in one direction or another. Column (1) of Table 8.5 summarizes our findings with regard to publication selection bias on estimated union effects, outcome by outcome. The absence of substantive publication bias is a sign of a relatively healthy empirical literature. Overall there is relatively little selection bias in the union effects literature. Nevertheless, there is substantial reporting bias

Table 8.5 Publication selection bias and endogeneity on estimates of union effects

Dimension	*Impact of publication selection bias (1)*	*Impact of failing to take account of endogeneity of unionism (2)*
Productivity – manufacturing	Substantial: preference for positive correlations	Larger adverse effects
Productivity – other industries	None	None
Productivity growth	Modest to substantial: preference for negative correlations	Not investigated
Physical capital investment	None	Not investigated
Intangible capital investment	Modest: preference for positive correlations	Not investigated
Job satisfaction	None	Larger adverse effects
Profitability	None	None
Turnover	Not investigated	Not investigated

Note: See individual chapters for details.

in favor of positive union effects in the correlation of unionism with productivity in manufacturing, a modest to substantial bias in favor of adverse union effects in the correlation with productivity growth, and a modest bias in the correlation with intangible investments in capital.

Doucouliagos and Stanley (2013) argue that strong and countervailing theoretical perspectives create space in academic journals for offsetting findings to be reported, which reduces publication selection bias. It may be that there is a time dimension to the reduction in publication bias. The earlier studies report larger positive (in the case of union productivity) or negative effects (on investment in physical or intangible capital, and profitability) and are then "reined" in by ensuing research that either would not have been done absent the initial strong claims, or would have had trouble being published. Under reasonable conditions, the research comes to the "right conclusion" through an increased sample size of studies set off by an initial strong claim.

Causal inference

Empirical research often starts with an observation that two variables are correlated, proceeding first to test whether the correlation stands up to multivariate analysis and then to a model that examines the causal connection between the variables. Most studies of unionism take union organization as given and treat the associations with economic outcomes as being caused by unionism. Some exploit longitudinal data that use the time sequence between unionism and outcomes to test causality (if unions cause higher wages, wages should rise when worker/firm moves from non-union to union status). But over a longer period, unionism is itself an endogenous economic choice, which blurs interpretation of the estimated parameters linking outcomes to unions. If unions positively affect an outcome and the outcome reduces unionism, least squares regressions understate the impact of unions on the outcome. If the outcome increases unionism, regressions will overstate the strength of the union impact.

Our approach to dealing with endogeneity moves from analyzing the association between unions and productivity (where virtually all studies take unions as exogenous or predetermined) to exploring the transmission channels through which unionization could potentially cause the observed associations. For most channels, researchers have lacked sufficient variation to assess endogeneity, so that the meta-analysis of the channels is largely built on associations as well. The associations are almost all partial associations obtained from regression calculations in which many factors that could confound causality are taken into account. But absent a genuine experiment, there invariably remains uncertainty whether estimates reflect causality properly.

Column (2) of Table 8.5 summarizes comparisons of estimated union effects from studies that make some effort to deal with endogeneity and those that do not. Correcting for endogeneity makes no difference in estimates of productivity outside of manufacturing. However, meta-regression reveals that estimates that do not deal with endogeneity produce larger negative or smaller positive effects on productivity in manufacturing industries and on job satisfaction. In these cases, OLS estimates are likely to misrepresent the magnitude of the union effect, inflating negative correlations between unionization and productivity and job satisfaction.

Challenges for future research and policy

It is often said that research that advances knowledge raises more questions than it answers. Stipulating that our meta-analysis of research findings post *What Unions Do?* and assessment of the impact of methods of analysis on the findings are valid, how might future research proceed so that the next decades' meta-analyses will yield stronger and deeper conclusions than those in this book?

We identify four challenges for future primary studies and meta-analyses.

Challenge 1: Expanding scope to test robustness

Due to inherent variation in institutions, people, and environments, generalizations about union effects, as with other social outcomes, come not from experimental replication that yield the same results across space and time as in physics, but rather from the *robustness* of findings across firms, sectors, economies, over time, and across data sets and model specifications, which are more mindful of biomedical sciences.

The importance of robustness calls for expanding the scope of union research *to more countries, sectors, and time periods, historical as well contemporary*. A bigger data base of union estimates would give the next meta-analyses inputs for generalizations under a wider span of economic conditions. This would let researchers move from our conclusion that union effects differ across units of analysis to discovering much more about the causes/moderator variables for the differences – for instance, why estimated union effects on productivity are negative in the United Kingdom, average zero in most other countries, and positive in the few developing countries for which we have evidence; and why effects are positive in education, construction, and nursing but negligible elsewhere. The employment shifts from industry to services require studies of union effects in wholesale and retail trade, various services, banking and finance, and the public sector to give a complete picture of the union impact.

Challenge 2: Widening the measures of collective voice/worker power

The second challenge is to expand analysis of collective voice beyond the unions/collective bargaining versus non-union management decision-making dichotomy specified in most countries' labor law, to the changing work arrangements and channels by which workers seek to affect workplace outcomes. On the employer side, the growth of multinational companies operating with extensive supply chains and outsourcing and of alternative work arrangements, where some workers are on call or independent contractors while others have temporary contracts, would seem to require voice channels beyond traditional trade unions or works councils. At the other side of the organizational structure, the large number of workplaces where employees have ownership stakes in their firms or are part of company profit-sharing adds another channel by which workers can influence firms, but also where their ownership stake will influence their views of workplace issues.

Unions have adjusted slowly to new technology, but the development of social media and web-based technologies that link workers together creates potential for new forms of voice through cyber unionism (Diamond and Freeman, 2002; Freeman and Rogers, 2002; Freeman, 2005). In China, which nominally has the world's greatest 'union' membership, the only legal unions are controlled by the party-run All China Federation of Trade Unions (ACFTU) that nominally organizes every workplace in the country, with the result that workers use social media to learn about labor developments and engage in huge numbers of wildcat strikes. Despite the ACFTU's lack of independence, workplaces with ACFTU chapters are associated with higher wages and benefits for workers, posing the challenge of how a government agency union affects outcomes.

Challenge 3: Getting more causal and policy relevant

The third challenge is to obtain better estimates of the extent to which changes in unionism change the outcomes associated with unionism when unionism is endogenously affected by the outcome variables. Studies deal with endogeneity in various ways: through before/after longitudinal analyses, by instrumenting unionism on exogenous factors, through propensity score comparison of persons with similar likelihoods of being unionised, and so on. A large sample of studies with estimates of these kinds would allow meta-analysts to contrast the impact of different types of adjustments for endogeneity that we could not do in Table 8.5. But even if these adjustments gave estimates that came close to those from a random assignment controlled experiment, researchers would not provide more guidance to decision-makers on policies toward unions. Changes in policies do not occur in a *ceteris paribus* random assignment world. The variation in union effects found in meta-analysis reflects in part random variation but in part also variation in context. And the effects of policies often depend on the details of the policy. A law that sought to make it easier for workers to unionize through harsh legal penalties on employers might backfire, just as a law that made union organization illegal might do the same.

To move from studies of union effects to policy advice requires analysis of actual labor policies, private as well as public and of labor laws and regulations. There is sufficient variation and changes in laws and regulations worldwide that could generate sufficient primal studies for meta-analysis generalizations. Debates in the United States over "right to work" (laws that forbid unions and employers from signing contracts that require workers opposed to joining a union to pay an agency fee for union services) have generated studies across states on their impact on unionism. The often quirky differences and timing of changes in labor laws and regulations not only in the United States but in countries worldwide and changes in policies among firms provides, moreover, instrumental variables for estimating union causal effects. Meta-analysis of an evidence base of the outcomes of policies is arguably the most useful way to help decision-makers assess future policies.

Challenge 4: Going beyond firm/economic measures

Assume that future research widened the scope of union studies, measured collective voice of workers more broadly, and did a better job in pinning down causal impacts not only of unionism but of policies to change unionism. Would that be enough to determine whether society should encourage or discourage more union activity, and if so, how?

We think that estimates of the impact of unions on the microeconomic performance measures on which quantitative studies of union effects focus are necessary but far from sufficient for societal assessment of unions and policies toward them. The more positive and less negative union effects on productivity and growth and the less costly to firms union increases in wage and benefits, the greater the rationale for policies tilted toward unions. But the opposite holds true if unions have large adverse or small positive effects on firm-based outcomes. Further, the social context in which unions do what they do matters. In a time of high and rising inequality, union policies that reduce inequality have greater value than in a time of low or falling inequality. In a society where free markets and democracy are threatened by uncontrolled finance and crony capitalism, unions are presumptively more valuable than in a society where markets approach Adam Smith's Invisible Hand ideal, which the monopoly face of unions may upend.

Finally, union activities almost invariably trade off some economic efficiency for the greater justice at workplaces and reduced inequalities valued by persons on the left and almost invariably do so in ways that constrain the personal liberties and economic freedoms valued by libertarians on the right. This means that the scientific studies that provided the evidence base for this book and that will ideally give better evidence for future assessments of unions are only one part of a decision system. They must be judged relative to the social preferences and utility functions of persons.

Notes

1 A more geographically accurate title would have been *What Do American Unions Do?*

2 The United States, United Kingdom, and developing country estimates are conditional meta-averages that take account of specification, estimation, and other data differences.

3 See Foulke (1981), Lewin (1990), and Colvin (2012).

4 Absent such studies, more subtle forms of analysis might help us assess the reasons for changes over time – for instance, it is possible to backcast a counterfactual based on 'today's' structure and the outcomes to those in the past. If the structure was unchanged, the projections would fit the past. If the projections did not fit, this would be a sign of structural change.

Bibliography

Abelson, M.A. and Baysinger, B.D. (1984) Optimal and dysfunctional turnover: Toward an organizational level model, *The Academy of Management Review*, 9: 331–41.

Abraham, K.G. and Farber, H.S. (1987) Job duration, seniority, and earnings, *The American Economic Review*, 77: 278–97.

Acemoglu, D. and Pischke, J.-S. (1999a) The structure of wages and investment in general training, *Journal of Political Economy*, 107: 539–72.

Acemoglu, D. and Pischke, J.-S. (1999b) Beyond Becker: Training in imperfect labour markets, *The Economic Journal*, 109: 112–42.

Acharya, V.V., Baghai, R.P. and Subramanian, K.V. (2013) Labor laws and innovation, *Journal of Law and Economics*, 56: 997–1037.

Acs, Z.J. and Audretsch, D.B. (1987) Innovation in large and small firms, *Economics Letters*, 23: 109–12.

Acs, Z.J. and Audretsch, D.B. (1988) Innovation in large and small firms: An empirical analysis, *The American Economic Review*, 78: 678–90.

Addison, J.T. (1982) Are unions good for productivity? *Journal of Labor Research*, 3: 125–38.

Addison, J.T. (1985) What do unions really do? A review article, *Journal of Labor Research*, 6: 127–46.

Addison, J.T. and Barnett, A. (1982) The impact of unions on productivity, *British Journal of Industrial Relations*, 20: 145–62.

Addison, J.T. and Chilton, J.B. (1998) Self-enforcing union contracts: Efficient investment and employment, *Journal of Business*, 71: 349–69.

Addison, J.T. and Hirsch, B.T. (1989) Union effects on productivity, profits, and growth: Has the long run arrived? *Journal of Labor Economics*, 7: 72–105.

Addison, J.T., Kraft, K. and Wagner, J. (1993) German works councils and firm performance. In B.E. Kaufman and M.M. Kleiner (eds.), *Employee Representation: Alternatives and Future Directions*, Madison, WI: Industrial Relations Research Association, 305–35.

Addison, J.T., Schank, T., Schnabel, C. and Wagner, J. (2007) Do works councils inhibit investment? *Industrial and Labor Relations Review*, 60: 187–203.

Addison, J.T. and Schnabel, C. (1997) On the determinants of mandatory works councils in Germany, *Industrial Relations: A Journal of Economy and Society*, 36: 419–45.

Addison, J.T., Schnabel, C. and Wagner, J. (2001) Works councils in Germany: Their effects on establishment performance, *Oxford Economic Papers*, 53: 659–94.

Addison, J.T., Schnabel, C. and Wagner, J. (2004) The course of research into the economic consequences of German works councils, *British Journal of Industrial Relations*, 42: 255–81.

Addison, J.T. and Wagner, J. (1994a) UK unionism and innovative activity: Some cautionary remarks on the basis of a simple cross-country test, *British Journal of Industrial Relations*, 32: 85–98.

Addison, J.T. and Wagner, J. (1994b) US unionism and R&D investment: Evidence from a simple cross-country test, *Journal of Labor Research*, 15: 191–7.

Adler, P.S. and Cole, R.E. (1993) Designed for learning: A tale of two auto plants, *Sloan Management Review*, 34: 85–95.

Akerlof, G.A. and Yellen, J.L. (1990) The fair wage-effort hypothesis and unemployment, *The Quarterly Journal of Economics*, 105: 255–83.

Alesina, A., Battisti, M. and Zeira, J. (2015) Technology and Labor Regulations: Theory and evidence, NBER Working Paper 20841.

Allen, S.G. (1984) Unionized construction workers are more productive, *The Quarterly Journal of Economics*, 99: 251–74.

Allen, S.G. (1985) Why construction industry productivity is declining, *The Review of Economics and Statistics*, 67: 661–9.

Allen, S.G. (1986a) The effect of unionism on productivity in privately and publicly owned hospitals and nursing homes, *Journal of Labor Research*, 7: 59–68.

Allen, S.G. (1986b) Unionization and productivity in office building and school construction, *Industrial and Labor Relations Review*, 39: 187–201.

Allen, S.G. (1988a) Declining unionization in construction: The facts and the reasons, *Industrial and Labor Relations Review*, 41: 343–59.

Allen, S.G. (1988b) Further evidence on union efficiency in construction, *Industrial Relations: A Journal of Economy and Society*, 27: 232–40.

Anderson, M.H. (2006) How can we know what we think until we see what we said? A citation and citation context analysis of Karl Weick's *The Social Psychology of Organizing*, *Organization Studies*, 27: 1675–92.

Anwar, S. and Sun, S. (2015) Unionisation and firm performance in China's manufacturing industries, *Journal of Labor Research*, 36: 78–102.

Argys, L. and Rees D. (1995) Unionization and school productivity: A reexamination, *Research in Labor Economics*, 14: 49–68.

Arthur, J.B. (1994) Effects of human resource systems on manufacturing performance and turnover, *The Academy of Management Journal*, 37: 670–87.

Artz, B. (2008) The role of firm size and performance pay in determining employee job satisfaction brief: Firm size, performance pay, and job satisfaction, *Labour*, 22: 315–43.

Artz, B. (2010) The impact of union experience on job satisfaction, *Industrial Relations: A Journal of Economy and Society*, 49: 387–405.

Artz, B. (2012) Does the impact of union experience on job satisfaction differ by gender? *Industrial and Labor Relations Review*, 65: 225–43.

Artz, B. and Kaya, I. (2014) Job insecurity and job satisfaction in the United States: The case of public sector union workers, *Industrial Relations Journal*, 45: 103–20.

Asteriou, D. and Monastiriotis, V. (2004) What do unions do at the large scale? Macro-economic evidence from a panel of OECD countries, *Journal of Applied Economics*, 7: 27–46.

Audretsch, D.B. and Graf von der Schulenburg, J.M. (1990) Union participation, innovation, and concentration: Results from a simultaneous model, *Journal of Institutional and Theoretical Economics*, 146: 298–313.

Bae, J. and Lawler, J.J. (2000) Organizational and HRM strategies in Korea: Impact on firm performance in an emerging economy, *The Academy of Management Journal*, 43: 502–17.

Baldwin, C.Y. (1983) Productivity and labor unions: An application of the theory of self-enforcing contracts, *Journal of Business*, 56: 155–85.

Baldwin, J. (1992) Industrial efficiency and plant turnover in the Canadian manufacturing sector. In R.E. Caves (ed.), *Industrial Efficiency in Six Nations*, Cambridge, MA: MIT Press, 273–310.

Ballardini, F, Malipiero, A, Oriani, R, Sobrero, M. and Zammit, A. (2005) Do stock markets value innovation? A meta-analysis, Paper presented at the 2005 Academy of Management Meeting, Honolulu, HI.

Bamberger, P.A., Kluger, A.N. and Suchard, R. (1999) The antecedents and consequences of union commitment: A meta-analysis, *The Academy of Management Journal*, 42: 304–18.

Barney, J. (1991) Firm resources and sustained competitive advantage, *Journal of Management*, 17: 99–120.

Bartel, A.P. (1981) Race differences in job satisfaction: A reappraisal, *The Journal of Human Resources*, 16: 294–303.

Bartel, A.P. (1994) Productivity gains from the implementation of employee training programs, *Industrial Relations: A Journal of Economy and Society*, 33: 411–25.

Batt, R. (1999) Work organization, technology, and performance in customer service and sales, *Industrial and Labor Relations Review*, 52: 539–64.

Batt, R., Colvin, A. and Keefe, J. (2002). Employee voice, human resource practices, and quit rates: Evidence from the telecommunications industry, *Industrial and Labor Relations Review*, 55: 573–94.

Batt, R. and Welbourne, T.M. (2002) Performance and growth in entrepreneurial firms: Revisiting the union-performance relationship, In J.A. Katz and T.M. Welbourne (eds.), *Managing People in Entrepreneurial Organizations (Advances in Entrepreneurship, Firm Emergence and Growth, Volume 5)*, Bradford, UK: Emerald Group Publishing, 147–74.

Becker, B.E. and Olson, C.A. (1989) Unionization and shareholder interests, *Industrial and Labor Relations Review*, 42: 246–61.

Becker, B.E. and Olson, C.A. (1992) Unions and firm profits, *Industrial Relations: A Journal of Economy and Society*, 31: 395–415.

Becker, G.S. (1964) *Human Capital*, New York: Columbia University Press.

Belfield, C.R. and Harris, R.D.F. (2002) How well do theories of job matching explain variations in job satisfaction across education levels? Evidence for UK graduates, *Applied Economics*, 34: 535–48.

Belman, D. (1992) Unions, the quality of labor relations, and firm performance. In L. Mishel and P.B. Voos (eds.), *Unions and Economic Competitiveness*, New York: M. E Sharpe, 41–107.

Bemmels, B. (1987) How unions affect productivity in manufacturing plants, *Industrial and Labor Relations Review*, 40: 241–53.

Bender, K.A., Donohue, S.M. and Heywood, J.S. (2005) Job satisfaction and gender segregation, *Oxford Economic Papers*, 57: 479–96.

Bender, K.A. and Sloane, P.J. (1998) Job satisfaction, trade unions, and exit-voice revisited, *Industrial and Labor Relations Review*, 51: 222–40.

Bennett, J.T. and Kaufman, B.E. (2007) *What Do Unions Do? A Twenty-Year Perspective*, New Brunswick, NJ: Transaction Publishers.

Benson, J. (2006) Japanese management, enterprise unions and company performance, *Industrial Relations Journal*, 37: 242–58.

Berg, P. (1999) The effects of high performance work practices on job satisfaction in the United States steel industry, *Relations Industrielles/Industrial Relations*, 54: 111–35.

Betcherman, G. (1991) The effect of unions on the innovative behaviour of firms in Canada, *Industrial Relations Journal*, 22: 142–51.

Betts, J.R., Odgers, C.W. and Wilson, M.K. (2001) The effects of unions on research and development: An empirical analysis using multi-year data, *Canadian Journal of Economics*, 34: 785–806.

Bielby, W.T. and Baron, J.N. (1986) Men and women at work: Sex segregation and statistical discrimination, *American Journal of Sociology*, 91: 759–99.

Black, S.E. and Lynch, L.M. (1996) Human-capital investments and productivity, *The American Economic Review: Papers and Proceedings*, 86: 263–7.

Black, S.E. and Lynch, L.M. (2001) How to compete: The impact of workplace practices and information technology on productivity, *The Review of Economics and Statistics*, 83: 434–45.

Blanchflower, D.G. and Bryson, A. (2004) What effect do unions have on wages now and would Freeman and Medoff be surprised? *Journal of Labor Research*, 25: 383–414.

Blanchflower, D.G. and Oswald, A.J. (2000) Well-being over time in Britain and the USA. NBER Working Paper, 7487, National Bureau of Economic Research.

Blau, F.D. and Beller, A.H. (1988) Trends in earnings differentials by gender, 1971–1981, *Industrial and Labor Relations Review*, 41: 513–29.

Blundell, R., Griffith, R. and Van Reenen, J. (1999) Market share, market value, and innovation in a panel of British manufacturing firms, *The Review of Economics Studies*, 66: 529–54.

Boal, W.M. (1990) Unionism and productivity in West Virginia coal mining, *Industrial and Labor Relations Review*, 43: 390–405.

Böckerman, P. and Ilmakunnas, P. (2006) Do job disamenities raise wages or ruin job satisfaction? *International Journal of Manpower*, 27: 290–302.

Booth, A. (1995) *The Economics of the Trade Union*, New York: Cambridge University Press.

Borenstein, M., Hedges, L.V, Higgins, J.P.T and Rothstein, H.R. (2009) *Introduction to Meta-Analysis*, Chichester: Wiley.

Borgatti, S.P., Everett, M. G. and Freeman, L.C. (2002) *Ucinet for Windows: Software for Social Network Analysis*, Cambridge, MA: Analytic Technologies.

Borjas, G.J. (1979) Job satisfaction, wages, and unions, *The Journal of Human Resources*, 14: 21–40.

Bowling, N.A. (2007) Is the job satisfaction–job performance relationship spurious? A meta-analytic examination, *Journal of Vocational Behavior*, 71: 167–85.

Bronars, S.G. and Deere, D.R. (1993) Unionization, incomplete contracting, and capital investment, *Journal of Business*, 66: 117–32.

Bronars, S.G., Deere, D.R. and Tracy, J.S. (1994) The effects of unions on firm behavior: An empirical analysis using firm-level data, *Industrial Relations: A Journal of Economy and Society*, 33: 426–51.

Brown, C. and Medoff, J.L. (1978) Trade unions in the production process, *Journal of Political Economy*, 86: 355–78.

Brown, C. and Medoff, J.L. (1989) The employer size-wage effect, *Journal of Political Economy*, 97: 1027–59.

Brunello, G. (1992) The effect of unions on firm performance in Japanese manufacturing, *Industrial and Labor Relations Review*, 45: 471–87.

Bryson, A. (2007) The effect of trade unions on wages, *Reflets et Perspectives*, XLVI, 2–3: 33–45.

Bryson A., Cappellari, L. and Lucifora, C. (2004) Does union membership really reduce job satisfaction in Britain? *British Journal of Industrial Relations*, 42: 439–59.

Bryson, A., Cappellari, L. and Lucifora, C. (2010) Why so unhappy? The effects of unionization on job satisfaction, *Oxford Bulletin of Economics and Statistics*, 72: 357–80.

Bryson, A., Forth, J. and Kirby, S. (2005) High-involvement management practices, trade union representation and workplace performance in Britain, *Scottish Journal of Political Economy*, 52: 451–91.

Budd, J.W., Chi, W., Wang, Y. and Xie, Q. (2014) What do unions in China do? Provincial-level evidence on wages, employment, productivity, and economic output, *Journal of Labor Research*, 35: 185–204.

Budd, J.W., Gollan, P.J. and Wilkinson, A. (2010) New approaches to employee voice and participation in organizations, *Human Relations*, 63: 303–10.

Bulow, J.I. and Summers, L.H. (1986) A theory of dual labor markets with application to industrial policy, discrimination, and Keynesian unemployment, *Journal of Labor Economics*, 4: 376–414.

Bycio, P., Hackett, R.D. and Alvares, K.M. (1990) Job performance and turnover: A review and meta-analysis, *Applied Psychology: An International Review*, 39: 47–76.

Byrne, D., Dezhbakhsh, H. and King, R. (1996) Unions and police productivity: An econometric investigation, *Industrial Relations: A Journal of Economy and Society*, 35: 566–84.

Byrnes, P., Fare, R., Grosskopf, S. and Lovell, C.A.K. (1988) The effect of unions on productivity: U.S. surface mining of coal, *Management Science*, 34: 1037–53.

Cable, J.R. and Machin, S.J. (1991) The relationship between union wage and profitability effects, *Economics Letters*, 37: 315–21.

Calmfors, L. and Driffill, J. (1988) Bargaining structure, corporatism and macroeconomic performance, *Economic Policy*, 3: 13–61.

Cameron, A.C., Gelbach, J.B. and Miller, D.L. (2008) Bootstrap-based improvements for inference with clustered errors, *The Review of Economics and Statistics*, 90: 414–27.

Capon, N., Farley, J.U. and Hoenig, S. (1990) Determinants of financial performance: A meta-analysis, *Management Science*, 36: 1143–59.

Cappellari, L., Lucifora, C. and Piccirilli, G. (2004) Union activism, workers' satisfaction and organizational change, *Labour*, 18: 1–28.

Cappelli, P. and Sherer, P.D. (1991) The missing role of context in OB: The need for a meso-level approach, *Research in Organizational Behavior*, 13: 55–110.

Card, D. (1996) The effect of unions on the structure of wages: A longitudinal analysis, *Econometrica*, 64: 957–79.

Casey, D.L. and McMillan, G.S. (2008) Identifying the "invisible colleges" of the *Industrial & Labor Relations Review*: A bibliometric approach, *Industrial and Labor Relations Review*, 62: 126–32.

Cassoni, A., Labadie, G.J., and Fachola, G. (2005) The economic effects of unions in Latin America: Their impact on wages and the economic performance of firms in Uruguay. In P. Kuhn and G. Márquez (eds.), *What Difference Do Unions Make? Their Impact on Productivity and Wages in Latin America*, Washington, DC: Inter-American Development Bank, 101–42.

Cavalluzzo, L. and Baldwin, D. (1993) Unionization and productive efficiency. In F. Harold, C.A.K. Lovell and S. Schmidt (eds.), *The Measurement of Productive Efficiency*, Oxford: Oxford University Press, 210–20.

Cavanaugh, J.K. (1998) Asset-specific investment and unionized labor, *Industrial Relations: A Journal of Economy and Society*, 37: 35–50.

Caves, R.E. (1980) Productivity differences among industries. In R.E. Caves and L.B. Krause (eds.), *Britain's Economic Performance*, Washington, DC: The Brookings Institution, 135–99.

Caves, R.E. and Barton, D.R. (1990) *Efficiency in U.S. Manufacturing Industries*, Cambridge, MA: MIT Press.

Caves, R.E., Porter, M.E., Spence, A.M. and Scott, J.T. (1980) *Competition in the Open Economy: A Model Applied to Canada*, Cambridge, MA: Harvard University Press.
Chappell, W.F., Mayer, W.J. and Shughart, W.F. (1991) Union rents and market structure revisited, *Journal of Labor Research*, 12: 35–46.
Chen, Y.-S. and Chen, I.-J. (2013) The impact of labor unions on investment-cash flow sensitivity, *Journal of Banking and Finance*, 37: 2408–18.
Chezum, B. and Garen, J.E. (1998) Are union productivity effects overestimated?: Evidence from coal mining, *Applied Economics*, 30: 913–8.
Chiles, T.W. and Stewart, J.B. (1993) Union rent appropriation and ex-post analysis, *Journal of Labor Research*, 14: 317–33.
Chintrakarn, P. and Chen, Y.-Y. (2011) Do unions impact efficiency?: Evidence from the U.S. manufacturing sector, *Contemporary Economic Policy*, 29: 431–40.
Chirinko, R.S. (2008) σ: The long and short of it, *Journal of Macroeconomics*, 30: 671–86.
Chor, D. and Freeman, R.B. (2005) The 2004 global labor survey: Workplace institutions and practices around the world, NBER Working Paper No. 11598, National Bureau of Economic Research.
Clark, A.E. (1997) Job satisfaction and gender: Why are women so happy at work? *Labour Economics*, 4: 341–72.
Clark, A.E., Oswald, A. and Warr, P. (1996) Is job satisfaction U-shaped in age? *Journal of Occupational and Organizational Psychology*, 69: 57–81.
Clark, K.B. (1980a) The impact of unionization on productivity: A case study, *Industrial and Labor Relations Review*, 33: 451–69.
Clark, K.B. (1980b) Unionization and productivity: Micro-economic evidence, *The Quarterly Journal of Economics*, 45: 613–39.
Clark, K.B. (1984) Unionization and firm performance: The impact on profits, growth and productivity, *The American Economic Review*, 74: 893–919.
Clark, K.B. and Griliches, Z. (1984) Productivity growth and R&D at the business level: Results from the PIMS data base. In Z. Griliches (ed.), *R&D, Patents, and Productivity*, Chicago: University of Chicago Press, 393–416.
Coff, R.W. (1999) When competitive advantage doesn't lead to performance: The resource-based view and stakeholder bargaining power, *Organization Science*, 10: 119–33.
Cohen, A. (1993) Organizational commitment and turnover: A meta-analysis, *The Academy of Management Journal*, 36: 1140–57.
Cohen, J. (1988) *Statistical Power Analysis for the Behavioral Sciences*, 2nd ed., Hillsdale, NJ: Lawrence Erlbaum Associates.
Colvin, A. (2012) Participation versus procedures in non-union dispute resolution, *Industrial Relations: A Journal of Economy and Society*, 52: 259–83.
Connolly, R.A., Hirsch, B.T. and Hirschey, M. (1986) Union rent seeking, intangible capital, and market value of the firm, *The Review of Economics and Statistics*, 68: 567–77.
Conte, M.A. and Svejnar, J. (1988) Productivity effects of worker participation in management, profit-sharing, worker ownership of assets and unionization in U.S. firms, *International Journal of Industrial Organization*, 6: 139–51.
Conte, M.A. and Svejnar, J. (1990) The effects of worker participation in management, profits, and ownership of assets on enterprise performance. In K.G. Abraham and R.B. Mc Kersie (eds.), *New Developments in the Labor Market: Toward a New Institutional Paradigm*, Cambridge, MA: MIT Press, 59–84.
Conyon, M.J. and Freeman, R.B. (2002) Shared modes of compensation and firm performance: U.K. evidence. In D. Card, R. Blundell and R.B. Freeman (eds.), *Seeking a*

Premiere Economy: The Economic Effects of British Economic Reforms, 1980–2000, Chicago: University of Chicago Press, 109–46.

Conyon, M.J. and Machin, S. (1991a) Market structure and the empirical specification of profit margins, *Economics Letters*, 35: 227–31.

Conyon, M.J. and Machin, S. (1991b) The determination of profit margins in UK manufacturing, *Journal of Industrial Economics*, 39: 369–82.

Cook, T.D., Cooper, H., Cordray, D.S., Hartmann, H., Hedges, L.V., Light, R.J., Louis, T.A. and Mosteller, F. (1992) *Meta-Analysis for Explanation: A Casebook*, New York: The Russell Sage Foundation.

Cooke, W.N. (1994) Employee participation programs, group-based incentives, and company performance: A union-nonunion comparison, *Industrial and Labor Relations Review*, 47: 594–609.

Cooper-Harim, A. and Viswesvaran, C. (2005) The construct of work commitment: Testing an integrative framework, *Psychological Bulletin*, 131: 241–59.

Cotti, C.D., Haley, M.R. and Miller, L.A. (2014) Workplace flexibilities, job satisfaction and union membership in the US workforce, *British Journal of Industrial Relations*, 52: 403–25.

Cotton, J.L. and Tuttle, J.M. (1986) Employee turnover: A meta-analysis and review with implications for research, *The Academy of Management Review*, 11: 55–70.

Coutrot, T. (1996) Relations sociales et performance economique: Une première analyse du cas français, *Travail et Emploi*, 66: 39–66.

Cowling, K. and Waterson, M. (1975) Price-cost margins and market structure, *Economica*, 43: 267–74.

Craig, B. and Pencavel, J. (1995) Participation and productivity: A comparison of worker cooperatives and conventional firms in the plywood industry, *Brookings Papers: Microeconomics*, 121–60.

Damiani, M. and Ricci, A. (2011) Performance-related pay, unions, and productivity in Italy: Evidence from quantile regressions. In J. DeVaro (ed.), *Advances in the Economic Analysis of Participatory and Labor-Managed Firms*, vol. 12, 169–96.

Datta, D.K, Guthrie, J.P. and Wright, P.M. (2005) Human resource management and labor productivity: Does industry matter? *The Academy of Management Journal*, 48: 135–45.

Davies, S. and Caves, R.E. (1987) *Britain's Productivity Gap*, Cambridge: Cambridge University Press.

Davis, S.J. and Haltiwanger, J. (1991) Wage dispersion between and within US manufacturing plants, 1963–86, *Brookings Papers on Economic Activity. Microeconomics*: 115–200.

Delaney, J.T. and Huselid, M.A. (1996) The impact of human resource management practices on perceptions of organizational performance, *The Academy of Management Journal*, 39: 949–69.

Delery, J.E., Gupta, N., Shaw, J.D., Jenkins Jr., G.D. and Ganster, M.L. (2000) Unionization, compensation, and voice effects on quits and retention, *Industrial Relations: A Journal of Economy and Society*, 39: 625–45.

Denny, K. (1997) Productivity and trade unions in British manufacturing industry 1973–85, *Applied Economics*, 29: 1403–9.

Denny, K. and Nickell, S.J. (1991) Unions and investment in British manufacturing industry, *British Journal of Industrial Relations*, 29: 113 v21.

Denny, K. and Nickell, S.J. (1992) Unions and investment in British Industry, *The Economic Journal*, 102: 874 –87.

Department for Business Innovation and Skills (2015) *Trade Union Membership 2014*, June.

Diamond, W.J. and Freeman, R.B. (2002) Will unionism prosper in cyberspace? The promise of the Internet for employee organization, *British Journal of Industrial Relations*, 40: 569–96.

Dickerson, A.P., Geroski, P.A. and Knight, K.G. (1997) Productivity, efficiency and strike activity, *International Review of Applied Economics*, 11: 119–34.

DiNardo, J. and Lee, D.S. (2004) Economic impacts of new unionization on private sector employers: 1984–2001, *The Quarterly Journal of Economics*, 119: 1383–441.

Diodato, V. (1994) *Dictionary of Bibliometrics*, Binghamton, NY: Haworth Press.

Domowitz, I., Hubbard, R.G. and Petersen, B.C. (1986) The intertemporal stability of the concentration-margins relationship, *The Journal of Industrial Economics*, 35: 13–34.

Donohue, S.M. and Heywood, J.S. (2004) Job satisfaction and gender: An expanded specification from the NLSY, *International Journal of Manpower*, 25: 211–38.

Doucouliagos, C.(H.) (2011) How Large Is Large? Preliminary Guidelines for Interpreting Partial Correlations in Economics, School of Economics Working Paper 2011_5, Deakin University.

Doucouliagos, C.(H.) and Laroche, P. (2003a) What do unions do to productivity? A meta-analysis, *Industrial Relations: A Journal of Economy and Society*, 42: 650–91.

Doucouliagos, C.(H.) and Laroche, P. (2003b) Unions and productivity growth: A meta-analytic review. In T. Kato and J. Pliskin (eds.), *The Determinants of the Incidence and the Effects of Participatory Organization*, vol. 7, Bradford, UK: Emerald Group Publishing, 57–82.

Doucouliagos, C.(H.) and Laroche, P. (2003c) Unions and tangible investments: A review and new evidence in France, *Relations Industrielles/Industrial Relations*, 58: 314–37.

Doucouliagos, C.(H.) and Laroche, P. (2007) Human resource practices, unionization and the organizational efficiency of French industry. In D. Lewin and B.E. Kaufman (eds.), *Advances in Industrial and Labor Relations*, 15: 67–102.

Doucouliagos, C.(H.) and Laroche, P. (2009) Unions and profits: A meta-regression analysis, *Industrial Relations: A Journal of Economy and Society*, 48: 146–84.

Doucouliagos, C.(H.) and Laroche, P. (2013) Unions and innovation: New insights from the cross-country evidence, *Industrial Relations: A Journal of Economy and Society*, 52: 467–91.

Doucouliagos, C.(H.), Laroche, P. and Stanley, T. (2005) Publication bias in union-productivity research? *Relations Industrielles/Industrial Relations*, 60: 320–44.

Doucouliagos, C.(H.) and Stanley, T.D. (2013) Are all economic facts greatly exaggerated? Theory competition and selectivity, *Journal of Economic Surveys*, 27: 316–39.

Doucouliagos, C.(H.), Stanley, T.D and Giles, M. (2012) Are estimates of the value of a statistical life exaggerated? *Journal of Health Economics*, 31: 197–206.

Dowrick, S. (1990) Wage pressure, bargaining and price-cost margins in UK manufacturing, *Journal of Industrial Economics*, 38: 239–67.

Drago, R., Estrin, S. and Wooden, M. (1993) Pay for performance incentives and work attitudes, *Australian Journal of Management*, 17: 217–31.

Drakopoulos, S.A. and Theodossiou, I. (1997) Job satisfaction and target earnings, *Journal of Economic Psychology*, 18: 693–704.

Dube, A., Kaplan, E. and Thompson, O. (2016). Nurse unions and patient outcomes, *Industrial and Labor Relations Review*, 69: 803–33.

Dundon, T. and Gollan, P.J. (2007) Re-conceptualizing voice in the non-union workplace, *The International Journal of Human Resource Management*, 18: 1182–98.

Dworkin, J.B. and Ahlburg, D.A. (1985) Unions and productivity: A review of the research. In D. Lipsky (ed.), *Advances in Industrial and Labor Relations*, Greenwich, CT: JIA Press, 2: 51–68.

Eaton, A.E. and Voos, P.B. (1992) Unions and contemporary innovations in work organization, compensation, and employee participation. In L. Mishel and P.B. Voos (eds.), *Unions and Economic Competitiveness*, Armonk, NY: M. E. Sharpe, 173–211.

Eberts, R.W. (1984) Union effects on teacher productivity, *Industrial and Labor Relations Review*, 37: 346–58.

Edelman, L.B. (1990) Legal environments and organizational governance: The expansion of due process in the American workplace, *American Journal of Sociology*, 95: 1401–40.

Edelman, L.B. (1992) Legal ambiguity and symbolic structures: Organizational mediation of civil rights law, *American Journal of Sociology*, 97: 1531–76.

Edwards, L.N. and Field-Hendrey, E. (1996) Unions and productivity in the public sector: The case of sanitation workers, *Research in Labor Economics*, 15: 305–28.

Egger, M., Smith, G.D., Scheider, M. and Minder, C. (1997) Bias in meta-analysis detected by a simple, graphical test, *British Medical Journal*, 315: 629–34.

Ehrenberg, R.G., Sherman, D.R. and Schwarz, J.L. (1983) Unions and productivity in the public sector: A study of municipal libraries, *Industrial and Labor Relations Review*, 36: 199–213.

Evans, M.G. and Ondrack, D.A. (1990) The role of job outcomes and values in understanding the union's impact on job satisfaction: A replication, *Human Relations*, 43: 401–18.

Evans, W.R. and Davis, W.D. (2005) High-performance work systems and organizational performance: The mediating role of internal social structure, *Journal of Management*, 31: 758–75.

Everett, M.G. and Borgatti, S.P. (1998) Analyzing clique overlap, *Connections*, 21: 49–61.

Fairris, D. (2006) Union voice effects in Mexico, *British Journal of Industrial Relations*, 44: 781–800.

Fairris, D. and Askenazy, P. (2010) Works councils and firm productivity in France, *Journal of Labor Research*, 31: 209–29.

Fallick, B.C. and Hassett, K.A. (1999) Investment and union certification, *Journal of Labor Economics*, 17: 570–82.

Faragher, E.B., Cass, M. and Cooper, C.L. (2005) The relationship between job satisfaction and health: A meta-analysis, *Occupational and Environmental Medicine*, 62: 105–112.

Fiorillo, D. and Nappo, N. (2014) Job satisfaction in Italy: Individual characteristics and social relations, *International Journal of Social Economics*, 41: 683–704.

Fitzroy, F.R. and Kraft, K. (1985) Unionization, wages and efficiency, *Kyklos*, 38: 537–54.

Fitzroy, F.R. and Kraft, K. (1986) Profitability and profit sharing, *The Journal of Industrial Economics*, 35: 113–30.

Fitzroy, F.R. and Kraft, K. (1987) Cooperation, productivity, and profit sharing, *The Quarterly Journal of Economics*, 102: 23–36.

Fitzroy, F.R. and Kraft, K. (1990) Innovation, rent-sharing and the organization of labour in the Federal Republic of Germany, *Small Business Economics*, 2: 95–103.

Fitzroy, F.R. and Kraft, K. (1993) Economic effects of Codetermination, *Scandinavian Journal of Economics*, 95: 365–75.

Flaherty, S. (1987) Strike activity, worker militancy, and productivity change in manufacturing, 1961–1981, *Industrial and Labor Relations Review*, 40: 585–600.

Flanagan, R.J. (1999) Macroeconomic performance and collective bargaining: An international perspective, *Journal of Economic Literature*, 37: 1150–75.

Fleming, C.M. and Kler, P. (2008) I'm too clever for this job: A bivariate probit analysis on overeducation and job satisfaction in Australia, *Applied Economics*, 40: 1123–38.

Foulke, F. (1981) How top nonunion companies manage employees, *Harvard Business Review*, September.

Francois, P. and Roberts, J. (2003) Relationships, commitment, and labor productivity growth, *Journal of the European Economic Association*, 1: 612–20.

Freeman, R.B. (1976) Individual mobility and union voice in the labor market, *The American Economic Review: Papers and Proceedings*, 66: 361–8.

Freeman, R.B. (1978) Job satisfaction as an economic variable, *The American Economic Review: Papers and Proceedings*, 68: 135–41.

Freeman, R.B. (1980) Unionism and the dispersion of wages, *Industrial and Labor Relations Review*, 34: 3–23.

Freeman, R.B. (1981) The effect of unionism on fringe benefits, *Industrial and Labor Relations Review*, 34: 489–509.

Freeman, R.B. (1983) Unionism, price-cost margins, and the return to capital, NBER Working Paper No. 1164, National Bureau of Economic Research.

Freeman, R.B. (1984) Longitudinal analyses of the effect of trade unions, *Journal of Labor Economics*, 2: 1–26.

Freeman, R.B. (1985) Unions, pensions, and union pension funds. In D.A. Wise (ed.), *Pensions, Labor, and Individual Choice*, Chicago: University of Chicago Press, 89–121.

Freeman, R.B. (1988) Union density and economic performance: An analysis of U.S. States, *European Economic Review*, 32: 707–16.

Freeman, R.B. (2003) Varieties of labor market institutions and economic performance, in IRRA Session on Labor Market Institutions and Economic Outcomes. IRRA; 2003.

Freeman, R.B. (2005) From the Webbs to the Web: The contribution of the Internet to reviving union fortunes. In S. Fernie and D. Metcalf (eds.), *Trade Unions: Resurgence or Demise?* London: Routledge, 162–84.

Freeman R.B. and Medoff, J.L. (1979a) New estimates of private sector unionism in the United States, *Industrial and Labor Relations Review*, 32: 143–74.

Freeman, R.B. and Medoff, J.L. (1979b) The two faces of unionism, *The Public Interest*, 57: 69–93.

Freeman, R.B. and Medoff, J.L. (1981) The impact of the percentage organized on union and nonunion wages, *The Review of Economics and Statistics*, 63: 561–72.

Freeman, R.B. and Medoff, J.L. (1982) Substitution between production labor and other inputs in unionized and nonunionized manufacturing, *The Review of Economics and Statistics*, 64: 220–33.

Freeman, R.B. and Medoff, J.L. (1984) *What Do Unions Do?* New York: Basic Books.

Freeman, R.B. and Rogers, J. (2002) Open source unionism, *WorkingUSA*, 5: 8–40.

Fuchs, V.R., Krueger, A.B., and Poterba, J.M. (1998) Economists' views about parameters, values, and policies: Survey results in labor and public economics, *Journal of Economic Literature*, 36: 1387–425.

Furrer, O., Thomas, H. and Goussevskaia, A. (2008) The structure and evolution of the strategic management field: A content analysis of 26 years of strategic management research, *International Journal of Management Reviews*, 10: 1–23.

Gallet, C.A. and Doucouliagos, C.(H.) (2014) The income elasticity of air travel: A meta-analysis, *Annals of Tourism Research*, 49: 141–55.

García-Serrano, C. (2009) Job satisfaction, union membership and collective bargaining, *European Journal of Industrial Relations*, 15: 91–111.

García-Serrano, C. (2011) Does size matter? The influence of firm size on working conditions, job satisfaction and quit intentions, *Scottish Journal of Political Economy*, 58: 221–47.

Garfield, E. (1979) Is citation analysis a legitimate evaluation tool? *Scientometrics*, 1: 359–75.

Geroski, P.A. (1990) Innovation, technological opportunity, and market structure, *Oxford Economic Papers*, 42: 586–602.

Ghosal, V. (1989) Market structure, price-cost margins and unionism: An empirical note, *Economic Letters*, 29: 179–82.

Gill, C. (2009) Union impact on the effective adoption of High Performance Work Practices, *Human Resource Management Review*, 19: 39–50.

Gittell, J.H., von Nordenflycht, A. and Kochan, T.A. (2004) Mutual gains or zero sum? Labor relations and firm performance in the airline industry, *Industrial and Labor Relations Review*, 57: 163–80.

Gius, M. (2012) The effects of district-level union status on the job satisfaction of teachers, *The Economic and Labour Relations Review*, 23: 79–90.

Golden-Biddle, K., Locke, K. and Reay, T. (2006) Using knowledge in management studies: An investigation of how we cite prior work, *Journal of Management Inquiry*, 15: 237–54.

Gordon, M.E. and Denisi, A.S. (1995) A re-examination of the relationship between union membership and job satisfaction, *Industrial and Labor Relations Review*, 48: 222–36.

Gordon, M.E. and Ladd, R.T. (1990) Dual allegiance: Renewal, reconsideration, and recantation, *Personnel Psychology*, 43: 37–69.

Graddy, D.B. and Hall, G. (1985) Unionization and productivity in commercial banking, *Journal of Labor Research*, 6: 249–62.

Green, C.P. and Heywood, J.S. (2008) Does performance pay increase job satisfaction? *Economica*, 75: 710–28.

Green, C.P. and Heywood, J.S. (2015) Dissatisfied union workers: Sorting revisited, *British Journal of Industrial Relations*, 53: 580–600.

Gregg, P., Machin, S. and Stewart, D. (1993) Signals and cycles: Productivity growth and changes in union status in British companies, 1984–89, *The Economic Journal*, 103: 894–907.

Griffeth, R.W, Hom, P.W. and Gaertner, S. (2000) A meta-analysis of antecedents and correlates of employee turnover: Update, moderator tests, and research implications for the next millennium, *Journal of Management*, 26: 463–88.

Grimes, P.W. and Register, C.A. (1990) Teachers' unions and student achievement in high school economics, *The Journal of Economic Education*, 21: 297–306.

Grimes, P.W. and Register, C.A. (1991) Teacher unions and black students' scores on college entrance exams, *Industrial Relations: A Journal of Economy and Society*, 30: 492–500.

Grout, P.A. (1984) Investment and wages in the absence of binding contracts: A Nash bargaining approach, *Econometrica*, 52: 449–60.

Guest, D.E. (1995) Human resource management, trade unions and industrial relations. In J. Storey (ed.), *New Perspectives on Human Resource Management*, London: Routledge, 41–55.

Guest, D.E. and Conway, N. (2004) Exploring the paradox of unionized worker dissatisfaction, *Industrial Relations Journal*, 35: 102–21.

Guest, D.E., Michie, J., Conway, N. and Sheehan, M. (2003) Human resource management and corporate performance in UK, *British Journal of Industrial Relations*, 41: 291–314.

Guthrie, J.P. (2001) High-involvement work practices, turnover, and productivity: Evidence from New Zealand, *The Academy of Management Journal*, 44: 180–90.

Hall, B.H. (2000) Innovation and market value. In R. Barrell, G. Mason and M. O'Mahony (eds.), *Productivity, Innovation and Economic Performance*, Cambridge: Cambridge University Press, 177–98.

Hammer, T.H. and Avgar, A. (2005) The impact of unions on job satisfaction, organizational commitment, and turnover, *Journal of Labor Research*, 26: 241–66.

Hancock, J.I., Allen, D.G., Bosco, F.A., McDaniel, K.R. and Pierce, C.A. (2013) Meta-analytic review of employee turnover as a predictor of firm performance, *Journal of Management*, 39: 573–603.

Harter, J.K., Schmidt, F.L. and Hayes, T.L. (2002) Business-unit-level relationship between employee satisfaction, employee engagement, and business outcomes: A meta-analysis, *Journal of Applied Psychology*, 87: 268–79.

Haskel, J. (1991) Imperfect competition, work practices and productivity growth, *Oxford Bulletin of Economics and Statistics*, 53: 265–79.

Haskel, J. and Martin, C. (1992) Margins, concentration, unions and the business cycle: Theory and evidence for Britain. *International Journal of Industrial Organization*, 10: 611–32.

Heavey, A.L., Holwerda, J.A. and Hausknecht, J.P. (2013) Causes and consequences of collective turnover: A meta-analytic review, *Journal of Applied Psychology*, 98: 412–53.

Hedges, L.V. and Olkin, I. (1985) *Statistical Methods for Meta-Analysis*, London: Academic Press.

Hersch, J. and Stone, J.A. (1990) Is union job dissatisfaction real? *The Journal of Human Resources*, 25: 736–51.

Heywood, J.S., Siebert, W.S. and Wei, X. (2002) Worker sorting and job satisfaction: The case of union and government jobs, *Industrial and Labor Relations Review*, 554: 595–609.

Heywood, J.S. and Wei, X. (2006) Performance pay and job satisfaction, *The Journal of Industrial Relations*, 48: 523–40.

Hirsch, B.T. (1990a) Innovative activity, productivity growth, and firm performance: Are labor unions a spur or a deterrent? *Advances in Applied Micro-Economics*, 5: 69–104.

Hirsch, B.T. (1990b) Market structure, union rent seeking, and firm profitability, *Economics Letters*, 32: 75–9.

Hirsch, B.T. (1991a) *Labor Unions and the Economic Performance of Firms*, Kalamazoo: W.E. Upjohn Institute for Employment Research.

Hirsch, B.T. (1991b) Union coverage and profitability among U.S. firms, *The Review of Economics and Statistics*, 73: 69–77.

Hirsch, B.T. (1992) Firm investment behavior and collective bargaining strategy, *Industrial Relations: A Journal of Economy and Society*, 31: 95–121.

Hirsch, B.T. (1997) Unionization and economic performance: Evidence on productivity, profits, investment, and growth. In F. Mihlar (ed.), *Unions and Right-to-Work Laws*, Vancouver, BC: The Frazer Institute, 35–70.

Hirsch, B.T. (2007) What do unions do for economic performance? In J.T. Bennett and B. Kaufman (eds.), *What Do Unions Do? A Twenty-Year Perspective*, New Brunswick, New Jersey: Transaction Publisher, 193–237.

Hirsch, B.T. and Addison, J.T. (1986) *The Economic Analysis of Unions: New Approaches and Evidence*, London: Allen and Unwin.

Hirsch, B.T. and Connolly, R.A. (1987) Do unions capture monopoly profits? *Industrial and Labor Relations Review*, 41: 118–36.

Hirsch, B.T. and Link, A.N. (1984) Unions, productivity, and productivity growth, *Journal of Labor Research*, 5: 29–37.

Hirsch, B.T. and Link, A.N. (1987) Labor union effects on innovative activity, *Journal of Labor Research*, 8: 323–32.

Hirsch, B.T. and Prasad, K. (1995) Wage-employment determination and a union tax on capital: Can theory and evidence be reconciled? *Economics Letters*, 48: 61–71.

Hirschman, A.O. (1970) *Exit, Voice, and Loyalty*, Cambridge, MA: Harvard University Press.

Holland, P., Pyman, A., Cooper, B.K. and Teicher, J. (2011) Employee voice and job satisfaction in Australia: The centrality of direct voice, *Human Resource Management*, 50: 95–111.

Hornstein, A., Krusell, P. and Violante, G.L. (2007) Technology-policy interaction in frictional labour-markets, *Review of Economic Studies*, 74: 1089–124.

Hosios, A.J. and Siow, A. (2004) Unions without rents: The curious economics of faculty unions, *Canadian Journal of Economics*, 37: 28–52.

Hübler, O. and Jirjahn, U. (2003) Works councils and collective bargaining in Germany: The impact on productivity and wages, *Scottish Journal of Political Economy*, 50: 471–91.

Hunter, J.E. and Schmidt, F.L. (1990) *Methods of Meta-Analysis: Correcting Error and Bias in Research Findings*, California: Sage.

Huselid, M.A. (1995) The impact of human resource management practices on turnover, productivity, and corporate financial performance, *The Academy of Management Journal*, 38: 635–72.

Hyman, R. (2006) Marxist thought and the analysis of work. In M. Korcynski, R. Hodson and P.K. Edwards (eds.), *Social Theory at Work*, Oxford: Oxford University Press, 26–55.

Iaffaldano, M.T. and Muchinsky, P.M. (1985) Job satisfaction and job performance: A meta-analysis, *Psychological Bulletin*, 97: 251–73.

Ichniowski, C., Kochan, T.A., Levine, D., Olson, C. and Strauss, G. (1996) What works at work: Overview and assessment, *Industrial Relations: A Journal of Economy and Society*, 35: 299–333.

Ichniowski, C., Shaw, K. and Prennushi, G. (1997) The effects of human resource management practices on productivity: A study of steel finishing lines, *The American Economic Review*, 87: 291–313.

Idson, T.L. (1990) Establishment size, job satisfaction and the structure of work, *Applied Economics*, 22: 1007–18.

Ioannidis, J.P.A., Stanley, T.D. and Doucouliagos, C.(H.) (2017) The power of bias in economics research, *The Economic Journal*, forthcoming. Also as Economics Working Paper No. 2016/1, Deakin University.

Islam, Md. R., Madsen, J.B. and Doucouliagos, C.(H.) (2016) Does inequality constrain the power to tax? Evidence from the OECD. Department of Economics Discussion Paper 29/16, Monash University.

Jackson, S.E. and Schuler, R.S. (1995) Understanding Human Resource Management in the context of organizations and their environments, *Annual Review of Psychology*, 46: 237–64.

Jaramillo, F., Mulki, J.P. and Marshall, G.W. (2005) A meta-analysis of the relationship between organizational commitment and salesperson job performance: 25 years of research, *Journal of Business Research*, 58: 705–14.

Jarrell, S.B. and Stanley, T.D (1990) A meta-analysis of the union-nonunion wage gap, *Industrial and Labor Relations Review*, 44: 54–67.

Jirjahn, U. and Mueller, S. (2014) Non-union worker representation, foreign owners, and the performance of establishments, *Oxford Economic Papers*, 66: 140–63.

Johnson, H.G. and Mieszkowski, P. (1970) The effects of unionization on the distribution of income: A general equilibrium approach, *The Quarterly Journal of Economics*, 4: 539–61.

Johnson, W.R., Johnson, G.J. and Patterson, C.R. (1999) Moderators of the relationship between company and union commitment: A meta-analysis, *The Journal of Psychology: Interdisciplinary and Applied*, 133: 85–103.

Jones, R.J. and Sloane, P.J. (2009) Regional differences in job satisfaction, *Applied Economics*, 41: 1019–41.

Judge, T.A., Thoresen, C.J., Bono, J.E. and Patton, G.K. (2001) The job satisfaction–job performance relationship: A qualitative and quantitative review, *Psychological Bulletin*, 127: 376–407.

Kahn, L.M. (2000) Wage inequality, collective bargaining and relative employment from 1985 to 1994: Evidence from 15 OECD countries, *The Review of Economics and Statistics*, 82: 564–79.

Kalleberg, A.L. and Loscocco, K.A. (1983) Aging, values, and rewards: Explaining age differences in job satisfaction, *American Sociological Review*, 48: 78–90.

Kalleberg, A.L. and Mastekaasa, A. (1994) Firm internal labor markets and organizational commitment in Norway and the United States, *Acta Sociologica*, 37: 269–86.

Kanter, R.M. (1977) *Work and Family in the United States: A critical review and agenda for research and policy*, New York: Russell Sage Foundation.

Karahasan, N. (1995) The effect of unionization on the firm profitability: The U.S. manufacturing firms, 1986–1988, *The Journal of Economics*, 21: 71–9.

Karier, T. (1985) Unions and monopoly profits, *The Review of Economics and Statistics*, 67: 34–42.

Karier, T. (1988) New evidence on the effect of unions and imports on monopoly power, *Journal of Post Keynesian Economics*, 10: 414–27.

Katz, H.C., Kochan, T.A. and Keefe, J.H. (1987) Industrial relations and productivity in the U.S. automobile industry, *Brookings Papers on Economic Activity*, 3: 685–727.

Katz, L.F. and Summers, L.H. (1989) Industry rents: Evidence and implications, *Brookings Papers on Economic Activity. Microeconomics*, 209–90.

Kaufman, B.E. (1993) *The Origins and Evolution of the Field of Industrial Relations in the United States*, Ithaca, NY: Cornell University Press.

Kaufman, R.S. and Kaufman, R.T. (1987) Union effects on productivity, personnel practices, and survival in the automotive parts industry, *Journal of Labor Research*, 8: 333–50.

Kaufman, R.T. (1992) The effect of Improshare on productivity, *Industrial and Labor Relations Review*, 45: 311–22.

Kendrick, J.W. (1973) Postwar productivity trends in the U.S. 1948–1969, *National Bureau of Economic Research*, New York: Columbia University Press.

Kendrick, J.W. and Grossman, E.S. (1980) *Productivity in the United States*, Baltimore and London: The Johns Hopkins University Press.

Kersley, B., Alpin, C., Forth, J., Bryson, A., Bewley, H., Dix, G. and Oxenbridge, S. (2006) *Inside the Workplace: Findings from the Workplace Employment Relations Survey*, Oxford: Routledge.

Kim, D.-O. and Kim, H.-K. (2004) A comparison of the effectiveness of unions and non-union works councils in Korea: Can non-union employee representation substitute for trade unionism? *The International Journal of Human Resource Management*, 15: 1069–93.

Kim, J., MacDuffie, J.P. and Pil, F.K. (2010) Employee voice and organizational performance: Team versus representative influence, *Human Relations*, 63: 371–94.

Kinicki, A.J., McKee-Ryan, F.M., Schriesheim, C.A. and Carson, K.P. (2002) Assessing the construct validity of the job descriptive index: A review and meta-analysis, *Journal of Applied Psychology*, 87: 14–32.

Kizilos, M. and Reshef, Y. (1997) The effect of workplace unionization on worker responses to HRM innovation, *Journal of Labor Research*, 18: 641–56.

Klaas, B.S., Olson-Buchanan, J.B. and Ward, A.K. (2012) The determinants of alternative forms of workplace voice: An integrative perspective, *Journal of Management*, 38: 314–45.

Kleiner, M.M. and Ay, C.-R. (1996) Unionization, employee representation, and economic performance: Comparisons among OECD nations, In D. Lewin, B.E. Kaufman and D. Sockell (eds.), *Advances in Industrial and Labor Relations*, 7: 97–121.

Kleiner, M.M. and Lee, Y.-M. (1997) Work councils and unionization: Lessons from South Korea, *Industrial Relations: A Journal of Economy and Society*, 36: 1–16.

Kleiner, M.M. and Petree, D.L. (1988) Unionism and licensing of public school teachers: Impact on wages and educational output. In R.B. Freeman and C. Ichniowski (eds.), *When Public Sector Workers Unionize*, Chicago: University of Chicago Press, 305–21.

Koch, M.J. and McGrath, R.G. (1996) Improving labor productivity: Human resource management policies do matter, *Strategic Management Journal*, 17: 335–54.

Kochan, T.A., Katz, H.C. and McKersie, R.B. (1986) *The Transformation of American Industrial Relations*, New York: Basic Books.

Kochan, T.A. and Osterman, P. (1994) *The Mutual Gain Enterprise: Forging a Winning Partnership Among Labor, Management, and Government*, Boston, MA: Harvard Business School Press.

Koeller, C.T. (1996) Union membership, market structure, and the innovation output of large and small firms, *Journal of Labor Research*, 17: 683–99.

Koeniger, W., Leonardi, M. and Nunziata, L. (2007) Labor market institutions and wage inequality, *Industrial and Labor Relations Review*, 60: 340–56.

Koske, I., Fournier, J. and Wanner, I. (2012) Less Income Inequality and More Growth – Are They Compatible? Part 2. The Distribution of Labour Income. OECD Economics Department Working Papers, No. 925, OECD Publishing.

Kosteas, V.D. (2011) Job satisfaction and promotions, *Industrial Relations: A Journal of Economy and Society*, 50: 174–94.

Kraft, K., Stank, J. and Dewenter, R. 2011. Co-determination and innovation, *Cambridge Journal of Economics*, 35: 145–72.

Kruse, D. (1993) *Profit Sharing: Does It Make a Difference?* Kalamazoo, MI: Upjohn Institute.

Kuhn, P. (1985) Union productivity effects and economic efficiency, *Journal of Labor Research*, 6: 229–48.

Kuhn, P. (1998) Unions and the economy: What we know; what we should know, *Canadian Journal of Economics*, 31:1033–56.

Kuhn, T.S. (1962) *The Structure of Scientific Revolutions*, Chicago: University of Chicago Press.

Kurth, M.M. (1987) Teachers' unions and excellence in education: An analysis of the decline in SAT scores, *Journal of Labor Research*, 8: 351–67.

Laporta, P. and Jenkins, A.W. (1996) Unionization and profitability in the Canadian manufacturing sector, *Relations Industrielles/Industrial Relations*, 51: 756–77.

Laroche, P. (2004) Présence syndicale et performance financière des entreprises: Une analyse statistique sur le cas Français, *Revue Finance Contrôle Stratégie*, 7: 117–45.

Laroche, P. (2016) A meta-analysis of the union-job satisfaction relationship, *British Journal of Industrial Relations*, doi: 10.1111/bjir.12193.

Laroche, P. and Wechtler, H. (2011) The effects of labor unions on workplace performance: New evidence from France, *Journal of Labor Research*, 32: 157–80.

Lawler, E.E. and Mohrman, S. (1987) Unions and the new management, *The Academy of Management Executive*, 1: 293–300.

Lazear, E.P. (1981) Agency, earnings profiles, productivity, and hours restrictions, *The American Economic Review*, 71: 606–20.

Lee, D.S. and Mas, A. (2012) Long-run impacts of unions on firms: New evidence from financial markets, 1961–1999, *The Quarterly Journal of Economics*, 127: 333–78.

Lee, J. (2012) Labor unions and firm profitability under different political and economic environments: Evidence from Korea, *International Economic Journal*, 26: 727–47.

Lee, M.B. and Rhee, Y. (1996) Bonuses, unions, and labor productivity in South Korea, *Journal of Labor Research*, *17*: 219–38.

Leibenstein, H. (1966) Allocative efficiency vs. "X-efficiency", *The American Economic Review*, 56: 392–415.

Lewin, D. (1990) Grievance procedures in nonunion workplaces: An empirical analysis of usage, dynamics, and outcomes, *Chicago-Kent Law Review*, 66: 823–44.

Lewis, H.G. (1963) *Unionism and Relative Wages in the United States: An Empirical Inquiry*, Chicago: University of Chicago Press.

Lewis, H.G. (1986) *Union Relative Wage Effects: A Survey*, Chicago: University of Chicago Press.

Lillydahl, J.H. and Singell, L.D. (1993) Job satisfaction, salaries and unions: The determination of university faculty compensation, *Economics of Education Review*, 123: 233–43.

Lincoln, J.R. and Boothe, J.N. (1993) Unions and work attitudes in the United States and Japan, *Industrial Relations: A Journal of Economy and Society*, 32: 159–87.

Lindsey, D. (1989) Using citations counts as a measure of quality in science: Measuring what's measurable rather than what's valid, *Scientometrics*, 15: 189–203.

Link, A.N. (1981) Basic research and productivity increase in manufacturing: Additional evidence, *The American Economic Review*, 71: 1111–12.

Link, A.N. (1982) Productivity growth, environmental regulations and the composition of R&D, *The Bell Journal of Economics*, 13: 548–54.

Long, A. (2005) Happily ever after? A study of job satisfaction in Australia, *Economic Record*, 81: 303–21.

Lovell, C.A.K., Sickles, R.C. and Warren, R.S. (1988) The effect of unionization on labor productivity: Some additional evidence, *Journal of Labor Research*, 9: 55–63.

Lu, Y., Tao, Z. and Wang, Y. (2010) Union effects on performance and employment relations: Evidence from China, *China Economic Review*, 21: 202–10.

Lucifora, C. and Origo, F. (2015) Performance-related pay and firm productivity: Evidence from a reform in the structure of collective bargaining, *Industrial and Labor Relations Review*, 68: 606–32.

MacDuffie, J.P. (1995) Human resource bundles and manufacturing performance: Organizational logic and flexible production systems in the world auto industry, *Industrial and Labor Relations Review*, 48: 197–221.

MacKinnon, J.G. and Webb, M.D. (2015) Wild bootstrap inference for wildly different cluster sizes. Queen's Economics Department Working Paper No. 1314.

Machin, S.J. (1991) Unions and the capture of economic rents: An investigation using British firm level data, *International Journal of Industrial Organization*, 9: 261–74.

Machin, S.J. and Wadhwani, S. (1991) The effect of unions on organisational change and employment, *The Economic Journal*, 101: 835–54.

Madsen, J.B., Islam, Md. R. and Doucouliagos, C.(H.) (2016) Inequality, financial development and economic growth in the OECD, 1870–2011. Department of Economics Discussion Paper 18/16, Monash University.

Maki, D.R. (1983) Trade unions and productivity: Conventional estimates, *Relations Industrielles/Industrial Relations*, 38: 211–28.

Maki, D.R. and Meredith, L.N. (1986) The effects of unions on profitability: Canadian evidence, *Relations Industrielles/Industrial Relations*, 41: 54–68.

Mansfield, E. (1980) Basic research and productivity increase in manufacturing, *The American Economic Review*, 70: 863–73.

Marini, M.M. (1989) Sex differences in earnings in the United States, *Annual Review of Sociology*, 15: 343–80.

Marshall, A. (1961) *Principles of Economics*, 8th ed., London: MacMillan.

Martin, C. (2003) Explaining labour turnover from UK establishments, *Labour*, 17: 391–412.

Marwell, N.P. (2004) Privatizing the welfare state: Nonprofit community-based organizations as political actors, *American Sociological Review*, 69: 265–91.

Mathieu, J.E. and Zajac, D.M. (1990) A review and meta-analysis of the antecedents, correlates, and consequences of organizational commitment, *Psychological Bulletin*, 108: 171–94.

McDonald, I.M. and Solow, R.M. (1981) Wage bargaining and employment, *The American Economic Review*, 71: 896–908.

McDonald, J.T. (1999) The determinants of firm profitability in Australian manufacturing, *Economic Record*, 75: 115–26.

McDonald, J.T. and Bloch, H. (1999) The spillover effects of industrial action on firm profitability, *Review of Industrial Organization*, 15: 183–200.

McEvoy, G.M. and Cascio, W.F. (1987) Do good or poor performers leave? A meta-analysis of the relationship between performance and turnover, *The Academy of Management Journal*, 30: 744–62.

McKersie, R.B. and Klein, J.A. (1983) Productivity: The industrial relations connection, *National Productivity Review*, 3: 26–35.

Meador, M. and Walters, S.J.K. (1994) Unions and productivity: Evidence from academe, *Journal of Labor Research*, 15: 373–86.

Mefford, R.N. (1986) The effect of unions on productivity in a multinational manufacturing firm, *Industrial and Labor Relations Review*, 40: 105–14.

Menezes-Filho, N.A. (1997) Unions and profitability over the 1980s: Some evidence on union-firm bargaining in the United Kingdom, *The Economic Journal*, 107: 651–70.

Menezes-Filho, N.A., Ulph, D. and Van Reenen, J. (1998a) The determination of R&D: Empirical evidence on the role of unions, *European Economic Review*, 42: 919–30.

Menezes-Filho, N.A., Ulph, D. and Van Reenen, J. (1998b) R&D and unionism: Comparative evidence from British companies and establishments, *Industrial and Labor Relations Review*, 52: 45–63.

Menezes-Filho, N.A. and Van Reenen, J. (2003) Unions and innovation: A survey of the theory and empirical evidence. In J.T. Addison and C. Schnabel (eds.), *The International Handbook of Trade Unions*, Cheltenham: Edward Elgar, 293–335.

Menezes-Filho, N.A., Zylberstajn, H., Chahad, J.P., and Pazello, E. (2005) Unions and the economic performance of Brazilian establishments. In P. Kuhn and G. Márquez (eds.), *What Difference Do Unions Make? Their Impact on Productivity and Wages in Latin America*, Washington, DC: Inter-American Development Bank, 77–100.

Meng, R. (1990) The relationship between unions and job satisfaction, *Applied Economics*, 22: 1635–48.

Meyer, J.W. and Rowan, B. (1977) Institutionalized organizations: Formal structure as myth and ceremony, *American Journal of Sociology*, 83: 340–63.

Milkman, M. (1997) Teacher's unions, productivity, and minority student achievement, *Journal of Labor Research*, 18: 137–50.

Miller, P.W. (1990) Trade unions and job satisfaction, *Australian Economic Papers*, 29: 226–48.

Miller, P.W. and Mulvey, C. (1991) Australian evidence on the exit/voice model of the labor market, *Industrial and Labor Relations Review* 45: 44–57.

Mitchell, D.J.B., Lewin, D. and Lawler, E.E. III. (1990) Alternative pay systems, firm performance and productivity. In A.S. Blinder (ed.), *Paying for Productivity: A Look at the Evidence*, Washington, DC: Brookings Institution, 15–88.

Mitchell, M.W. and Stone, J.A. (1992) Union effects on productivity: Evidence from Western U.S. sawmills, *Industrial and Labor Relations Review*, 46: 135–45.

Mohr, R.D. and Zoghi, C. (2008) High-involvement work design and job satisfaction, *Industrial and Labor Relations Review*, 61: 275–96.

Monastiriotis, V. (2007) Union retreat and regional economic performance: The UK experience, *Regional Studies*, 41: 143–56.

Morikawa, M. (2010) Labor unions and productivity: An empirical analysis using Japanese firm-level data, *Labor Economics*, 17: 1030–7.

Morishima, M. (1991) Information sharing and firm performance in Japan, *Industrial Relations: A Journal of Economy and Society*, 30: 37–61.

Moshiri, S. and Simpson, W. (2011) Information technology and the changing workplace in Canada: Firm-level evidence, *Industrial and Corporate Change*, 20: 1601–36.

Muramatsu, K. (1984) The effect of trade unions on productivity in Japanese manufacturing industries. In M. Aoki (ed.), *The Economic Analysis of the Japanese Firm*, Amsterdam: Elsevier, 103–23.

Murnane, R. and Cohen, D. (1986) Merit pay and the evaluation problem: Why most merit pay plans fail and a few survive, *Harvard Educational Review*, 56: 1–18.

Nair-Reichert, U. and Pomery, J. (1999) International R&D rivalry and export market shares of unionized industries: Some evidence from the US manufacturing sector, *Journal of International Economics*, 49: 77–97.

Naus, F., van Iterson, A. and Roe, R. (2007) Organizational cynicism: Extending the exit, voice, loyalty, and neglect model of employees' responses to adverse conditions in the workplace, *Human Relations*, 60: 683–718.

Nelson, F.H. and Gould, J.C. (1988) Teachers' unions and excellence in education: Comment, *Journal of Labor Research*, 9: 379–87.

Nickell, S. (1997) Unemployment and labor market rigidities: Europe versus North America, *Journal of Economic Perspectives*, 11: 55–74.

Nickell, S. and Layard, R. (1999) Labor market institutions and economic performance. In O. Ashenfelter and D. Card (eds.) *Handbook of Labor Economics*, 3: 3029–84.

Nickell, S., Wadhwani, S. and Wall, M. (1992) Productivity growth in U.K. companies: 1975–86, *European Economic Review*, 36: 1055–85.

Noam, E.M. (1983) The effect of unionization and civil service on the salaries and productivity of regulators, *Research in Labor Economics, New Approaches to Labor Unions*, Supplement 2, 157–70.

Odgers, C.W. and Betts, J.R. (1997) Do unions reduce investment? Evidence from Canada, *Industrial and Labor Relations Review*, 51: 18–36.

OECD (2016), *Trade union density*, https://stats.oecd.org/Index.aspx?DataSetCode=UN_DEN#.

OECD Ministerial Statement, Building More Resilient and Inclusive Labor Markets, OECD Labour and Employment Ministerial Meeting, Paris, 15 January 2016.

Olson, M. (1965) *Logic of Collective Action: Public Goods and Theory of Groups*, Cambridge, MA: Harvard University Press.

Osterman, P. (1987) Turnover, employment security, and the performance of the firm. In S.G. Allen. and M. Kleiner (eds.), *Human Resources and the Performance of the Firm*, Madison, WI: Industrial Relations Research Association, 275–317.

Pantuosco, L.J., Parker, D., Seyfried, W. and Lyman, S. (2002) Macroeconomic differences in public and private union density: An analysis of U.S. state economies, *The Review of Regional Studies*, 32: 171–86.

Pantuosco, L.J, Parker, D. and Stone, G. (2001) The effect of unions on labor markets and economic growth: An analysis of state data, *Journal of Labor Research*, 22: 195–205.

Pantuosco, L.J. and Ullrich, L.D. (2010) The impact of teachers union on state-level productivity, *Journal of Education Finance*, 35: 276–94.

Park, T.-Y. and Shaw, J.D. (2013) Turnover rates and organizational performance: A meta-analysis, *Journal of Applied Psychology*, 98: 268–309.

Peltzman, S. (1993) The political economy of the decline of American public education, *Journal of Law and Economics*, 36: 331–70.

Peltzman, S. (1996) Political economy of public education: Non-college-bound students, *Journal of Law and Economics*, 39: 73–120.

Pencavel, J.H. (1977) Distributional and efficiency effects of trade unions in Britain, *British Journal of Industrial Relations*, 15: 137–56.

Pencavel, J.H. (1991) *Labor Markets Under Trade Unionism: Employment, Wages, and Hours*, Cambridge, MA: Basil Blackwell.

Petty, M.M., McGee, G.W. and Cavender, J.W. (1984) A meta-analysis of the relationships between individual job satisfaction and individual performance, *The Academy of Management Review*, 9: 712–21.

Pfeffer, J. and Baron, J.N. (1988) Taking the workers back out: Recent trends in the structuring of employment, *Research in Organizational Behavior*, 10: 257–303.

Pfeffer, J. and Davis-Blake, A. (1990) Unions and job satisfaction: An alternative view, *Work and Occupations*, 17: 259–83.

Phipps, A. and Sheen, J. (1994) Unionisation, industrial relations and labour productivity growth in Australia: A pooled time-series/cross-section analysis of TFP growth, *Labour of Economics and Productivity*, 6: 54–77.

Pohler, D.M. and Luchak, A.A. (2014) Balancing efficiency, equity, and voice: The impact of unions and high-involvement work practices on work outcomes, *Industrial and Labor Relations Review*, 67: 1063–94.

Pouliakas, K. and Theodossiou, I. (2009) Confronting objections to performance pay: The impact of individual and gain-sharing incentives on job satisfaction, *Scottish Journal of Political Economy*, 56: 662–84.

Powdthavee, N. (2011) Anticipation, free-rider problems, and adaptation to trade unions: Re-examining the curious case of dissatisfied union members, *Industrial and Labor Relations Review*, 64: 1000–19.

Premack, S.L. (1984) Prediction of employee unionization from knowledge of job satisfaction: A meta-analytic investigation, *Academy of Management Proceedings*, 1: 279–83.

Prendergast, C. (1999) The provision of incentives in firms, *Journal of Economic Literature*, 37: 7–63.

Prendergast, C. and Topel, R.H. (1996) Favoritism in organizations, *The Journal of Political Economy*, 104: 958–78.

Reed, C.S., Young, W.R. and McHugh, P.P. (1994) A comparative look at dual commitment: An international study, *Human Relations*, 47: 1269–93.

Rees, A. (1962) *The Economics of Trade Unions*, Chicago: University of Illinois Press.

Rees, D.I. (1991) Grievance procedure strength and teacher quits, *Industrial and Labor Relations Review*, 45: 31–43.

Register, C.A. (1988) Wages, productivity, and costs in union and nonunion hospitals, *Journal of Labor Research*, 9: 325–45.

Register, C.A. and Grimes, P.W. (1991) Collective bargaining, teachers, and student achievement, *Journal of Labor Research*, 12: 99–109.

Renaud, S. (2002) Rethinking the union membership/job satisfaction relationship: Some empirical evidence in Canada, *International Journal of Manpower*, 23: 137–50.

Riketta, M. (2002) Attitudinal organizational commitment and job performance: A meta-analysis, *Journal of Organizational Behavior*, 23: 257–66.

Roberts, C.J. and Stanley, T.D. (2005) *Meta-Regression Analysis: Issues of Publication Bias in Economics*, London: Basil Blackwell.

Robinson, A.M. and Wilson, N. (2006) Employee financial participation and productivity: An empirical reappraisal, *British Journal of Industrial Relations*, 44: 31–50.

Rose, M. (2003) Good deal, bad deal? Job satisfaction in occupations, *Work, Employment and Society*, 17: 503–30.

Rose, N.L. (1987) Labor rent sharing and regulation: Evidence from the trucking industry, *Journal of Political Economy*, 95: 1146–78.

Rosen, S. (1982) Authority, control, and the distribution of earnings, *The Bell Journal of Economics*, 13: 311–23.

Rosenthal, R. (1984) *Meta-Analytic Procedures for Social Research*, Beverly Hills, CA: Sage.

Ruback, R.S. and Zimmerman, M.B. (1984) Unionization and profitability: Evidence from the capital market, *Journal of Political Economy*, 92: 1134–57.

Rusbult, C.E., Farrell, D., Rogers, G. and Mainous III, A.G. (1988) Impact of exchange variables on exit, voice, loyalty, and neglect: An integrative model of responses to declining job-satisfaction, *The Academy of Management Journal*, 31: 599–627.

Saavedra, J. and Torero, M. (2005) Union density changes and union effects on firm performance in Peru. In P. Kuhn and G. Márquez (eds.), *What Difference Do Unions Make? Their Impact on Productivity and Wages in Latin America*, Washington, DC: Inter-American Development Bank, 33–76.

Salinger, M.A. (1984) Tobin's q, unionization, and the concentration-profits relationship, *The RAND Journal of Economics*, 15: 159–70.

Schmalensee, R. (1989) Inter-industry studies of structure and performance. In R. Schmalensee and R.D. Willig (eds.), *Handbook of Industrial Organization*, vol. 2, Amsterdam: North-Holland, 951–1009.

Schmidt, F.L. and Hunter, J.E. (2015) *Methods of Meta-Analysis: Correcting Error and Bias in Research Findings*, 3rd ed., Thousand Oaks, CA: Sage.

Schnabel, C. and Wagner, J. (1992a) Unions and innovative activity in Germany, *Journal of Labor Research*, 13: 393–406.

Schnabel, C. and Wagner, J. (1992b) Unions and innovation: Evidence from German micro data, *Economic Letters*, 39: 369–73.

Schnabel, C. and Wagner, J. (1994) Industrial relations and trade union effects on innovation in Germany, *Labour*, 8: 489–503.

Schnabel, C., Zagelmeyer, S. and Kohaut, S. (2006) Collective bargaining structure and its determinants: An empirical analysis with British and German establishment data, *European Journal of Industrial Relations*, 12: 165–88.

Schulenburg, J.M. Graf von der and Wagner, J. (1990) Advertising, innovation and market structure: A comparison of the United States of America and the Federal Republic of Germany. In Z. Acs and D.B. Audretsch (eds.), *Innovation and Technological Change: An International Comparison*, Ann Arbor: University of Michigan Press, 160–82.

Schuster, M. (1983) The impact of union-management cooperation on productivity and employment, *Industrial and Labor Relation Review*, 36: 415–30.

Shapiro, C. and Stiglitz, J.E. (1984) Equilibrium unemployment as a worker discipline device, *The American Economic Review*, 74: 433–44.

Shaw, J.D., Delery, J.E., Jenkins, D.G., Gupta, N. (1998) An organization-level analysis of voluntary and involuntary turnover, *The Academy of Management Journal*, 41: 511–25.

Shaw, J.D., Gupta, N., and Delery, J.E. (2005) Alternative conceptualizations of the relationship between voluntary turnover and organizational performance, *The Academy of Management Journal*, 48: 50–68.

Slichter S.H., Healy, J.J. and Livernash, R.E. (1960) *The Impact of Collective Bargaining on Management*, Washington DC, The Brookings Institution.

Sloane, P.J. and Williams, H. (2000) Job satisfaction, comparison earnings, and gender, *Labour*, 143: 473–502.

Small, H. (2004) Why authors think their papers are highly cited, *Scientometrics*, 60: 305–16.

Smerek, R.E. and Peterson, M. (2007) Examining Herzberg's theory: Improving job satisfaction among non-academic employees at a university, *Research in Higher Education*, 48: 229–50.

Sojourner, A.J., Frandsen, B.R., Town, R.J., Grabowski, D.C. and Chen, M.M. (2015) Impacts of unionization on quality and productivity: Regression discontinuity evidence from nursing homes, *Industrial and Labor Relations Review*, 68: 771–806.

Sousa-Poza, A. and Sousa-Poza, A.A. (2000) Well-being at work: A cross-national analysis of the levels and determinants of job satisfaction, *The Journal of Socio-Economics*, 29: 517–38.

Sousa-Poza, A. and Sousa-Poza, A.A. (2003) Gender differences in job satisfaction in Great Britain, 1991–2000: Permanent or transitory?, *Applied Economics Letters*, 10: 691–94.

Standing, G. (1992) Do unions impede or accelerate structural adjustment? Industrial versus company unions in an industrialising labour market, *Cambridge Journal of Economics*, 16: 327–54.

Stanley, T.D. (2001) Wheat from chaff: Meta-analysis as quantitative literature review, *The Journal of Economic Perspectives*, 15: 131–50.

Stanley, T.D. (2005) Beyond publication bias, *Journal of Economic Surveys*, 19: 309–45.

Stanley, T.D. (2008) Meta-regression methods for detecting and estimating empirical effects in the presence of publication selection, *Oxford Bulletin of Economics and Statistics February*, 70: 103–27.

Stanley, T.D. and Doucouliagos, C(H.) (2012) *Meta-Regression Analysis in Economics and Business*, Oxon: Routledge.

Stanley, T.D. and Doucouliagos C.(H). (2014) Meta-regression approximations to reduce publication selection bias, *Research Synthesis Methods*, 5: 60–78.

Stanley, T.D. and Doucouliagos, C.(H.) (2015) Neither fixed nor random: Weighted least squares MRA, *Statistics in Medicine*, 34: 2116–27.

Stanley, T.D. and Doucouliagos, C.(H.) (2016) Neither fixed nor random: Weighted least squares meta-regression, *Research Synthesis Methods*, in press. DOI: 10.1002/jrsm.1211.

Stanley, T.D., Doucouliagos, C.(H.), Giles, M., Heckemeyer, J., Johnston, R.J., Laroche, P., Pugh, G., Nelson, J., Paldam, M., Poot, J., Rosenberger, R. and Rost, K. (2013) Meta-analysis of economics research reporting guidelines, *Journal of Economic Surveys*, 27: 390–4.

Stanley, T.D. and Jarrell, S.B. (1989) Meta-regression analysis: A quantitative method of literature surveys, *Journal of Economic Surveys*, 3: 54–67.

Steelman, L.C., Powell, B. and Carini, R.M. (2000) Do teacher unions hinder educational performance? Lessons learned from state SAT and ACT scores, *Harvard Educational Review*, 70: 437–66.

Stewart, M.B. (1995) Union wage differentials in an era of declining unionization, *Oxford Bulletin of Economics and Statistics*, 57: 143–66.

Storm, S. and Naastepad, C.W.M. (2009) Labor market regulation and productivity growth: Evidence for twenty OECD countries (1984–2004), *Industrial Relations: A Journal of Economy and Society*, 48: 629–54.

Sveikauskas, C.D. and Sveikauskas, L. (1982) Industry characteristics and productivity growth, *Southern Economic Journal*, 48: 769–74.

Szymanski, D.M., Bharadwaj, S.G. and Varadarajan, P.R. (1993) An analysis of the market share-profitability relationship, *Journal of Marketing*, 57: 1–18.

Tachibanaki, T. and Noda, T. (2000) *The Economic Effects of Trade Unions in Japan*, New York: St. Martin's Press.

Tauman, Y. and Weiss, Y. (1987) Labor unions and the adoption of new technology, *Journal of Labor Economics*, 5: 477–501.

Taymaz, E. (1991) The impact of trade unions on the diffusion of technology: The case of NC machine tools, *British Journal of Industrial Relations*, 29: 305–11.

Terleckyj, N. (1980) What do R&D numbers tell us about technological change? *The American Economic Review: Papers and Proceedings*, 70: 55–61.

Terleckyj, N. (1984) Comment on R&D and productivity growth at industry level. In Z. Griliches (ed.), *R&D, Patents, and Productivity*, Chicago: The University of Chicago Press, 496–501.

Theodossiou, I. and Vasileiou, E. (2007) Making the risk of job loss a way of life: Does it affect job satisfaction? *Research in Economics*, 61: 71–83.

Theodossiou, I. and Zangelidis, A. (2009) Career prospects and tenure–job satisfaction profiles: Evidence from panel data, *The Journal of Socio-Economics*, 38: 648–57.

Torii, A. (1992) Technical efficiency in Japanese industries. In R.E. Caves (ed.), *Industrial Efficiency in Six Nations*, Cambridge, MA: MIT Press, 31–120.

Tullock, G. (1967) The welfare costs of tariffs, monopolies, and theft, *Western Economic Journal*, 5: 224–32.

Turnbull, P.J. (1991) Trade unions and productivity: Opening the Harvard "Black Boxes", *Journal of Labor Research*, 12: 135–50.

Turnbull, P.J. (2003) What do unions do now? *Journal of Labor Research*, 24: 491–527.

Ulph, A. and Ulph, D. (1988) Bargaining structures and delay in innovation, *The Scandinavian Journal of Economics*, 90: 475–91.

Ulph, A. and Ulph, D. (1989) Labor markets and innovation, *Journal of the Japanese and International Economies*, 3: 403–23.

Ulph, A. and Ulph, D. (1994) Labour markets and innovation: Ex-post bargaining, *European Economic Review*, 38: 195–210.

Ulph, A. and Ulph, D. (1998) Labour markets, bargaining and innovation, *European Economic Review*, 42: 931–9.

United States Bureau of Labor Statistics. (2016) *Union Affiliation Data from the Current Population Survey*. http://data.bls.gov.

Uppal, S. (2005) Disability, workplace characteristics and job satisfaction, *International Journal of Manpower*, 26: 336–49.

Urízar, H. and Lée, S. (2005) The effects of unions on productivity: Evidence from large coffee producers in Guatemala. In P. Kuhn and G. Márquez (eds.), *What Difference Do Unions Make? Their Impact on Productivity and Wages in Latin America*, Washington, DC: Inter-American Development Bank, pp. 143–73.

Valadkhani, A. (2003) An empirical analysis of Australian labour productivity, *Australian Economics Papers*, 42: 273–91.

Van der Ploeg, F. (1987) Trade unions, investment, and employment: A non-cooperative approach, *European Economic Review*, 31: 1456–92.

Verma, A. and McKersie, R.B. (1987) Employee involvement: The implications of noninvolvement by unions, *Industrial and Labor Relations Review*, 40: 556–68.

Vernon, G. and Rogers, M. (2013) Where do unions add value? Predominant organizing principle, union strength and manufacturing productivity growth in the OECD, *British Journal of Industrial Relations*, 51: 1–27.

Volpe, R. (2014) Supercenters, unionized labor, and performance in food retail, *Industrial Relations: A Journal of Economy and Society*, 53: 325–55.

Voos, P.B. and Mishel, L.R. (1986a) The union impact on profits: Evidence from industry price-cost margin data, *Journal of Labor Economics*, 4: 105–33.

Voos, P.B. and Mishel, L.R. (1986b) The union impact on profits in the supermarket industry, *The Review of Economics and Statistics*, 68: 513–7.

Voss, K. and Sherman, R. (2000) Breaking the iron law of oligarchy: Union revitalization in the American labor movement, *American Journal of Sociology*, 106: 303–49.

Walder, A.G. (1992) Property rights and stratification in socialist redistributive economies, *American Sociological Review*, 57: 524–39.

Wall, T.D., Michie, J., Patterson, M., Wood, S.J., Sheehan, M., Clegg, C.W. and West, M. (2004) On the validity of subjective measures of company performance, *Personnel Psychology*, 57: 95–118.

Wallerstein, M. (1999) Wage-setting institutions and pay inequality in advanced industrial societies, *American Journal of Political Science*, 43: 649–80.

Warren, R.S. (1985) The effect of unionization on labor productivity: Some time-series evidence, *Journal of Labor Research*, 6: 199–207.

Webb, S.J. and Webb, B. (1920) *The History of Trade Unionism*, London: Longmans Green and Co.

Weeden, K.A. (2002) Why do some occupations pay more than others? Social closure and earnings inequality in the United States, *American Journal of Sociology*, 108: 55–101.

White, H.D. and Griffith, B.C. (1981) Author cocitation: A literature measure of intellectual structure, *Journal of the American Society for Information Science*, 32: 163–71.

White, H.D. and McCain, K.W. (1998) Visualizing a discipline: An author co-citation analysis of information science, 1972–1995, *Journal of the American Society for Information Science*, 49: 327–55.

Whitman, D.S., Van Rooy, D.L. and Viswesvaran, C. (2010) Satisfaction, citizenship behaviors, and performance in work units: A meta-analysis of collective construct relations, *Personnel Psychology*, 63: 41–81.

Wilkinson, A. and Fay, C. (2011) New times for employee voice? *Human Resource Management*, 50: 65–74.

Williams, C.R. and Livingstone, L.P. (1994) Another look at the relationship between performance and voluntary turnover, *The Academy of Management Journal*, 37: 269–98.

Williams, M. and Moomaw, R.L. (1989) Capital and labour efficiencies: A regional analysis, *Urban Studies*, 26: 573–85.

Wilson, K.G. (1995) *The Impact of Unions on United States Economy-Wide Productivity*, New York and London: Garland.

Wilson, N. and Cable, J.R. (1991) Unions, wages and productivity: Some evidence from U.K. engineering firms, *Applied Economics*, 23: 219–27.

Wilson, N. and Peel, M.J. (1991) The impact on absenteeism and quits of profit-sharing and other forms of employee participation, *Industrial and Labor Relations Review*, 44: 454–68.

Withey, M.J. and Cooper, W.H. (1989) Predicting exit, voice, loyalty, and neglect, *Administrative Science Quarterly*, 34: 521–39.

Wolf, E. and Zwick, T. (2008) Reassessing the productivity impact of employee involvement and financial incentives, *Schmalenbach Business Review*, 60: 160–81.

Wood, S.J. and Wall, T.D. (2007) Work enrichment and employee voice in human resource management-performance studies, *The International Journal of Human Resource Management*, 18: 1335–72.

Wooden, M. and Warren, D. (2004) Non-standard employment and job satisfaction: Evidence from the HILDA survey, *The Journal of Industrial Relations*, 46: 275–97.

Yellen, J. (1984) Efficiency wage models of unemployment, *The American Economic Review: Papers and Proceedings*, 74: 200–5.

Yu, G.-C. and Park, J.-S. (2006) The effect of downsizing on the financial performance and employee productivity of Korean firms, *International Journal of Manpower*, 27: 230–50.

Zagler, M. (2000) On the sources of high growth experience in Austria, *International Advances in Economic Research*, 6: 210–20.

Zeytinoglu, I.U., Yilmaz, G., Keser, A., Inelmen, K., Uygur, D. and Özsoy, A. (2013) Job satisfaction, flexible employment and job security among Turkish service sector workers, *Economic and Industrial Democracy*, 34: 123–44.

Zigarelli, M.A. (1994) The linkages between teacher unions and student achievement, *Journal of Collective Negotiations in the Public Sector*, 23: 299–319.

Zuckerman, H. (1987) Citations analysis and the complex problem of intellectual influence, *Scientometrics*, 12: 329–38.

Zwick, T. (2004) Employee participation and productivity, *Labour Economics*, 11: 715–40.

Zwick, T. (2006) The impact of training intensity on establishment productivity, *Industrial Relations: A Journal of Economy and Society*, 45: 26–46.

Index

For Product Safety Concerns and Information please contact our EU representative GPSR@taylorandfrancis.com Taylor & Francis Verlag GmbH, Kaufingerstraße 24, 80331 München, Germany